Disturbing Indians

Disturbing Indians

The Archaeology of Southern Fiction

Annette Trefzer

THE UNIVERSITY OF ALABAMA
Tuscaloosa

The University of Alabama Press
Tuscaloosa, Alabama 35487-0380
uapress.ua.edu

Hardcover edition published 2007.
Paperback edition published 2016.
eBook edition published 2011.

Typeface: Minion

Manufactured in the United States of America
Cover image: Detail of *Master Development Plan of the Natchez Trace Parkway*, National Park Service, US Department of Interior, 1940; courtesy of the Mississippi Department of Archives and History.
Cover design: Paul Moxon

∞

The paper on which this book is printed meets the minimum requirements of American National Standard for Information Science–Permanence of Paper for Printed Library Materials, ANSI Z39.48-1984.

Paperback ISBN: 978-0-8173-5881-5
eBook ISBN: 978-0-8173-8153-0

A previous edition of this book has been catalogued by the Library of Congress as follows:
Library of Congress Cataloging-in-Publication Data
Trefzer, Annette, 1960–
Disturbing Indians : the archaeology of southern fiction / Annette Trefzer.
p. cm.
Includes bibliographical references and index.
ISBN-13: 978-0-8173-1542-9 (alk. paper)
ISBN-10: 0-8173-1542-X
1. American fiction—Southern States—History and criticism. 2. Indians in literature. 3. Southern States—In literature. 4. American fiction—20th century—History and criticism. 5. Lytle, Andrew Nelson, 1902—Criticism and interpretation. 6. Gordon, Caroline, 1895–1981—Criticism and interpretation. 7. Welty, Eudora, 1909–2001—Criticism and interpretation. 8. Faulkner, William, 1897–1962—Criticism and interpretation. I. Title.
PS374.I49T74 20z07
813'.52—dc22
2006017246

To my parents,
Christel and Hans Trefzer

There was a time when archaeology, as a discipline devoted to silent monuments, inert traces, objects without context, and things left to the past, aspired to the condition of history, and attained meaning only through the resituation of a historical discourse; it might be said, to play on words a little, that in our time history aspires to the condition of archaeology, to the intrinsic description of the monument.

—Michel Foucault, *The Archaeology of Knowledge*

Precious lamb, take the pencil,
mark your colonial fields,
your revolutionary storage bins and pantry
Your whole map.

—Diane Glancy, "Cartography," in *The Relief of America*

Contents

Maps

Acknowledgments

I never could have written this book without my time in Oklahoma. I want to thank my colleagues at Southeastern Oklahoma State University in Durant and the Nation Representatives of the Choctaw Nation of Oklahoma and the Chickasaw Nation for giving their energy, time, and support to the creation of a Native American Symposium that afforded me valuable insights into Native American life and cultural politics. Thanks to everyone who supported this effort, particularly to my colleagues on the planning committee: Robin Murray, James Pate, Elbert Hill, Andrew Robson, Corie Delashaw, Brad Cushman, Jane Alrujoub, Chad Litton, Elizabeth Kennedy, Chun Mei You, Sue Folsom (Choctaw Nation) and Jefferson Keele (Chickasaw Nation).

The book owes a great deal to the support of friends and colleagues at the University of Mississippi, whose thoughtful suggestions and careful readings have much improved it. I would particularly like to thank Ivo Kamps, for believing I could start and finish this book on the tenure clock; Deborah Barker, Karen Raber, Kathryn McKee, Ann Fisher-Wirth, Ethel Young-Minor, and David Galef, for reading early chapter drafts; Joseph Urgo and Doug Robinson, for commenting on the introduction; Robbie Ethridge, my colleague in anthropology, for discussions of the issues raised here; and Jacqueline Foertsch, for long-distance support and interest in my project. I am particularly grateful to Eric Gary Anderson for his careful attention and insightful criticism of the manuscript. Eric and a second reader for the press, who remains anonymous, have much improved this work. Thanks also to the staff of The University of Alabama Press, whose expert guidance was invaluable to the completion of this book.

Some sections of *Disturbing Indians* have appeared elsewhere. I am grateful for permission to reprint a section of chapter 4 that appeared as "Tracing the Natchez Trace: Native Americans and National Anxieties in Eudora Welty's 'First Love'" in *Mississippi Quarterly* 55.3 (2002): 419–40; a section of chapter 5 that was first published as "Postcolonial Displacements in Faulkner's Indian Stories of the 1930s" in *Faulkner in the Twenty-First Century,* edited by Robert Hamblin and Ann J. Abadie (University Press of Mississippi, 2003), 68–88; and a section of chapter 3 that was published as "Imperial Discourses in Caroline Gordon's *Green Centuries*" in the *Mississippi Quarterly* 57.1 (2003–4): 113–22.

Finally, I want to thank my parents, Christel and Hans Trefzer, who have inspired me with their lives, and my sisters, Bianca Hippach and Christine Rödling, for their unwavering love and support. Very special thanks go to my husband, Mickey Howley, whose belief in me sustains me.

Disturbing Indians

Introduction

The year 1930 marked the centenary of the Indian Removal Act, which had given the federal government the power to force Native Americans living east of the Mississippi River to move to a designated Indian territory in the West. The passage of the act and its traumatic and far-reaching consequences for the Native Americans who were thus dispossessed of their lands and belongings is a familiar if discomforting chapter in American history. The physical removal of Indians from the South resulted, whether intentionally or not, in their discursive removal as well.[1] What was often considered their "fated disappearance" opened up a space in the white literary and scientific imagination for the construction and exploration of the Indian other. In the South, the crisis of the depression in the 1930s and the resulting governmental intervention created popular and scholarly interest in the region's Native American heritage. During this time, the "vacated" space of Native Americans was examined for traces of their presence in the signifiers that remained embedded in local history and lore and in the landscape itself. Among the various relief programs of Franklin D. Roosevelt's New Deal, federally sponsored archaeology in the South played a significant role in recovering a sense of the Native American presence that marked the land. During the New Deal, massive archaeological excavations were undertaken all over the South. The Tennessee Valley Authority (TVA) alone spanned a huge area covering portions of Tennessee, Virginia, North Carolina, Georgia, Alabama, and Mississippi. It created dams to control flooding in some of the poorest areas in the South, but in the process it would inundate many archaeological sites; as a result, archaeological work had to progress swiftly over a very large area with the help of hundreds of workers.[2] These major civil works brought to the fore thousands of Native American artifacts and remains from historic and so-called "prehistoric" times as archaeologists cataloged, photographed, recorded, and excavated a large number of sites, including stone mounds, burial mounds, earth mounds, caves, cemeteries, and village sites.

These large-scale physical excavations also resulted in fictional excavations of Indian "remains" that brought forth, one hundred years after their removal, the Indian presence in the southern literary imagination. While New Deal archaeologists were digging into Indian mound graves all over the southeastern United States, southern writers of the 1930s were undertaking textual digs into the colonial histories of the South and its Native American heritage. William Faulkner's *Go Down, Moses* (1942) contains such a reference to New Deal archaeology in the South when Lucas Beauchamp tries to hide his whiskey still in an Indian mound.

> Then he saw the place he sought—a squat, flat-topped, almost symmetrical mound rising without reason from the floor-like flatness of the valley. The white people called it an Indian mound. One day five or six years ago a group of white men, including two women, most of them wearing spectacles and all wearing khaki clothes which had patently lain folded on a store shelf twenty-four hours ago, came with picks and shovels and jars and phials of insect repellent and spent a day digging about it, while most of the people, men and women, came at some time during the day and looked quietly on; later—within the next two or three days, in fact—he was to remember with almost horrified amazement the cold and contemptuous curiosity with which he himself had watched them. (37)

Faulkner positions his narrative consciousness with the black spectators who watch and witness with "contemptuous curiosity" the "scientific" excavation of Native American graves for treasures from the past. Through the marginalized perspective of his African-American characters, archaeology emerges as a white hegemonic enterprise, a new science that probes into secrets of racial others. Faulkner mocks the scientists and professionals with their new khakis and their spectacles, symbols not only of the investigating white intellectual gaze but of the new large-scale scientific effort of New Deal archaeology in the South. He explores this scene for comic effect when Lucas returns to the mound six years later with the intention of burying his still in it. It is then that the mound collapses on top of him, and in an avalanche it comes to life,

> hurling clods and dirt at him, striking him a final blow squarely in the face with something larger than a clod—a blow not vicious so much as merely heavy-handed, a sort of final admonitory pat from the spirit of darkness and solitude, the old earth, perhaps the old ancestors themselves. . . . His hand found the object which had struck him and learned it in the blind dark—a fragment of an earthenware vessel which, intact, must have been as big as a churn and which even

as he lifted it crumbled again and deposited in his palm, as though it had been handed to him, a single coin.

He could not have said how he knew it was gold. (38)

Struck in the head by the past and haunted by the spirit of "the old ancestors," Lucas becomes obsessed with his search for gold in Faulkner's humorous revision of America's colonial and capitalist fantasy. The "spirit of darkness and solitude" that strikes Faulkner's non-native inhabitants of the South from the vacated place of the Indian grave is a familiar one. The Native American presence is eclipsed and yet rendered in the signifier of the mound grave as a historical spirit that leaves its imprint on the land and its people. This "spirit" distinctly echoes D. H. Lawrence's prophetic warning that the ghosts of dispossessed Indians will inhabit and haunt America. "A curious thing about the Spirit of Place," Lawrence wrote in 1923, "is the fact that no place exerts its full influence upon a new-comer until the old inhabitant is dead or absorbed. So America" (35). And so the South. In the 1930s, Indian ghosts are as powerful as ever, and their presence as textual signifiers is haunting the literature and the consciousness of the American South. The exercise of archaeology plays a major role in awakening this ghost and in recovering in literature the traces of an Indian presence.

Faulkner's scene captures this book's inquiry in two crucial ways. First, it features the surfacing of the Native American signifier in the textual landscape of the South as a historically marked "place" that signifies a lack. The Indian mounds that dot the fictional terrain of the post-removal South testify to the imagined bygone presence of Indians in the mute cultural monuments that remain. Second, it shows that for southern writers, the Native American signifier is for the most part embedded in the scientific framework of archaeology and the Works Progress Administration excavations that were undertaken everywhere, often not very far from the southern writers' homes. Situated contextually in the depression South, this study examines the archaeological site quite literally as a reference to the ethnographic and historical activities taking place in the southern landscape under the New Deal. But beyond that, archaeology provides a metaphorical entry point into the interior mode of a discourse that engages the place and significance of Native Americans in the southern imagination. Anchored in the archaeological metaphor, this study focuses on a variety of discursive constructions of Native Americans in southern texts and addresses several questions: How does southern literature participate in and reflect on the modernist construction of Native Americans? How do southern writers constitute Native Americans as signifiers in discourses of regionalism and nationalism? How do these discourses link up with the fields of archaeology, anthropology, and history whose specific domain is the recovery of Indian bodies and a (Native) American past?

In this study, as in the archaeological enterprise more generally, I will examine a small piece of ground as an opening into these questions about southern writers' construction of the Native American signifier. I privilege the term *Native American signifier* in the poststructuralist sense of reading language as consisting only of signifiers engaged in an endless chain of signification in order to foreground this discursive construction of Native American identity. This is not to eclipse the "real" Indians behind the text but rather to reveal the textual politics that participate in the construction of any identity. As Native American critics remind us, the textual construction of Indians has been historically employed to define and regulate their identities and to justify violence against them. The American Indian "is a treasured invention," writes Louis Owens, a cultural product that "often bears little resemblance to actual, living Native American people" (4). The term *Indian* itself "came into being on this continent simply as an utterance designed to impose a distinct 'otherness' upon indigenous peoples," and it continues to function for non-Indians as "a signifier that comprehends Euramerican responses to the 'New World'" (7). My choice of the term "Native American signifier" therefore is an attempt to lay bare the very constructedness in language of the idea of "Indians."[3]

A number of scholars have focused on representations of Indians in American literary and political culture, among them Robert Berkhofer, Brian Dippie, Leslie Fiedler, Richard Drinnon, Walter Benn Michaels, Lucy Maddox, and most recently Philip Deloria, Renee Bergland, Shari Huhndorf, Helen Carr, Sherry Smith, and Joshua Bellin. Building on these studies, this book examines the cultural and symbolic significance of the Indian figure. I share with Berkhofer's project the task of investigating anthropological, literary, and political constructions of Indians, but unlike Berkhofer, who traces a relatively stable image of the Indian over time, I foreground its literary production at a particular historical moment. I share with Michaels a focus on a specific decade, but unlike him, I center my study in the prewar decade in order to examine the reverberations of policy changes such as the Indian Reorganization Act (1934) on the southern literary imagination. As such, my project marks a significant departure from prior studies in terms of time and place, inviting the reader to contemplate the discursive recirculation of Indians in the South one hundred years after their removal. Like Fiedler, Dippie, Maddox, and Bergland, I situate this study within the tradition of the "vanishing Indian," grounded in the physical act of removal and its haunting psychological, political, and literary effects. Seeking to recover the significance of the Indian body that slumbers as a ghost in the (textual) landscape, Renee Bergland, for example, shows how this ghost works both to "establish American nationhood and to call it into question" (5). In my analysis of the South's participation in the transformation of Indian space into both white national and regional territory, I am not on the lookout for nineteenth-century ghosts but rather for the modernist forces that shape the discursive constructions of the Native American signifier.

In the South, this Native American signifier is often buried under a symbolic creation of the region that minimizes its importance or even negates its presence altogether. Southern literature, it is commonly believed, seems to lack a significant concern with Native American life and history because, as Richard Slotkin argues, southern writers were largely unable to "deal with the West as a psychological problem of immense national significance" (*Regeneration* 463). This "lack," Slotkin writes, "restricted the southern author's artistic vocabulary and frame of reference to contemporary thought and current literary trends." Unlike writers from the Northeast or the West, those of the South had to create a tradition through "retrospective views of southern history, based inevitably on contemporary social and literary conventions" (460). By examining the discursive appearance of Indians precisely within the context of these conventions, this study responds to this perceived lack of creative and critical attention to Indians in southern texts and argues that they are in fact essential to the southern writers' understanding of region and nation. Although there are a few studies of Faulkner's fictional treatments of Indians,[4] there is of yet no systematic critical analysis of the discursive construction of Native Americans in the South at the time of its most self-conscious articulation of regional identity. *Disturbing Indians: The Archaeology of Southern Fiction* attempts to fill this lack.

1

Excavating the Sites

Indians in Southern Texts and Contexts

> For decades, thousands of skeletons were gathered systematically and shipped away to be displayed and warehoused in museums. By the early twentieth century, it was grimly joked that the Smithsonian Institution in Washington had more dead Indians than there were live Indians.
>
> —Jace Weaver, *Other Words: American Indian Literature, Law, and Culture*

Considering the long-standing critical tradition in American studies that scrutinizes literary and cultural representations of Native Americans for their ideological and creative functions, it is surprising that no such enterprise exists yet in southern studies. Although scholars are beginning to gesture toward the Native American presence in southern literature, this inquiry remains in its initial stages. Houston Baker and Dana Nelson have recently pointed out that "the South is thick with civilly disappeared history," including that of indigenous peoples, but their own volume ironically reflects rather than remedies this disappearance. Noticing the "disappeared bodies" of Native Americans from the southern landscape, Baker and Nelson write: "we know that the murder, displacement, and relocation of thousands of Native American bodies from the same geographies in which enslaved Africans in the United States worked the land is a critical area of investigation for a new Southern studies" (233). And yet, despite this acknowledgment of the Native American presence in the South, Native Americans—both as authors and subjects—are conspicuously absent from their volume, which renders the southern racial geography yet one more time as a prominently "black and white" territory.

Map 1. "Southern States and Mississippi Territory, 1816." Attributed to Mathew Carey and Son, ca. 1816. Courtesy of the Mississippi Department of Archives and History

This study responds to such a lack of critical attention by examining the discursive appearance of Indians in southern texts and by reinserting their presence into scholarly discussions about the South. Not only do Native Americans play an active role in the construction of the cultural landscape of the South—despite a history of colonization, dispossession, and removal aimed at rendering them "invisible"—but their so-far-underexamined presence in southern literature provides a crucial avenue for a new post-regional understanding of the American South. Centering on the textual construction of Native Americans in the South, this study seeks to participate in the articulation of a new American studies project that focuses comparatively on the intersection of two cultures marginal to the nation: "the South" and "Native America."

Not only do Native American signifiers appear in southern texts during times of violent cultural conflict, such as during the colonial period or the removal period, but they also appear frequently in the literature of the post-removal

South. This study focuses on the imaginative reconstruction of the Native American past during the Southern Renaissance, when southern writers—among them William Faulkner, Eudora Welty, Andrew Lytle, and Caroline Gordon—turned to Indians in their fiction. Writing between 1930 and 1942, these authors created works about the Spanish conquest of the New World, the Cherokee frontier during the Revolutionary period, the expansionist schemes in Mississippi Territory, and the slaveholding Indian societies of the American Southeast. Together these texts map a Native American South that stretches from Virginia to Kentucky, from Mississippi to Florida, and from Tennessee to present-day Peru. One hundred years after the forced removal of Native Americans from the Southeast, these writers return to an "Indian frontier" marked by colonial struggles and imperialist power. In the process of exploring colonial history from their position in the modern South, they engage with a variety of discourses about Native Americans: some celebrate Native American cultures as seemingly more wholesome and "civilized" than modern Anglo-American industrial culture; others reject concepts of cultural hierarchy and racial purity for a sense of the hybridity of modern identities; all of them respond to discourses of Manifest Destiny and the idea of the "vanishing Indian," concepts that lingered in historical and political discussions about Native Americans well into the 1930s. Through the discursive construction of Indians, these writers also participate in the ethnological debates of mainstream American modernism and in a kind of primitivism they share with writers outside the South.

In exploring the Native American signifier, southern writers engage in a double discourse about region and nation. On the one hand, discourses about Indians articulate a regionalist, if not nativist, thesis about the American South. Writing during the decade that began with the publication of the southern manifesto *I'll Take My Stand* (1930), these writers respond to and participate in the fabrications of regional identity by invoking the idea of the South's "native" heritage. The authors examined here engage in a kind of local particularism by using the Indians as a root discourse for the creation of a specifically southern landscape and ideology. On the other hand, their discourses about Indians point well beyond regional concerns, because the Native American signifier is always also anchored in national and international history. Through their Indian treatments, these writers participate in the shaping of American national ideology even as they seek to place themselves in a dialectic regionalist perspective to the nation. That is, these southern writers, far from merely acting as apologists and perpetrators of an insular local southernness, explicitly engage an international history of imperial expansion through the Indian figure. Haunted by the history of American colonization and plagued by questions of national guilt, the authors of these texts dip into the mythology of westward expansion and into the history of American and European imperialism. In doing so, they reflect not only on the imperialist past but also on the rising national anxieties of their own contemporary political moment, which is marked by the appearance of a "new nationalism" during the depression and by growing concerns over the increasing power of fascism abroad during the prewar years.

In order to examine how the Indian signifier contributes to the shaping of regional and national self-definitions as well as to the corresponding production of cultural, racial, and national others, I situate the discursive appearance of Indians in southern texts in the national and international climate of imperial expansion. I am particularly interested in how literary texts by white southerners characterize those "others" and how, through the discursive construction of the Native American presence, these writers condense the contradictory political, cultural, and psychological effects of colonial conquest. Faulkner, Welty, Lytle, and Gordon are particularly important precisely because they are entrenched in the hegemonic construction of a white South and a southern literary tradition whose precepts we know so well: the centrality of place, a respect for the past, a love for and hate of the South. I want to pry these writers from these old precepts of critical analysis and, by focusing a postcolonial lens on their work, examine them through new paradigmatic frameworks.

This study borrows from Foucault the archaeological metaphor, from Derrida its concern with textual traces, from postcolonialism its attention to imperial forces and colonial encounters, and from Native American studies its critical interest in the discursive construction of the Indian other. The concept of archaeology functions in two ways. First, it refers quite literally to the excavation of cultural artifacts in the South during the New Deal of the 1930s. New Deal archaeology, I argue, provides a crucial disciplinary context for the reappearance of the Native American signifier in the cultural consciousness of the South, a "surfacing" to which the southern writers are responding. Second, archaeology serves as a method that characterizes my theoretical approach for exploring the literary texts. Methodologically, I want to stress two intersecting discursive levels in my textual excavations. "Digging down" vertically, each text marks a trace (in the Derridean sense) into the rhetorical constructions of Native Americans at a particular, historically remote time. From the present moment of excavation in the prewar decade, these traces lead all the way back to the discursive construction of the Indian signifier during the Age of Discovery. Collectively, these texts offer a historical trajectory that leads from the sixteenth-century conquest of the Incan empire to Hernando de Soto's exploration of the American South; from the Indian wars during the American Revolution to the expansionist schemes of Aaron Burr; from the extermination of the Natchez Indians to the Indian removal under Andrew Jackson—and on into the present. In short, each vertical "dig" into the textual strata opens up a diachronic perspective and a deep historical range. Each horizontal "dig" lays bare the broad structure of (southern) culture and the texts' intersections with intellectual and ideological discourses of the same period to which the Native American textual trace points. Such an exploration will reveal, for example, the countercultural and critical function that Native American discourses carry for some of the writers examined here and the degree to which the fictional texts intersect with contemporary racial and cultural theories, with Native American policy, and with popular culture.

Digging Up: Contemporary Contexts

Before digging into these cultural contexts, I want to acknowledge the warning of cultural archaeologists against a simple understanding of surface and depth: the layers of discourse about Native Americans run deep and broad, vertical and horizontal, synchronically and diachronically. But they are also hybridized so that it becomes difficult to say which discourses are contemporary to the time period depicted and which are particular to the current understanding. Acknowledging this hybridization, I begin with a broad mapping of the contemporary inscriptions of Native Americans in the textual landscapes of the national culture during the depression and prewar years. The texts I will be examining are anchored in rhetorical constructions of Native Americans as part of a larger pervasive public discourse conducted in various disciplines, including literature, politics, and science. First, I want to situate these discourses as part of a modernist aesthetic that offers an ambiguous view of Native Americans suspended between celebration and condemnation and their usefulness for constructions of regionalist and nationalist identities. Second, I want to briefly examine the political rhetoric of the depression years and Franklin D. Roosevelt's New Deal administration, which supported not only dramatically new Indian legislation but also the recirculation of the (old) frontier thesis in politics and media. As we will see, federal intervention in American cultural space helped trigger the growth of a new cultural nationalism at the same time that southern writers were articulating their own regionalist theories. Finally, I want to turn to the archaeological and historical constructions of Native Americans in the source materials that were available to Faulkner, Welty, Lytle, and Gordon in order to examine how the proliferation of these studies under the New Deal helped shape their ideas about Indians.

When southern writers turned to Native American signifiers in their fiction, they were in many ways part of an intellectual mainstream of modern Americans who protested what they perceived as the increasing materialism of the United States. In southern texts, the cultural differences articulated through Native American figures offer at least a small degree of resistance to the hegemonic national culture of industrialism and capitalism. It is from the nation's southern fringe that these writers participated in such modernist resistance by positively identifying a Native American cultural difference in order to launch a critique of the colonizing and mechanizing impulses of U.S. capitalism. But this resistance is often double-edged, as the case of Andrew Lytle makes abundantly clear: born out of a conservative, universalizing humanism, his fiction critiques U.S. imperialism and the international operations of capitalism, but it turns a blind eye to southern segregation and exploitative labor politics in his own backyard. In short, the modernist "resistance" offered in the Native American figure of some of these southern texts may sometimes turn out to be fundamentally conservative.

In the national context, Native American culture has frequently served the same purpose as a counterpoint to hegemonic culture. In modern American society, the so-called pre-industrial lifestyle of Native American cultures was often used as a standard by which national progress could be measured. But for many American intellectuals, such "progress" based on materialism and the culture of capital became increasingly suspect during the ostentatious celebration of the national business culture in the 1920s. During this decade of high modernism, America's cultural climate led to a sense of alienation and fragmentation that prompted many writers to flee into European exile and others into a search for a new spiritual and cultural grounding. The collective intellectual critique of the United States' commercial priorities incited an interest in Indian cultures as a sanctuary for artistic and spiritual values.[1] "Let us try to adjust ourselves again to the Indian outlook, to take up an old dark tread from their vision, and see again as they see, without forgetting we are ourselves," urged D. H. Lawrence (qtd. in Dippie 281). Many modernists shared this agenda and engaged the myth of a more harmonious, natural Indian culture in their fiction. They saw in Native American culture a cure for the malaise of modern civilization and those "false standards of measurement"—power, success, and wealth—that Freud had pointed out in *Civilization and Its Discontents* (1930). Modernists in the United States now celebrated "primitive" cultures as an antidote to bourgeois modernity, and they increasingly perceived Native Americans as "inheritors of ancient wisdom" (Carr 200). This wisdom was to be found among the Pueblo cultures of the Southwest.

The revival of interest in Native American cultures began with the migration of intellectuals, writers, and public policy makers to the Southwest in the early 1920s, some of whom had gathered there to prevent the passing of the Bursum bill, which was endangering the land claims of Pueblo Indians in New

Mexico. The list of artists and writers who congregated in Taos included D. H. Lawrence, Willa Cather, Mary Austin, and Mabel Dodge Luhan, as well as John Collier, who would later become commissioner of the Bureau of Indian Affairs (BIA). One of the most powerful men to influence Indian policy in the twentieth century, Collier was born in Georgia. But it was not the South that shaped the romantic vision of Indian life that underpinned his policies; it was his stay among the Pueblo peoples in the Southwest, where he discovered in the 1920s a healthy alternative to the "sickness" of his own capitalist and industrialist society. Deeply concerned about the lack of community in American life as a whole, Collier mourned what he perceived as "the lost reverence and passion for the earth and its web of life" (*Indians* 15). He was passionate about preserving Native American cultures, and even before becoming involved with the BIA he believed, like many other American intellectuals, that modern societies were fundamentally flawed. For Collier, Native American cultures held truths that could help heal modern Western societies. He saw Native Americans as "repudiating the materialism, the secularism, and the fragmentation of modern White life under industrialism for a simpler, more beautiful way of life that emphasized the relationship of humans with one another, with the supernatural, and with land and nature" (qtd. in Berkhofer 178).

Native Americans of the Southwest, particularly the Pueblos and the Navajos, were often portrayed as "an ancient people, peaceable cultivators, paragons of domestic virtue, deeply religious, hospitable, and patriotic" (Dippie 277). Promising spiritual and cultural renewal, Indians were now integrated into the national narrative by writers, artists, social activists, politicians, and even commercial marketers. Clear signs of this trend are not only the burgeoning tourism in the western United States but the passage of the Indian Citizenship Act in 1924, which sought to include into the concept of American national identity formerly excluded native populations.[2] In short, Native Americans, now increasingly perceived as a potential source for American cultural identity, were seen as having a rich and distinct culture. When Collier and his contemporaries turned to the Pueblo Indians as examples for an alternate cultural history, they did so partially because the Pueblos were sedentary, agricultural, and democratic, but also because they had preserved a degree of cultural authenticity that southeastern Indians seemed to lack. "Vanished" from the South, the eastern tribes had been transplanted to Oklahoma and in the process variously assimilated into the mainstream culture. As "civilized tribes" they could not provide the desired model of primitive genuineness and cultural tradition.

The new ethnological view of the Indian as a "comparatively peaceful, industrious figure, a child of nature, close to the soil from which he wins his living, cultivating the earth with a rough hoe" (Carr 207) particularly appealed to white southern writers who sympathized with agrarianism and celebrated in backward glance a time when the world seemed more wholesome. Americans everywhere were troubled by what they perceived as the nation's celebration of capital and commodity, but white southern writers in particular tried to imagine a community different from American mainstream industrialism. Their sense of alienation was very much reinforced by the economic crisis of the depression, which served only to confirm the much larger cultural crisis in the United States. In many ways the agrarian manifesto *I'll Take My Stand*—often read as the most famous paradigm of regionalism during the first half of the twentieth century—participates in and responds to the very same sense of modernist dissatisfaction with American capitalism and industrialization. The theses of this regionalist manifesto—the return to the soil, the centrality of spirituality, the sense of the importance of nature as "something mysterious and contingent," the desire for community and tradition—all resonate with the ideals upheld by those writers all over the nation who traveled to the Southwest in order to find spiritual and communal wholeness among the Indians.

But the southern writers examined here did not travel to the Southwest to witness the Native American cultural revival; they sought to locate these values in the soil of a rural South and in a community ideal of a time prior to industrialization. As a result, they were guided by a very different spatial logic, as far as Native American cultures are concerned, from that of their contemporaries who undertook the trip. While southern writers did participate in a kind of modernist primitivism and in discourses of nationalism through the Native American signifier, they imagined otherness not through the modern colonial fantasies of travel and tourism in the Southwest but through a return to the frontier days of the Old Southwest. It is in the southern past and in the paradigm of the frontier that they encounter the valuable lessons of the nation's Native American heritage. This difference in access to Indian culture—through the record of history and archaeology rather than through tourism and travel—also accounts for the different regionalist nuances in the discourse about Native Americans that we find in their texts. Southern writers center primarily on a perceived lack of those Indians who once populated the woodlands of the Southeast. The familiar idea of the "vanishing"—and in this case "vanished"—Indian finds thematic expression in the return to the frontier and finds stylistic expression in the mode of mourning and elegy. Whereas such mourning and haunting is also part of the national metaphor—the idea of America as a nation—the tone and purpose of such nostalgia serve both regionalist and nationalist agendas.[3] Collectively these texts by southern writers respond to debates about the social, cultural and political climate of the United States between the stock market's crash in 1929 and America's entry into World War II. By returning to foundational moments in the nation's remote past, these texts engage national history from a southern locale as a form of sectional imperialism.

In terms of its regionalist importance, the decade is framed by *I'll Take My Stand* (1930) and Wilbur Cash's *The Mind of the South* (1941), both of which seek to outline a regional difference by which the South defines its cultural specificity in opposition to the nation. Whether it is the theory of agrarianism delineated in the first text or the theory of the southern frontier that had discouraged intellectualism and favored a "savage ideal," as the second text proclaims, southern writers looked at modern American life through regional eyes. What they saw before the stock market's crash must have troubled them as much as the depression afterward. Southern literature of the 1930s centers on this regional difference and tries to forge the "mind" of the South as a concept substantially different from that of other regions and from the nation-state more generally. In his meditation on the relationship between region and nation in *The Attack on Leviathan* (1938), Donald Davidson refuses to prioritize the role and rank of nation and region: "I can't conceive of our country as offering a fixed hierarchy of values: 1. Something called a nation, of which you must think first; 2. Something called a region, of which you are privileged to think" (qtd. in O'Brien, *Idea* 196). He writes that "without elevating one above the other," regionalism provides a useful perspective because it helps to position the nation in its proper place.

But while southern writers attempted to tell their regional story, they also participated in a national trend. The exploration of a specific region's history, folklore, art, literature, and people was very much part of the larger national effort under Roosevelt's New Deal administration of the depression years. Alfred Kazin has characterized the years between 1930 and 1942 as a time of "national self-discovery" for American writers. In *On Native Grounds* (1942) he argues that "underlying the imaginative life in America all through the years of panic, depression and the emergence of international civil war was an enormous body of writing devoted to the American scene" (485). During the New Deal, a national effort to chart and document American culture was under way, and the Works Progress Administration (WPA) projects played a major role in this national rediscovery. The WPA provided jobs for hundreds of intellectuals, among them writers, documentary reporters, photographers, filmmakers, archivists, folklorists, historians, geographers, and archaeologists who participated in the documentation of American life by establishing a national inventory that led to what Kazin calls a "new nationalism." Some writers who participated in the WPA, like Eudora Welty, found themselves explicitly contributing to the national effort of cataloging and narrating regional experience and "history" as part of a larger national story. Other writers, like Lytle, saw their emphasis on regional as opposed to national directives and trends, specifically the tendency in the United States toward urbanization and industrialization. Either way—by collaborating or by resisting—these southern writers engage with a form of American literary nationalism.[4]

As a response to the domestic crisis, the WPA's large-scale research effort strengthened the national consciousness specifically by reawakening an interest in American history. "The past now lay everywhere ready to be reclaimed, waiting to be chanted and celebrated," writes Kazin (509). Indeed, under the surface of industrial life, a different America was to be discovered. Kazin waxes poetic as he provides this archaeological picture:

> Road by road, town by town, down under the alluvia of the industrial culture of the twentieth century, lay an America that belied many of the traditional legends about itself. For here under the rich surface deposits of the factory and city world, lay the forgotten stories of all those who had failed rather than succeeded in the past, all those who had not risen on the steps of the American dream from work bench to Wall Street, but had built a town where the railroad would never pass, gambled on coal deposits where there was no coal, risked their careers for oil where there was no oil: all the small-town financiers who guessed wrong, all those who groped toward riches that never came. And here, too, was the humorous, the creepy, the eccentric life of the American character: the secret rooms and strange furtive religions; the forgotten enthusiasms and heresies and cults; the relics of fashion and tumbling mansions that had always been someone's folly. (502)

And here, too, was the colonial frontier and the Indians, ready for rediscovery. When southern writers dug through the "rich surface deposits" of their landscape they encountered the traces of previous cultural inscriptions by Native Americans that had been "overwritten" by the dominant white settler culture. By excavating the layered cultural strata of their region, they accessed the Native American signifier in three crucial ways: the contemporary historical discourse of the frontier, popular representations in film and print, and archaeological and ethnographic research.

The discourse of the frontier was an important part of a national debate during the 1930s. The new historical and national consciousness, propelled by the Great Depression, brought sharply into focus the failure of the American dream of prosperity. It was during this time that debates about the frontier rose again. The depression brought on a "peak interest" in ideas presented decades earlier by sociologist William Graham Sumner and historian Frederick Jackson

Turner about the frontier as the basis for the American democratic principle and its function as a "safety valve" in times of economic stagnation (Alexander 3). President Franklin D. Roosevelt used this renewed interest in the frontier as a powerful argument for government action in a speech in 1932: "Our last frontier has long since been reached, and there is practically no more free land. More than half of our people do not live on the farms or on the lands and cannot derive a living by cultivating their own property. There is no safety valve in the form of a Western prairie to which those thrown out of work by the Eastern economic machines can go for a new start" (qtd. in Alexander 4). For many the implication of this was that the United States' economic and technological frontiers were exhausted and a new era had begun. During the depression, "the very usefulness of the Turner thesis lay in the fact that it told you something not only about the past but about the present as well" (Kesselman 256). This renewed preoccupation with the frontier and its impact on national character and destiny was part of a national conversation, but it was also important for the writers in the South who espoused regional concerns. During this time "the old ballads began to come back, all the dear familiar legends, all the fine rawboned heroes of the frontier epic" (Kazin 509). All of the writers examined here participated in this recovery of frontier materials by collectively reviving its protagonists, including Mississippi's tall-tale hero Mike Fink, Kentucky's legendary Daniel Boone, and Florida's conqueror Hernando de Soto. All these frontier "heroes"—fabricated giants whether mythical or historical—reveal the writers' participation in America's invention of a national heritage, a "usable past."[5] The Indians, of course, are an essential ingredient in this frontier history.

Not only did the renewed public attention of the frontier thesis help reinforce discourses of Manifest Destiny and a view of the "Indian" as an anachronism, but mainstream movies also helped to solidify the image of the doomed Indian. Centering on Native Americans as obstacles to the civilizing of the continent, many Hollywood scripts brought back into circulation Turner's frontier thesis and a view of Native Americans as relics of the past. Even at the close of the decade, Westerns such as *Allegeny Uprising* (1939) and *Stage Coach* (1939) continued to display a bluntly colonialist vision of Indians as obstacles to the exploration of "uncharted territory." Westerns were particularly popular and important during the depression because people wanted a fantasy "of a time when all it took to 'make it' was hard work and courage" (Kilpatrick 39). The frontier was crucial to this myth and the shaping of nationalist sentiment. Kilpatrick writes that "modern mass media, including cinema, have played a major part in the production of national symbols. As these symbols become part of each individual through the media, they effectively break down the separation between public and private, local and national. This produces a nationalist discourse, a primary function of which is to develop a national mythology of historical origin. In America, it is the myth of 'How the West Was Won'" (5). What this meant in the cinematic world of the 1930s was that the frontier had to be made safe from the Indians. Both *Geronimo* (1936) and *Stage Coach,* for example, conveyed this message by portraying ominous and aggressive Indians (Apaches) whose resistance to white civilization must be squashed. This depiction begins to change only slowly as the United States is entering into World War II, a time when discourses of Manifest Destiny are slowly being checked because "a national campaign to purge the land of its Indian inhabitants smacked of fascist genocide" (Aleiss 27).

Southern writers did not create their Indians in a cultural vacuum; on the contrary, they, too, were influenced by mainstream cultural discourses and images produced by Hollywood's Westerns, news reports, and the popular press. They were certainly aware of articles and cartoons of Indians in the *Saturday Evening Post,* a magazine in which Faulkner, for example, published a number of his stories. One of the most popular and influential magazines during the first half of the twentieth century, the *Saturday Evening Post* alone featured hundreds of references to Indians in fiction and news, art and cartoons, feature columns and photographs that helped to guide public perception of Native Americans for better or worse depending on editorial policy and the cultural and racial climate of the time.[6] This included, of course, stereotypical representations of Indians as savage or benign, exotic or extinct, as these images befitted the narrative of the nation.

In addition to popular magazines, local newspapers also played a powerful role in shaping the public perception of Indians. In the national arena, the biggest news about Native Americans concerned the new Indian policy, presented as the Indian New Deal of 1934, whose landmark legislation was the Indian Reorganization Act (IRA). Proposed by John Collier, who was then the commissioner of the BIA, the Wheeler-Howard Bill marked a major change in Indian policy toward Native American self-determination. Collier writes that before 1934, "Indian tribes rarely had been consulted on the legislation introduced for their supposed benefit" (*Indians* 264). In order to remedy this situation, his bill originally contained six parts, including provisions for political and economic self-government, Indian civil service training, termination of Indian land allotment, establishment of agricultural and industrial credit, civil and criminal law enforcement, and the consolidation of fractional allotted lands (264). The first four parts of the bill became law in 1934 and are known as the Indian Reorganization Act. This act is of immense importance because it sought to reverse the assimilation policies of the past decades and to restore to Native Americans a communal land base. Regardless of how much of this national policy change and its powerful impact on native cultures actually arrived in the daily news in the living rooms of Faulkner, Welty, Lytle, and Gordon, none of them explicitly remark on it. And yet coverage of the debates surrounding Collier's bill was both national and local, and it was part of the discursive environment in which these writers lived and wrote, no matter how far from the centers of national politics they lived. Researching the press coverage of events involving Native Americans, Mary Ann Weston writes that "audiences far from an event [like the writers examined here], reading about it in a national publication, were more likely to get an account colored by distorted, stereotypical images. This was particularly unfortunate because these audiences were also less likely to have first-hand knowledge of the real people who had been edited out of the national stories" (57). If we assume with Weston that Native Americans in news reports became more lurid the more the distance between the events and the location of the paper, the writers in the South were in a disadvantaged place for receiving fair and balanced coverage on national Indian issues. But of course, the press and popular media were neither the only nor the most important sources for information about Native Americans for these writers. Faulkner, Welty, Lytle, and Gordon, I believe, were not so much interested in contemporary Native American communities as in their "ancestors" who once populated the South.

The discourse of "ancestry" ascribed to the Native American signifier is central for these southern writers' "discovery" of a "usable past" that is part of the archaeological deep structure of the land itself. As I have already mentioned, these writers' reconstruction of a national past anchored in its regional "native" heritage was inspired by major archaeological efforts that began in the southern states under the New Deal.[7] Governmental intervention created archaeological reform with the help of relief agencies such as the WPA, the Civil Works Administration (CWA), and the Tennessee Valley Authority (TVA), resulting in enormous archaeological excavations all over the South. These major civil works projects redefined the landscapes close to the homes of Gordon, Welty, Lytle, and Faulkner and raised their awareness of the South's historic Indian roots. The WPA excavations stimulated scholarly and popular interest in southern ethnology and history and in the activity of archaeology itself. Jace Weaver reminds us that even before the systematic efforts of WPA archaeology, "thousands of skeletons were gathered systematically and shipped away to be displayed and warehoused in museums. By the early twentieth century, it was grimly joked that the Smithsonian Institution in Washington had more dead Indians than there were live Indians" (158). Archaeologist Neal Judd said in 1929 that "public interest in archaeology is deep and firmly rooted. No other subject surpasses archaeology in popular appeal; none so quickly awakens the lay imagination" (qtd. in Lyon 51). And Samuel Dickinson remarked that "the

Depression set many a man dreaming of gold and silver supposedly buried by Indians and de Soto's men. Equipped with forked peach tree or willow divining sticks or mail-order mineral rods, they went at night to dig for treasure" (qtd. in Lyon 52). The result was widespread "amateur archaeology," or to put it more bluntly, vandalism and looting. Native American critics speak of a "massive theft" that included thousands of human remains and "millions of funerary, ceremonial and cultural objects" (Weaver 158). News of such treasure hunts and major ecological transformations of their environments did not escape these writers. The imaginative shift to the claims of monuments from the distant and even archaic cultural past that we witness in the texts of the writers examined here reveals the contemporary urgency and relevance of the "unearthed" Native American presence. The extensive excavations of Native American mounds, villages, and burial sites all over the South moved the Indian presence into conscious awareness. As material evidence was recovered from various periods, allowing archaeologists and anthropologists to trace Native American life and history, these writers, too, trace the past all the way back to the discovery histories of the New World and to the "contact zones" and ethnic frontiers of colonial history.

In order to sketch these historical encounters, southern writers relied on new scientific inquiries that began to have institutional lives in archaeology, anthropology, and ethnology departments. Among scholars of southeastern ethnology, John Swanton had the most wide-ranging contemporary reputation, and his prolific work provided ample source material for the fiction writers examined here. First published in 1911, Swanton's study *Indian Tribes of the Lower Mississippi Valley and Adjacent Coast of the Gulf of Mexico* contains important information on the Natchez Indians that resonates with Welty's depictions of them. Later Swanton became interested in the de Soto exploration, and as a result of his archaeological research on de Soto's route he was appointed by President Roosevelt to the United States de Soto Expedition Commission in 1935. Under Swanton's direction, this work resulted in the official publication of the report of the de Soto commission in 1939, only two years before Andrew Lytle's fictional treatment of de Soto's exploration of "La Florida" was published. Swanton's seminal work *The Indians of the Southeastern United States* (1942) is a collection of ethnological information on modern southeastern Indians, including the Cherokees, whom Gordon was writing about; the Choctaws and Chickasaws, whom Faulkner was working into the genealogical foundations of his Yoknapatawpha landscape; the Natchez, who captured Welty's imagination; and the Indians of Florida, Georgia, Alabama, and Mississippi, whom de Soto would have encountered in 1541. In addition to Swanton's work, James Adair's classic *History of the American Indians* (1775), regarded as an early authoritative source text on southeastern Indians, was brought back into print in 1930 by the National Society of Colonial Dames of America just as these southern writers were turning to Native American topics. Among Adair's vivid descriptions of life among the Indians of the South they found information on rituals of purification, burial, and marriage; on feasts, sacrifices, and religious rites; and specific information on individual tribes such as the Cherokee, Muskogee, Choctaw, and Chickasaw Indians.

Among contemporary historians working on southern Indians during the 1930s, there was a clear sense of the historical centenary of the Indian removal. John P. Brown, whose *Old Frontiers* (1938) provided one of the main sources on Cherokee history for Caroline Gordon's novel *Green Centuries* (1941), begins his study with a remark about the timing of his publication: "Exactly one hundred years ago the Cherokee Indians were removed from their ancestral homes to what was then Arkansas" (vii). And the title of Angie Debo's *The Rise and Fall of the Choctaw Republic* (1934), a contemporary history important to all of the writers here, captures (somewhat unfortunately) the ideological and discursive force imposed by the removal, which resulted in the idea that Indians had "fallen." The removal of the "Five Civilized Tribes" from the South seemingly left a "vacuum" that could be filled with the archaeological "discoveries" of Native American artifacts and with the historical and fictional narratives of white southern writers, who now occupied and re-imagined the "vacated" landscapes.

It is not surprising, therefore, that the Indian presence in the South is often seen as embedded in the landscape itself. Giving rise to the archaeological imagination, the Indian mounds that can be found all over the South play a significant role in this understanding. Calvin S. Brown's *Archeology of Mississippi* (1926) describes and catalogs the different Indian mounds and earthworks in Mississippi (including Faulkner's Lafayette County) and indexes the kinds of artifacts found in the soil. These artifacts range from pre-Columbian arrowheads to pipes and pottery. Faulkner, who owned a copy of Brown's book, no doubt was influenced by its descriptions and photographs. Indian mounds would have been familiar not only to Faulkner and Welty but also to Gordon and Lytle, who spent much time in Tennessee. The Pinson Indian Mound complex in Tennessee is one of the largest mound areas testifying to ancient Indian towns. These mounds in the southern landscape might have quite naturally provoked curiosity and evoked lore and legend, but the activities of the New Deal excavations quickened that interest. Relief archaeology in Kentucky, Gordon's home state, specifically the discovery of two mounds on the Big Sandy River in eastern Kentucky that were excavated in 1938 and 1939, contributed, I believe, to Gordon's decision to focus on the exact same area in her captivity narrative.[8]

Just how deeply the rediscovery of the Indian presence in the South was embedded in the activity of archaeology can also be seen in *Mississippi: The WPA Guide to the Magnolia State* (1938). In the section "Before the White Man Came," Indians and archaeology appear in the same chapter as part of the "Natural Setting." Based on the work of Calvin S. Brown, the *WPA Guide* states that "the State is rich in aboriginal remains in the form of mounds and village sites" and mentions the need for preservation and surveying of the rich mound landscape in order to "bring the life of the primitive Indian to light" (46). It also lists the best collections of Native American artifacts in Mississippi, a concern in keeping with the nationwide interest of Americans in collecting Americana and the importance of historic preservation that began to take shape during the 1920s and 1930s (Kammen 315). Even though the *WPA Guide* references the serious academic work of Brown and Swanton, it also engages in popular myths and stereotypes about Native Americans when it describes, for example, Choctaw and Chickasaw women as "Indian maidens, however small and beautifully formed, with sparkling eyes and black hair, [who] lost their charm while young and were deteriorated utterly by middle age" from hard labor and their general state of "degradation" (50). Even in federally sponsored work, in academic, scientific, and historical studies, Indians still belonged to a cultural register of "others" around which old and new mythologies were gathered. These narratives of otherness were constructed all the more fantastically and luridly the further away Indians were in time and space. In the South, a landscape visibly marked by the mounds and artifacts of Indian life of a much earlier pre-contact period, such narratives readily sprang up to fill the place that the Indians had seemingly left.

This brief mapping of the Native American signifier in the broad structures of American culture of the 1930s illustrates the "recovery" of Native American presences in various disciplines and discourses. The resurfacing of this signifier may be seen as rooted in domestic developments, including American policy that shaped the WPA, a federal movement that launched a major reinvestigation of local knowledge—specifically history, art, literature, music and other cultural expressions—as part of a larger national(ist) project. In many ways, the southern writers' rediscovery of the Indian presence is part of such a national conversation about Native Americans in American literary modernism, in national policy and law, in government-sponsored studies, in history and archaeology, and in popular culture and the media more generally. This national conversation about Indian cultures had regional ramifications that may be seen as directly related to the development of southeastern archaeology and the appearance of regional ethnological and anthropological treatises as well. As we will see, in the context of the South, the physical and discursive removal of Indians resulted in acts of ideological and imaginative recovery that face two ways: toward a kind of nativization of the South for which the imagined Indian presence is claimed in an act of local identification, and toward a kind of nationalization for which the Native American signifier participates in the construction of the American national imaginary. In southern writing of the 1930s, these signifiers appear foremost in narratives of colonialism, nationhood, and cultural dispossession.

Digging Down: Historical Deep Structures

How these southern texts engage with histories of colonialism and imperialism becomes evident in a textual dig that lays bare the diachronic structures of place. In an archaeological framework, a place such as the South can be re-imagined not simply as surface topography but as "deep structure." This means that place is no longer simply a more or less stable geographical surface marked by cultural essences and practices different from those of other regions. Nor is it any longer primarily defined by a history centered in the Civil War and the institution of slavery. Instead, the location of the South as "deep structure" is embedded in discursive practices involving resistance to, affirmation of, or participation in the global history of colonialism. In the spirit of probing place for depth, I want to dig all the way down into the layers of stratification that reveal the colonial, imperial, and early nationalist encodings of a southern past that is embedded in the Native American signifier. I have arranged the chapters that follow according to a historical trajectory, outlined in the fictional texts examined here, beginning with the deepest layer of historical stratification anchored in the period of "discovery."

In chapter 2, I place Lytle's fictional histories of sixteenth-century European imperialism into the framework of postcolonial analysis. I examine in *Alchemy* (1942) and *At the Moon's Inn* (1941) the tropes of imperialism—particularly the controlling metaphors of alchemy in the novella of the same name and of cannibalism in *At the Moon's Inn*—as well as the ethnographic and anthropological discourses about native populations that Lytle attributes to the genre of the "discovery narrative." We will see that Lytle unexpectedly shares his critique of capitalist modernity that drives the colonialist enterprise with other modernist writers such as Joseph Conrad and with policy makers of the 1930s such as John Collier. Lytle, perhaps more than any of the other writers examined in this study, was interested in the moral dimensions of the global colonial imaginary: alchemy announces the desperate capitalist pursuit of gold, and cannibalism metaphorically characterizes the imperialist enterprises of Spain seeking to devour the New World. By uncovering a colonialist past embedded into the local geography of what was then "La Florida," Lytle launches his imperialist critique in which the Indians become a discursive venue for romantic, nativist, and regionalist identification as well as a springboard to topics of colonialism and global imperialism that connect the American South with the Incan empire and with the world.

In chapter 3, I examine how Caroline Gordon picks up the European colonial trace leading into the Kentucky frontier during the Revolutionary period. The imperialist struggles between and among European and Native American nations serve as a setting for her exploration of the social and legal mechanisms of race and gender differentiation. From her position as a white woman living in the segregated South of the 1930s, Gordon explores Native American "contact" in the framework of racial and sexual anxieties that she projects back into the colonial past. In both "The Captive" (1932) and *Green Centuries* (1941) she traces the origins of modern southern whiteness back into the beginnings of the nation, thus locating the production of whiteness and its relation to the maintenance of social power not in regional history but in national history. Excavating the gendered inscriptions in Gordon's textual landscape, I argue that her Indian frontier provides the place for an investigation of flawed notions of Anglo-American patriarchy in an unfavorable contrast to a more wholesome matrilinear Cherokee society. In Gordon's captivity narrative, white female sexuality functions as a locus for discourses about racial purity, blood, and genealogy. In *Green Centuries,* published a decade later, these biologically inspired discourses shift to a concern with "race" as a cultural and political construction. Through the figure of the (white male) American outlaw, Gordon examines those laws on which the American nation was based at its inception, and she traces the interpretation of "law" as it applies to women, blacks, and Indians to show how the cultural politics of the early national environment eventually resulted in a definition of citizenship as white and male. I explore this crucial discursive shift from "race" to "culture" by examining the Indian signifiers in Gordon's fiction and in her historical and ethnographic source materials. Gordon's shifting Indian signifier is linked to a larger scientific discourse that repudiates evolutionism and raciology under the growing influence of new anthropological concepts of "culture" that began to take shape in the United States in the 1930s, not incidentally at the same time that theories of "blood and soil," now of fascism, also began circulating again.

In chapter 4, I seek to uncover the shadowy outlines of an Indian presence in Eudora Welty's short-story collection *The Wide Net* (1941) and her novella *The Robber Bridegroom* (1942). Although Welty cautions us against reading her fiction historically, my analysis of the Indian signifiers buried in her texts reveals that her historical and political commentary is not less important or "present" than that of the other writers examined here, but that the presence history assumes in her writing is precisely over things that are left out. In Welty's short story "First Love," set in Natchez in 1807, Indians are subtly integrated into the story of Aaron Burr, a historical character who serves as a symbol of national expansionism, and a young deaf boy, who represents the nation's inability to listen to Native American interests and needs. In her novella *The Robber Bridegroom*, an imperial romance that merrily mixes myth, fairy tale, and history, Welty leads us back to the traumatic beginnings of the nation. In her version of colonial history, Indian violence puts a "mark" on white settlers in their succession from pioneer to planter to merchant. Linking the rise of the southern plantation economy with the discourse of Manifest Destiny, Welty's narrative mocks the national promise of free agency and the capitalist desires that serve as the driving force for westward expansion. Welty's playful celebration of historical pastiche sharply contrasts with Lytle's and Gordon's earnest desire to turn History into historical fiction, and her irreverent attitude toward "the violent Indians" contrasts with their elegiac mood.

In chapter 5, I return to William Faulkner's Indian country, Yoknapatawpha, a landscape dotted with ancient Indian mounds, testimony to a once-thriving culture that provides the historical sediment for his famous saga. It is also from Faulkner's reference to New Deal archaeology in *Go Down, Moses* (1942) that my study borrows one of its main metaphors for examining the Native American presence in modern southern literature. Faulkner's Indians, loosely based on the Chickasaws and Choctaws of Mississippi, first appear in the 1930s in his short stories of the "Wilderness" section of *Collected Stories*. These stories, I argue, do not participate in a mimetic rendering of cultural and ethnographic reality outside the text, but instead in the distortion and displacement of such realities. With respect to Native Americans, Faulkner's texts do not produce mimesis but mimicry; they hold up a skewed mirror to national history as it reflects Indian removal, plantation economy, and a fantasy of spiritual and cultural ancestry. Indians in Faulkner's texts become signifiers of cultural hybridity—slaveholding societies—who by the time of removal (which Faulkner re-creates in "Lo!") have become decadent colonial hybrids. Like Lytle, Faulkner uses the Indian signifier in some of his stories to critique the capitalist underpinnings of American civilization by recirculating the discourse of cannibalism (as in "Red Leaves"), but like Welty, Faulkner forsakes historical transparency for multi-layered irony as he rehearses discourses of Manifest Destiny.

Through the Postcolonial Lens

Excavating Native American presences in southern texts results in an intervention not only in existing literary and critical discourses but also in both canonical and theoretical work. Considered from the standpoint of literary history, my argument in *Disturbing Indians: The Archaeology of Southern Fiction* aligns the study of twentieth-century southern literature in a new and provocative way by reintroducing writers such as Lytle and Gordon, who have been much neglected, and by repositioning a "minor work" (*The Robber Bridegroom*) by an acclaimed writer. By exposing what has until now been the discipline's blind spot around the Native American presence and by shedding new light on this topic, this study reconfigures some of the political outlines of the movement known as the Southern Renaissance.

Considered from a theoretical angle, my project participates in a critical paradigm shift in American and southern studies. As scholars in American literature are beginning to break up monolithic constructions of region and nation, many understand their task as a form of border crossing, of forming new cross-disciplinary and transnational coalitions. Part of such a border crossing, I believe, is approaching the task from the "inside." I agree with John Carlos Rowe that new coalitions—such as between Native American and southern studies, for example—must be accompanied by a deconstruction of the internal social relations of geopolitical units such as region or nation (*New American* xv). My primary goal is to begin such a "deconstruction" of the narrowly constructed textual field of southern literature. By analyzing the function of the Native American signifier in the discipline's locally based texts for broader cultural and political meanings, my study reveals the southern writers' participation in discourses about colonialism, and it examines those national anxieties about imperialist expansion, past and present, that are gathered in the Native American signifier.

In the wake of poststructuralism and deconstruction, scholars of southern literature are currently debunking the grand narratives of southern identity that seek to locate particular cultural or geographical essences in the South.[9] They are questioning the binary frameworks that locked the South for decades into an oppositional relationship with the "North" and seek to "chart new connections with other Souths."[10] In contemporary efforts to reread, re-imagine, and to some extent decenter the American South, there is a marked trend "outward" across canonical boundaries toward the inclusion of previously omitted writers of various ethnic groups and genders and across national borders to Mexico, the Caribbean, Cuba, and Latin America, and other Souths globally.[11] But as we hurry across national borders—borders that are still very much politically patrolled and economically controlled—we might think for a moment about the extent to which these border crossings might not themselves represent colonizing moves by a U.S. academic elite. The problematics of location, privilege, and access pertaining to the postcolonial critic in the field of "New American" studies and his or her possible co-optation by globalization is not the only concern. What happens at "home" is an equally important question. Under postcolonial critical scrutiny the "home" often appears uncanny—"unheimlich," as Freud calls it—in the double sense of being simultaneously familiar and unfamiliar, comforting and alienating. Where the southern home is located and what it means to its different constituencies, including Native Americans, often equally destabilizes the material and emotional securities that "home" connotes. In the postcolonial analysis of the pre–World War II South offered in this book, I want to crack open traditional understandings of the "home place" by laying bare its colonial deep structure and by engaging the South in a dialectical perspective: looking both outward across regional and national borders and inward at borders drawn around racial and gendered identities and geographies, I want to see how southern texts intersect with national and global interests as well as with local politics and regional specificity. This shuttling move among the global, the national, and the local is centered in the analysis of the Native American signifiers that appear in the literature of the Southern Renaissance.

As scholars are beginning to investigate what it would mean to situate southern literature within theories of postcolonialism, as well as what repercussions such a theoretical shift might have for what we have called "southern literature" specifically and for cultural and historical constructions of "the South" more broadly, I want to emphasize the importance of "local knowledge" for such an investigation. The question of postcoloniality is increasingly examined with respect to the United States, although critics have warned particularly of the term's unnuanced use in the U.S. context and of the danger of using "postcolonial" as a catch-all term that erases historical differences and obliterates continued practices of colonial oppression.[12] But the United States, and the American South more specifically, can certainly be characterized not only as a specific form of postcolonial society but as participating in colonialist and postcolonialist discourses. When examining such discourses, it is essential, as Anne McClintock argues in "The Angel of Progress," to discriminate between the very different circumstances and struggles of colonial societies, and to avoid homogenizing the histories of very different nations under the concept "postcolonial." Among those nations, the United States appears to present a special case of postcoloniality as a territory that is simultaneously colonized and colonizing. Formerly colonized by European nations, the United States in turn not only colonized Native American populations in its interior but also became (and some would argue that it still is), by participating in the slave trade and assuming possession and control of other foreign dominions, an imperial force with a colonizing agenda abroad and at home. As Native American critic Jace Weaver reminds us, "American Natives are not *post*-colonial peoples. Instead, today they remain colonized, suffering from internal colonialism" (11). And by extension, the "current state of Native literature," as Craig Womack believes, is "at least partially a colonized one" (7). In sum, for many critics, especially Native American critics, the United States cannot be said to be properly postcolonial.

But there is also a way of reading U.S. history that would allow us to view the nation as postcolonial. Critics have made a convincing case that the United States went through its own version of the colonial/postcolonial transition (Barker, Hulme, and Iversen, *Colonial Discourse* 3). Linking the postcoloniality of the United States specifically to the American Revolution, Helen Carr suggests that "perhaps it is significant that in the United States the dominant group could only successfully incorporate a positive identification with the 'subaltern' Native American at the moment when in relation to Britain, they themselves were an emergent, subaltern group" (11). But, in another way the United States may be less exceptional in its history than earlier historians have believed. Critiquing "our national habit of seeing U.S. history as being so exceptional as to be unique" (xii), Richard Drinnon traces the mental patterns of colonialism and imperialism that the United States shares with its European neighbors, patterns that have remained more or less constant from the colonization of America to U.S. foreign politics in the Philippines, Indochina, and Vietnam in the mid-twentieth century and more recently in Iraq. Certainly, the postcolonial condition—both as a temporal marker as implied in Carr's definition and as a discursive cultural marker—finds its expression in American literature that inscribes, transforms, and reinscribes colonial and imperial discourses. This is not only the case in the texts of the colonialist period proper but every time interior and exterior colonial relations are addressed or alluded to in America's literary heritage.[13]

By shifting the discussion of postcolonialism to a southern locale, I follow Peter Hulme's invitation to pay more attention to "local knowledge" and treat the southern texts examined here with a great amount of historical and local specificity. In training a postcolonial lens onto the American South, I want to affirm local cultural differences that colonialist discourse characteristically tends to homogenize. By examining the ways in which southern writers engage in discourses of colonialism and imperialism through the Native American signifier in the years preceding World War II and in relation to a particular "place," I seek to work against a reduction of postcolonial discourse generally. Barker, Hulme, and Iversen highlight the importance of the local context for postcolonial work:

> In the postcolonial context, the arguments for giving due consideration to the local are firstly that the discourse of colonialism has always operated by making the local (colonized) place secondary to the metropolitan center, its history calibrated according to an external norm; and secondly that the stereotyping simplification of colonial discourse works by a similarly reductive dismissal of "local" distinctions: its theatre is populated by figures like "the Oriental," "the savage," and "the Indian," who have been divorced from particular times and places. Postcolonial work is, then, to a degree re-constitutive: to begin to understand local geographies and histories and to allow them to count in a way previously denied, are crucial counter-hegemonic moves. (*Colonial Discourse* 10)

This study examines the realm of "local knowledge" and focuses on the racial, cultural, and gendered construction of the Indian in the texts under scrutiny, and to a lesser degree on the reconstitution of the specific identities and local cultures behind this figure. In the following chapters I investigate how local, national, and global discourses about Indians are woven into these southern texts and what the ideological positions toward Native Americans are that emerge from them.

Exploring "local geographies" in the context of the American South is both familiar and unfamiliar work. It is familiar in the sense that the South has always tried to imagine itself as a unique place, a region different from a hegemonic national culture, and it has insisted and capitalized on its "local" difference. This was particularly so during the Southern Renaissance, when the separatist manifesto *I'll Take My Stand* was issued and the "Mind of the South" was up for examination. In the South this sense of place has been linked to a literary tradition of regionalism that imagines "place" as intricately bound up with history, memory, and identity. In her well-known essay "Place in Fiction," Eudora Welty addresses the fear of losing this distinct imprint of place on local knowledge and identity: "It is not only too easy to conceive that a bomb that could destroy all traces of places as we know them, in life and through books, could also destroy all feelings as we know them, or irretrievably and so happily are recognition, memory, history, valor, love, all instincts of poetry and praise, worship and endeavor, bound up in place" (qtd. in Erdrich 47). Anishinaabe writer Louise Erdrich reminds us that Welty's speculation about the loss of place is a grim reality for almost all Native Americans who experienced the trauma of removal, migration, and resettlement: "to American Indians it is as if the unthinkable has already happened, and relatively recently" (48). Place, Erdrich says, is equally important to Native American writers, who, like southern writers, need "a place to love and be irritated with" (49). But place is nothing apart from its people. Welty and Erdrich agree that the stories and chronicles of the population—their migrations, displacements, and cultural residues—are deeply embedded in a place and that this is what gives "place" supreme significance.

How place is constructed is a question not only for writers and scholars of literature but also for archaeologists of landscape, who are increasingly speaking of "lived space" as opposed to "geometric space." "A place is not a thing or an entity," writes archaeologist Julian Thomas. "Place is a relational concept, since locations are always drawn to our attention through what happens there or through the things we expect to find there. . . . A place is always the place *of* something" (173). When place is as complex and ideologically charged as the "South," the layers of cultural stratification concerning Native Americans are often buried under the symbolic weight of the meaning of the region. Therefore I want to activate a postcolonial concept of place as a palimpsest, a space that bears the traces of previous cultural inscriptions that have been "overwritten" and rewritten.[14] Working against the idea of the tabula rasa, the empty space, a postcolonial reading of the southern landscape allows us to see the complex textuality of its cultural traces and renders visible the histories of marginalized and colonized peoples. By combining a form of local postcolonial inquiry that centers on the political and cultural colonization of Native Americans in the South with a method of textual archaeology, I hope to produce a critical perspective that can substantially change the way we read the literature of the American South.

Last, I should address what this book is and what it is not. Overall, this book is an exercise in the joys of textual archaeology, that is, practical literary criticism. As such it seeks to stimulate and redefine literary interpretation of these texts, some of which, though somewhat obscure, have considerable pedagogical and aesthetic value. I want to locate these texts historically and culturally and see what each contributes to the public debates that are constructed around the native figure as a key to regional and national identity. In the histories the authors dig up and in the Native American signifier they present, I want to study both the authors' individual articulations and the collective cultural expressions of the contemporary moment. By digging up the disappeared presences of Native Americans in the literature of the depression South and by asking how critics have managed to perpetuate this blind spot, my study seeks to make a new contribution to American and southern studies. As such this book is a "case study" marking a departure from the familiar precepts of southern literature and criticism. It is not, however, a full-scale reading of the Native American presence in southern letters from the beginning on. It is also not a study of Native American writers' contributions to southern literature. A next step might be to examine the Native American contribution to southern literature, not with the intention of "colonizing" the field of Native American studies,[15] but to see how productive such an interchange might be for both disciplines.

2

Colonialism and Cannibalism

Andrew Lytle's Conquest Narratives

> Appeals to the past are among the commonest of strategies in interpretations of the present. What animates such appeals is not only disagreement about what happened in the past and what the past was, but uncertainty whether the past is really past, over and concluded, or whether it continues, albeit in different forms, perhaps.
>
> —Edward Said, *Culture and Imperialism*

The history of first contact between Native Americans and European explorers was an event of public interest in 1939 when the four hundredth anniversary of Hernando de Soto's march through the American Southeast was celebrated. Confronted with national celebrations of the "discovery" of the American South, Andrew Lytle and his contemporaries must have thought about the politics of such commemorative events: Are de Soto's exploratory forays to be celebrated or condemned? Should the work of "discovery" be defended or criticized? While the United States may have been in a celebratory mood as the government was marking this historical milestone, Lytle was certainly aware of major flaws in national narratives of "discovery" that thinly mask the long and brutal conquests of native peoples of the New World. Reexamining the great history of exploration, Lytle produced two works about the Spanish conquest of the New World that both criticize *and* perpetuate colonial paradigms. In 1941 he published his historical novel *At the Moon's Inn,* which is about de Soto's conquest of "La Florida," and in 1942 he published *Alchemy,* a novella about Francisco Pizarro's conquest of the Incan empire. Opening upon a colonial "contact zone," these two narratives interrogate the systems of belief and the epistemological assumptions with which Native Americans and Renaissance Spaniards encountered each other: What did each group know, and what did they believe in?

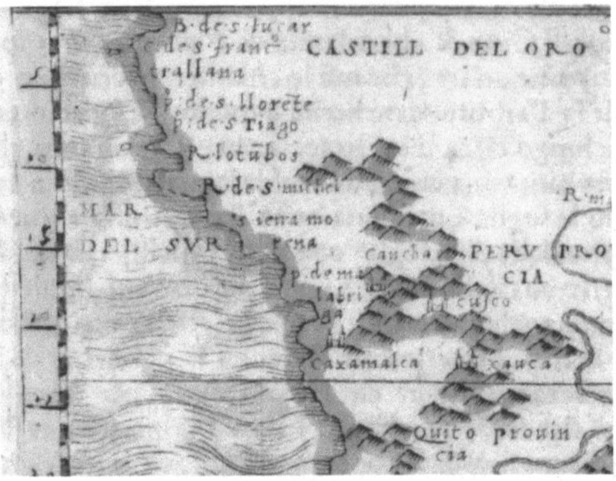

Map 2. Detail of Giacomo Gastaldi's map "Tierra Nova" of 1548, showing the cities of Caxamalca and Cusco in Peru. Courtesy of Rucker Agee Map Collection, Birmingham Public Library.

What made Spanish conquest possible? And what is the meaning of such conquest in the sixteenth and the twentieth century? Both *Alchemy* and *At the Moon's Inn* attempt to answer these questions by illuminating the political and moral meanings of conquest. For Lytle, the history of Western expansion in the sixteenth century is not primarily about the battle for political inscriptions of geographical space; it is about the rise of capitalism and individualism and the economic and religious ideologies that underpin and seek to justify the modern history of colonialism. Viewed in this light, Lytle's work is part of a larger discourse of colonialism; these texts are squarely situated at the heart of what Peter Hulme calls "the classic colonial triangle" spanning the relationships among colonizer, native, and the land. As such, Lytle's texts excavate and re-create colonial discourses from the Enlightenment period that reflect on Native Americans and the significance of the New World to European empires.

Lytle's interest in the history of Western imperialism was prompted by the nation's excitement around the historical anniversary and the archaeological excavations in the Southeast that supported it. In 1935, President Franklin D. Roosevelt had appointed a federal commission to study the de Soto expedition and to report to Congress its recommendations for a suitable commemoration of the event. The report was published in 1939 under the leadership of archaeologist John Swanton as *The Final Report of the United States de Soto Expedition Commission.*[1] Swanton and his team pieced together documentary, historical, and archaeological evidence in an attempt to mark the historic discovery route.[2] The recovery of historical and material residue dating back to the early sixteenth century brought forth new information on Native Americans of the Southeast that was collected and interpreted with great interest by scholars of archaeology, anthropology, and history.[3] The archaeological work of the de Soto commission also evoked the curiosity of southern writers and motivated their own textual digs into the narratives of the exploration period. Swanton's contributions to scholarship on Native Americans of the Southeast did not escape Lytle's notice. By the time the *Final Report* appeared, Lytle's own work on de Soto was well under way, as his letters show.[4] Reporting excitedly about his research, Lytle told his friend Allen Tate in 1938 that he had the unique opportunity to learn about the expedition from "an old gentleman who has studied de Soto for twenty-five years in close communication with Swanton of the Smithsonian" and who had access to "old maps, original editions, and special translations of authorities" (Young and Sarcone 119). The national work of "discovery" yielded new archaeological and historical information crucial to Lytle's own research on the early social history of the American South. Lytle's research on de Soto's exploration of the South had intellectual ramifications, however, much beyond his own region. From Lytle's contemporary moment, defined by brewing international conflicts leading to World War II, a clear global connection emerges among discourses of nationalism, ethnography, and Western imperial expansion.

Despite Lytle's obvious interest in these topics, it is not really surprising that his conquest narratives have not yet been rediscovered as part of a postcolonial discourse. His relative canonical obscurity, his contribution to the well-known southern manifesto *I'll Take My Stand* (1930), his biography on Nathan Bedford Forrest and other texts purporting to investigate a particularly "southern" culture, and the critical construction of him as a "southern writer" interested in regional topics have so far prevented our recognition that Lytle is a sharp critic of the capitalist underpinnings of empire. Elizabeth Sarcone agrees that critical understanding of his work has been "misled by Lytle's contribution to Agrarianism, distracted by his use of the South, and confused by inadequate understanding of his terms" (162). Sarcone is right. Lytle is overdue for a critical reassessment that broadens the frame of inquiry. Responding to the critical failure to see the postcolonial dimensions of Lytle's work, I argue in this chapter that Lytle is a participant in a postcolonial discourse that reaches well beyond regional boundaries.

Lytle's dissatisfaction with the evils of materialism and industrialism is well known. As a southern intellectual who "took his stand" against industrialized capitalism in 1930, Lytle deplored the "triumph of industry" and believed that "since 1865 an agrarian Union has been changed into an industrial empire bent on the conquest of the earth's goods and ports to sell them in. This means warfare, a struggle over markets, leading in the end, to actual military conflicts between nations" (*I'll Take My Stand* 202). As this prophecy came true in December 1942, Lytle was recasting his earlier ideas about the threat of technology to human life in both his novella about the Incas and in his novel about de Soto.

When the atomic bomb destroyed Hiroshima in 1945, Lytle's 1930s jeremiad rang quite true: "since a power machine is ultimately dependent upon human control, the issue presents an awful spectacle: men, run mad by their inventions, supplanting themselves with inanimate objects. This is, to follow the matter to its conclusion, a moral and spiritual suicide, foretelling an actual physical destruction" (202–3). The escape from the dilemma of technology, Lytle says, is not in socialism or communism—"these change merely the manner and speed of the suicide; they do not alter its nature"—but in a return to an agrarian society (203).

Because Lytle used agrarian terminology, his critics have concluded that his concern with materialism and spiritual self-destruction was "an outgrowth of the author's southern sensibility" (Lucas 85). In the slender critical response to Lytle's historical novels, the larger colonial context and the global political framework are typically displaced in favor of a reading of the agrarian paradigm. Lytle is so thoroughly mediated as an orthodox white conservative southern writer that other reading strategies seem near impossible. He is so anchored within a traditional understanding of a regional culture—and within it the conservative agrarian camp—that even recent efforts at reviving these texts have failed to wrest them free from the ideologies that typically define and confine them. In his recent rereading of Lytle in *Southern Aberrations*, Richard Gray focuses on Lytle's celebration of the rural community in which the farmer is the "true keeper of the agrarian faith" (135). This thesis easily extends to Lytle's conquest narratives, in which he rehearses "a contrast familiar to any reader of fiction from the South: between the capitalist and the agrarian" (135). In these narratives, the capitalists are the Spanish conquistadores and the agrarians are the Native Americans who "become the first agrarian victims of the forces of progress and capital" (137). The agrarian theme is a continuous concern for Lytle and certainly one that operates in his conquest narratives. However, I believe that the critical tendency to highlight the regional concerns of Lytle's work results in a reading that superimposes the southern history of agrarianism onto the global history of colonialism in an act that displaces the latter. In such a reading, Native Americans emerge as figures of agrarian identification and are significant only as placeholders in a familiar paradigm of agrarianism and political conservatism. "What is particularly remarkable about Lytle's portrait of Native American culture in this novel," writes Gray about *At the Moon's Inn*, "is the way it reveals, again, the profoundly conservative nature of his thinking" (137). Lytle's conservatism, however, masks another story: his didactic critique of the nationalist project of "discovery" highlights the capitalist agenda of colonial exploitation and the resulting anxiety about the moral imperatives of imperialism more generally.

Lytle achieves this critique of empire through the Native American signifier in *Alchemy* and *At the Moon's Inn*. The pre-industrial Indian figure—though anchored in Lytle's regional agenda, as critics have pointed out—is discursively part of the national movement of anti-industrial modernism and an increasingly widespread global anti-imperial attitude. Native Americans are double-edged signifiers in Lytle's texts: they provide at once a strategy for regionalist identification and global imperial critique. But ultimately Lytle's conquest narratives are caught between two incompatible interests: on the one hand, his critique of colonial exploitation and imperialist greed; on the other, his own blind spot around the oppressive practices of racial exploitation. These conflicting interests open a field of textual and political tension. How, we may ask, can Lytle possibly critique Western imperialism without criticizing at the same time slavery, Jim Crow laws, Indian removals, and other forms of social and political oppression? What blocks his vision? I propose that his attempts at criticizing Native American oppression are weakened by a modernist ethnographic nostalgia that he shared with many other writers of the period, including John Collier, the commissioner of the Bureau of Indian Affairs. These modernist ethnographic discourses, which include in Lytle's texts echoes of Manifest Destiny and orientalism, interfere with his critique of colonialist paradigms; in fact, they threaten to perpetuate them. The flawed success of Lytle's critique of empire is reminiscent of Joseph Conrad, with whom Lytle shares a strong critique of the capitalist motivation of Western imperialism and an indictment of the Christian colonizers' moral bankruptcy, but also a racist blindness to the "natives" in his narratives. In the end, Lytle's focus on the politics *of* colonial exploitation prevents a more politically effective argument *against* exploitation.

Native Americans and Modernist Nostalgia: Andrew Lytle and John Collier

Lytle's political vision functions not only in a southern paradigm. Put into a larger modernist trajectory, his texts cease to be "regional aberrations" and begin to be participants in national and international discourses. Lytle's anti-materialist critique was shared not only by fellow conservative agrarians but by many left-leaning intellectuals such as John Collier and other writers from different regions and professions who were equally disillusioned with capitalism and industrialism. They, too, were searching for alternative political models and recognized in the apparently more "simple" lifestyle of Indians an alternative to the neuroses of civilization. As a young man, Collier left the South to study literature and biology at Columbia University, where he attended lectures of the Socialist League and became attracted to ideas of a classless society. Later he worked in New York City with immigrants at the People's Institute in order to stem the powerful wave of Americanization by helping to persuade immigrants to "keep their national dress, their customs, and their diets, their religion, and all their folk ways" (Philip 17). Unlike Lytle, Collier moved in a social circle that included many radical leftist intellectuals of the time, such as "Max Eastman and John Reed, the editors of the *New Masses;* Walter Lippmann, a well-known socialist critic from Harvard" and the dancer Isadora Duncan (Philip 17). And yet, despite their different political backgrounds, the left-leaning Collier and the right-wing Lytle share some important social concerns. Both deplore the "sickness" of post–World War I American culture, and both see in Native American culture a viable alternative to industrial life. In Collier's critique of American culture as driven by its "externalism and receptive sensualism, its hostility to human diversity, its fanatical devotion to down-grading standardization, its exploitative myopia, and that world fascism and home fascism which the boundless, all haunting insecurity and the consequent lust for personal advantage were bringing to fatal power" we can hear echoes of Lytle's own sense of what is wrong with America (*Indians* 18). Collier shares with Lytle not only a sense of national anxiety and world crisis but also the deep belief that lingering nineteenth-century industrialist assumptions about "the nature of economic and political man" are harmful if not destructive for life in the twentieth century. Collier argues that the Industrial Revolution created the idea that wealth is a means to power and that in its wake have come "the uprooting of populations, the disintegration of neighborhoods, the end of home and handcrafts, the supremacy of the machine over man, the immense impoverishment of the age-old relationships between generations, the increased mobility of the individual, the enormous expansion of commercialized recreation, the quest by mass-circulating newspapers, the movies and radio for the lowest common denominators. All this confused, degraded and sometimes destroyed the societies utterly" (25). If this list sounds like the agrarians' complaint of the ills of modern civilization, it is because it is based on a similar need for a stability of social traditions and the impulse to return to a seemingly more simple pre-industrial lifestyle. In his contribution to *I'll Take My Stand,* written seventeen years earlier, Lytle anticipates Collier's critique when he urges his readers to return to "our looms, our handcrafts, our reproducing stock. Throw out the radio and take down the fiddle from the wall. Forsake the movies for play-parties and square dances" ("Hind Tit" 244).

Lytle and Collier, although from opposing political perspectives, share a vibrant critique of modern materialism; they turn away from industrial "progress" and proclaim their strong preference for societies rooted in tradition and ritual. And both writers find such societies among the American Indians. Lytle and Collier perceive in Indian societies an organic inwardness, power, and resourcefulness that modern American society lacks. Collier argues that native societies had preserved a deep spirituality expressed in an essential reverence for the earth: "They had what the world has lost. They have it now" (*Indians* 15). Lytle similarly idealizes the spiritual essence of the Indians, which he describes as "spirit indwelling, not transubstantial" (*A Wake* 53), and he, too, thinks that something important and powerful was lost when Indian civilizations were forced to assimilate or die. Both writers invoke a nostalgic vision of a spiritual society not dominated by capitalism and industry, and in doing that they are part of a larger American ethnographic, artistic, and political trend that viewed Indian cultures as remedies for what ailed the modern world.

Beginning in the 1920s, many Anglo-American writers and intellectuals romanticized the beauty and spirituality they perceived in Indian lives. This value system "appealed to them precisely because of its apparent divergence from Anglo-American emphases on possessive individualism, conformity, rationality, scientific determinism, materialism, and corruption" (S. L. Smith 9). Celebrations of Native American culture as more wholesome, spiritual, and communal than Anglo-American industrial life were mostly inspired by "a nostalgia for a real or imagined past" (9). Lytle and Collier, too, were in the grip of such a nostalgia when they turned to Indian life as an expression of their discontent with commercially driven life in the United States.[5] Both participate in a celebration of the spirituality, community, and "ancient wisdom" of Indian societies, and in doing so, both construct an "imagined past." There is, however, an essential difference. One of the most important premises of Collier's Indian New Deal legislation was the recognition that Indian societies continue to exist in the present, that despite a long history of conquest, extermination, and assimilation, they had not "vanished." "As we traverse Indian history from the Conquest down to their present-day strivings," Collier writes, we see that "through all the slaughter of American Indian biological stocks, the slaughter of their societies and trampling upon their values, strange as it may seem, they have kept the faith. The inner core-value, complex and various, had not been killed" (*Indians* 22).

Whereas Collier celebrates the continued survival of native core values despite all odds, Lytle deplores the gradual loss of those values. Unlike Collier, Lytle freezes Native American life in the past. For Lytle, the Indians once had an authenticity and a power that they lost to the conquering cultures. In his memoir, *A Wake for the Living*, Lytle imagines Native America prior to European conquest as a largely ceremonial society, where war, like other events in life, was part of a social ritual that kept the cosmic balance (42). In the histories and travelogues of James Adair and William Byrd, Lytle found information on ceremonial aspects of Indian life in the southeastern United States, including planting and harvesting rituals, the rites of purity, the rules of war, and the role of spirituality. Here he also found origin stories that told of a rich and thriving native culture, a deep spirituality, and a cosmological order full of mystery and beauty. When, during the settlement period, Lytle's own ancestors first came to live on Cherokee land, "the Cherokee," he writes, were a "formidable" society marked by a social order and supported by a mythological and spiritual world that still functioned (42). Lytle emphasizes the importance of cultural wholeness and spiritual heritage by showing that the clan structure was still intact and by naming the seven traditional Cherokee clans: "These tribes were the Ani-waya, or Wolf People. The wolves were never hunted, being the hounds of the Spirit hunter. . . . The Ani-wadi, Paint People; Ani-gilahi, Long Hair People; Ani-sahini, Blue People; and finally the Ani-gatu-ge-u-e, the Kituwah, or Beloved Town People, for the Kituwah was the first Cherokee settlement near the Smokies. This was the oldest name for the tribe. Later . . . they called themselves the Real People" (49).

Lytle adds that there was one more tribe: the Ani-tsaguhi, who lived in the woods like animals and became the Yanu, or bears. "Even as bears they did not forget what they had been nor the sorrows of tribal life. Out of compassion they taught the Cherokee two songs to sing when they were hungry: Hearing the music, the Yanu would come forward and offer his body, his hide for cover, and his sweet fat reduced to oil to make the squaws and young men shine at the dances" (*A Wake* 49). Lytle includes these origin stories as examples of a deeply spiritual native culture that gave a sense of order and identity to the Cherokee world prior to European conquest and colonization. When the Europeans happened upon the southeastern Indians, they found, in Lytle's words, "a Stone Age people in full bloom, hunters all, nothing pastoral, although certain tribes were fairly extensive farmers. They were good fishermen, both in salt and tame water, as early accounts and shell mounds show" (44).

Lytle's celebration of traditional Cherokee culture is not so much surprising as it is strategic. It is part of a historical narrative that seeks to demonstrate that with increasing contact native cultures were disrupted, transformed, and destroyed. Lytle cites Cherokee oratory as an example of what he calls "the decline" of a native culture by its slow adoption of the language of the colonizer. The rhetorical appeal of Cherokee chief Old Tassel is "the speech of a defeated people. It is cast, even, in the language less that of the old beloved tongue than that of the enemy" (*A Wake* 52).[6] By the time of removal, writes Lytle, the Cherokees "had almost entirely taken on our 'civilized ways,' living in houses, owning slaves, and operating farms and plantations, learning our speech and writing their own, which Sequoya had made possible by composing a Cherokee alphabet" (52). This forced adoption of "civilized ways," in conjunction with centuries of European warfare and a capitalistic surplus trade system foreign to traditional Cherokee economy, constituted their ultimate "defeat" and led to the loss of spirituality—in fact, to a downright "religious failure." Lytle explains that "the respect the Indian had for the animal clans, killing only for food and clothing and doing this with a ritual respecting all life, mitigated the brutal facts of living, antagonistic and cannibalistic" (53). When the traditional spiritual vision of the Cherokees, which "did not conceive of the spirit as apart from the object" (53), gave way to an admiration for the "magic" of the Europeans, their spiritual and physical decline began. For Lytle, this "decline" not only signifies a human tragedy for native populations in the colonial "contact zone" but also stands as a warning for the colonizing cultures: "One wonders, is magic indigenous to the world we took from the Indians? Is our economy of profane possession more proficient in its technology? Will our magical belief in matter as the only value not bring us to a disaster as final as the Indians received?" (53). Whether the Incas of *Alchemy*, the ancient southeastern chiefdoms of *At the Moon's Inn*, or the Cherokees of his memoir, Indians in Lytle's historical paradigm are part of a pattern of cultural conquest and "decline" that serves as a warning to the forces of industrial materialism currently in power. In each case, the Native American signifier is ideologically coded to signal a nostalgic wish for a more wholesome, pre-capitalist lifestyle and a need for communal and agricultural values.

Lytle's perspective essentially looks backward to a moment of native cultural authenticity that has long passed, whereas for John Collier that native authenticity, while endangered, is still alive and was never entirely conquered. Ultimately, the writers' messages are very different: for Lytle, European conquest, whether of the Incas or the southeastern chiefdoms, provides a warning to those in power now as it tells a story of cultural "succession" and defeat; for Collier, Native American culture provides a positive example of vibrant cultural survival and continuity that European conquest could not squash. In Collier's understanding, Native American culture is not a pre-stage to industrialization but an alternative that should be acknowledged and protected. This difference in point of view might be the result of many factors, not the least of which is that Lytle lived and worked most of his life in the southeastern United States, from which Native Americans had been largely removed by 1850 and Anglo-Americans—his own family included—literally took the place and the land that they were forced to vacate. Collier, on the other hand, was most inspired by the Pueblo cultures of the Southwest, which had not been driven from their native land and which evidenced a high degree of cultural independence compared with the relative loss of cultural integrity of the southeastern Indians. Lytle's focus on the Cherokees might be a case in point: after their removal to Oklahoma, many of the so-called Civilized Tribes yielded to the pressures of assimilation; they accepted individual land allotments and largely gave up tribal self-government. Not surprisingly, it was from American Indians who were most assimilated, such as the Cherokees, that Collier's 1934 Indian Reorganization Act met with the greatest opposition. According to Philip, "They objected to relinquishing individual allotments for community ownership and feared that the creation of self-governing communities would restore outdated traditions" (138). Even though Lytle's access to native culture was primarily through ethnographies and history books and Collier's work as commissioner of Indian Affairs brought him in constant contact with living native culture and politics, this alone is not the reason for their differences in perspective. Lytle's vision of "cultural defeat" was inspired by the Cherokees, who were seen as part of the more assimilated southeastern Indians, whereas Collier's celebration of "cultural survival" was prompted by the southwestern tribes, who were believed to have kept more of their ancient traditions alive.

Despite these differences, however, it is clear that Lytle's ethnographic vision was, like Collier's, part of a larger anti-industrial modernist discourse that they shared with many other American intellectuals. The soil-oriented philosophy of the agrarians is not separate from but part of American celebrations of primitivism in art and culture, and it coincides with a critique of modern economic self-interest that was not only rooted in the South. Of course, Lytle did write the history of western expansion from a southern locale, but he did not only do it, as Lucas claims, "in a passionate defense of his region's demonstratable difference from the aggressive nation as a whole" (88). On the contrary, by setting his colonial histories in the South, Lytle represents the South not as exempt from or opposed to the violence of capitalism and colonialism but rather as part of it. From the beginning, the landscape that became imagined as "the South" was marked by an aggressive materialism that cannot be blamed on the North, the nation, or a remote international community. In *Alchemy* and *At the Moon's Inn*, "the South" emerges as part of rather than an exception to larger, global patterns of colonial conquest.

Lytle's fictional representations of the destructive power of a capitalist-driven imperialism in his conquest narratives present a grim picture of modern society's "heart of darkness." It is largely because of this didactic impulse that Lytle focuses on the violent encounters between premodern Indian societies and industrialized modernity in the sixteenth century. And it is partially because of this overriding didactic design that he gathers all Indians—whether Incas, southeastern chiefdoms, or modern Cherokees—into a totalizing picture: all Indians in Lytle's fiction are part of the continuous history of Western imperialism. Essentially, Lytle's totalizing view of Native Americans is tied to an evolutionary narrative—a narrative of cultural development and decline that anthropologists like Franz Boas were increasingly beginning to challenge.[7] Although Lytle distinguishes to some extent between different circumstances and struggles of different native peoples and makes an effort at including correct ethnographic and historical information, his goal remains the same: an illustration and prophetic warning that civilizations "fall." For Lytle, the Enlightenment period—the beginning of secular history in the sixteenth century—marks the crucial beginning of such a "fall." The execution of Sir Thomas More, writes Lytle, "marks the second fall of man, the fall into history." Lytle explains the shift into secular modernity as the gradual substitution of theology with history when "the world came to be looked upon not as grounds for the drama of the soul, but as the end in itself" (*Hero* 28). With the Christian vision dimming, historical vision took shape around the time of the Spanish conquests of the Americas. The violent Spanish encounter with native people provides a vehicle for Lytle to address the dark side of "Western progress" in narratives marked by a palpable anxiety about the dangers of imperialism and nationalism, past and present.

In these conquest narratives, Lytle's own contemporary moment is only slightly masked by the more remote time period that his narratives purport to address. In both *Alchemy* and *At the Moon's Inn,* the New World emerges as a projection and as an extension of the imperial heritage of the Old World. From Lytle's own vantage point in the early 1940s, America's own imperial desires, techniques of colonization, and emphasis on commerce and technology must have come into view as an outgrowth of European Enlightenment thought and those original motives that got the Spanish and other colonizing powers under way to begin with. John Carlos Rowe believes that "it is fair to conclude that U.S. imperialism extends the established practices of European exploration, conquest, and colonization against which the United States struggled in its own anti-colonial revolution" (*Literary Culture* 11). But if Lytle alludes to U.S. imperialism, he does so only obliquely by admitting to a continuous history of capitalist imperialism that moves from Europe to America, where it is embraced. Covering up this anxiety by reinscribing it in a different historical moment, Lytle's narratives safely foreground events in the history of European imperialism, removed in time and space from mounting anxieties about an expanding German Reich and America's entry into World War II. Such a temporal removal of Western imperialism that faces outward toward a global colonial situation in the past also ensures that the history of the present internal colonization of Native Americans and African Americans does not come into view except as an oblique narrative undercurrent. Although Lytle acknowledges the continuum of Western imperial exploitation, he gets caught up in a Eurocentric perspective that has dramatic limitations as it keeps writing History from the seat of Empire and from the perspective of troubled but powerful first-world nations.

The Conquest of the Incas: The Alchemy of Colonization

In *Alchemy*, Lytle fictionalizes the historical account of Francisco Pizarro's famous 1532 conquest over the Incan empire. Turning to Latin American history, he sketches the outlines of a political geography that had been settled and "civilized" for many centuries by highly sophisticated Mayan, Aztecan, and Incan cultures at the time of European invasion. Upon the arrival of the Spanish, the Americas were no "virgin land" but rather nations with long histories prior to European conquest and colonization.[8] Like many of its historical sources, Lytle's novella reconstructs the dramatic encounter between Pizarro, the Spanish conqueror, and Atahuallpa, the Incan emperor.[9] Narrated from the perspective of an eyewitness and participant in the Spanish conquest, Lytle's narrative follows Pizarro's men in their search for gold all the way from their coastal landing into the mountainous interior of the Incan empire. Each geographical move brings new challenges to the Spanish exploring group, but it also brings them closer to their goal of sacking Incan gold. The story's suspense arises from the dangers of the foreign terrain and the apparent unpredictability of the Incan emperor. The further the emperor lets the conquering party advance, the more they fear that they are being trapped by "the Indian's cunning," and the more the reader wonders why the Spanish are allowed to advance into the inner sanctum of Incan society. Was it Incan ignorance of the Europeans and their technology? Was it military misjudgment, human error, complacency, or pride? Was it foolish trust in words promising friendship, or acceptance of "fate"? What could have led to the conquest of the powerful Incan empire by a mere 168 Spaniards?

What is most startling about the Spanish conquest of the Incan empire is also what drew Lytle into its fictional re-creation: in manpower the Incas outweighed the Spanish several thousand times, but the invaders were nevertheless able to win the battle. Jared Diamond attributes the Spanish conquest to technological imbalances between Europeans and Native Americans: "Pizarro's military advantages lay in the Spaniards' steel swords and other weapons, steel armor, guns, and horses. To those weapons, Atahuallpa's troops, without animals on which to ride into battle, could oppose only stone, bronze, or wooden clubs, maces, and hand axes, plus slingshots and quilted armor" (74). The Spaniards, Diamond argues, gained a tremendous advantage from their use of steel weapons and guns against native populations lacking steel, guns, and horses. While not solely responsible for the ability of early modern industrialized societies to conquer agricultural societies like the Incas, superior weapons and war technology certainly assured good odds even against thousands of well-trained native foot soldiers. For Lytle, this imbalance in technology, which resulted in the bloody slaughter of ancient Indian civilizations, is characteristic of the continued threat posed by technological societies. His vivid exposure of such technologically driven conquest may be seen as part of his regionalist political agenda, but I would argue that it also expresses his global international concerns.

Reflecting on his own historical moment—a time when World War II began to involve the United States, fascism reigned in Europe, and familiar political world orders were once again reshuffled—Lytle, in his correspondence with Allen Tate, reveals how disturbed he is by the possibility of a German victory. He wrote on May 27, 1940, that "even if in the intoxication of victory Hitler does not try to establish a military hegemony of the world . . . it's going to be like Rome with all of the loot of the world passing into Berlin, and you will find the loot come very quickly and thoroughly" (Young and Sarcone 156). Lytle was worried about the kind of society that would support a military hegemony based on its technology and superior means of warfare. "It always worried me how an agrarian society could be maintained in the face of the necessity for a mechanized army and navy. You can have a Republic when the smooth bore rifle is an effective weapon. But when you've got tanks and antiaircraft and machine guns, you will bring about the kind of organization to maintain such an army. Nationalism has played Judas to Christendom" (156). In Lytle's view, nationalism splinters the human community, "the brotherhood of man," into different political entities that supersede larger communal values. In his conclusion to the letter, Lytle establishes a clear connection between twentieth-century nationalism and sixteenth-century imperialism. Showing the confluence of past and present, he promises: "I'm going to stop thinking about this thing [Hitler's nationalism] until events become more urgent. After all the damage was done in the 16th century, and I'd better try to return to that" (156). Lytle's present historical moment certainly gave pause to contemplate the large-scale national conflicts and the often violent ways in which societies "succeed" one another on a global scale. It also gave rise to a suspicion of the rhetoric of empire and the economic self-interest that accompanies it, and that is what concerned Lytle in both of his conquest narratives.

But there are other reasons for Lytle's interest in the Incas, including the agricultural basis of their society, the social fabric of their communities, and their high standard of "civilization" that "fell" to the power of capitalist imperialism. Read as a regional allegory of the agrarian South and its "fall" to the industrial North, Lytle's motivation in *Alchemy* appears similar to his intention in *The Velvet Horn* (1957), a novel he characterized as "a long piece of fiction on a society that was dead" (*Hero* 178). Although Lytle refers to the pre–Civil War southern society of *The Velvet Horn* here, the same spirit of eulogy for an older and seemingly more civilized culture also operates in *Alchemy*. His desire to "resuscitate a dead society" applies equally to both works (*Hero* 181). His choice of present-day Peru, a land "south of South," provides a certain discursive analogy to the U.S. South, at least in terms of a rhetoric that celebrates its once glorious but vanquished culture. In such a reading, which foregrounds Lytle's regionalist politics, writing about Peru is not a flight from the South, as it may seem at first, but precisely a way of writing (about) the South.

Alchemy performs well as an agrarian text with a regionalist political agenda as Lytle is voicing anxieties about industrial modernity that he shared with many fellow southern writers. But the novella also intersects with a number of national and international discourses. *Alchemy*, for example, shares the neoromantic mood of many historians and archaeologists working on Mexico and Central America during this time, who produced histories of primitive societies that were eulogized for their supposed innocence and simplicity.[10] The interesting political and rhetorical construction of Incan society during the 1930s and 1940s might begin to explain why Lytle centers on the conquest of the Incas and not that of the Aztecs or Maya, for example. Why write about Pizarro's conquest rather than Hernán Cortés's similarly spectacular exploits among the Aztecs? The answer lies in the very curious contemporary ethnographic construction of the Incas as an agricultural "socialist" society. In the Western imagination, writes Benjamin Keen, Incan society has always been more favorably regarded than Aztecan society, because the Incas were a highly successful communal empire that did not practice ritual human sacrifice. The rarity of this gruesome practice makes the Incas by comparison more "civilized" and better known for "promoting peace, good order, and the prosperity of their subjects" (155). In addition, the Incan empire is often described as a communal, socialist, and agrarian society in the historical sources that were available to Lytle.[11] For example, A. Hyatt Verrill points out in *Great Conquerors of South and Central America* (1929) that "the empire was socialistic, practicing the most complete and successful socialism the world has ever known" (229). This "socialism," which led to Incan social order and wealth, was based on an agricultural economy. William H. Prescott's 1847 classic *History of the Conquest of Peru*, with which Lytle was familiar, also pays tribute to the Incan "spirit of economical husbandry." "Without the use of tools or the machinery familiar to the European," Prescott writes, "each individual could have done little; but acting in large masses, and under a common direction, they were enabled by indefatigable perseverance to achieve results, to have attempted that which might have filled even the European with dismay" (134).

This discourse of socialism and agrarianism in contemporary characterizations of the Incan social order remained a persistent part of historical and ethnographic descriptions. Even John Collier, writing in the 1940s, does not remain unaffected by such peculiar ethnographic constructions of the Incas. Turning his eyes south to Latin America in *The Indians of the Americas* (1947), Collier concurs on the significance of their agricultural achievements, which are "their living, increasing meaning to the world" (72). The political rhetoric that characterized the Incan state as "socialist" took shape from the mid-nineteenth century on and continued well into the 1920s and beyond. Keen explains that European historians of the 1920s, responding to the threat posed by the Russian Revolution, often used the Incan state to "prove the dehumanized, animal-like condition to which Soviet communism would reduce its subjects" (156).[12] In 1942, when the United States entered the war not only against the axis powers of Germany, Italy, and Japan but also against the Russian Communist system, Lytle's focus on Incan society seems rather deliberate with respect to these social constructions, anchored not only in regional polemics but in larger Western ethnographic and political discourses. In other words, while the agrarian achievements of Incan society may have rendered them particularly suitable as doppelgängers of Lytle's own South, as Richard Gray suggests, the contemporary perception of Incan political order extends beyond such regional significance. Lytle's turn South to the Incas in 1942 provides the backdrop to an ideologically motivated critique of both European imperialism in the Americas five hundred years ago and contemporary imperial politics that would soon involve the United States in World War II and fundamentally and irreversibly change the economic and social structure of the South. Read against its conspicuous publication date, *Alchemy* extends its critique of imperialism and materialism well beyond regional borders. It is a story about the rise of capitalism and colonialism written at a time when Europe and the United States still owned colonies abroad and when Indians in the United States, although citizens since 1924, were frequently still wards of the federal government and could not vote in at least three states (Collier, *Indians* 29). Pointing simultaneously outward to global imperialism, present and past, and inward to a history of "internal colonization" of Native Americans, Lytle's narrative traces the disastrous effects of imperialist politics on both the colonized and the colonizers.

Lytle expresses his critique of capitalist imperialism in the central metaphor of his novella: alchemy. This metaphor is more than "an inert sign or emblem" for Lytle, whose New Critical dictum demands that "where symbols appear

. . . they represent the entire action by compressing into a sharp image or succession of images the essence of meaning" (*Hero* 185). The title of his narrative does exactly that; it symbolically condenses the plot and announces the coming of what it performs: an alchemical transformation. Poised between the concepts of "discovery" and "invention," *Alchemy* oscillates between the unveiling of colonial history and its imaginative (re)production.[13] In the act of writing about the discovery and conquest of the Incas, Lytle produces the historical "reality" he seeks to describe, and in this sense *Alchemy* can be read as the performance of a discourse to which any such description always already belongs. As a metaphor, alchemy bluntly announces that the fundamental motif of sixteenth-century imperial expansion is materialism. The Spaniards' desire for gold turns the missionary work of Christianity into a cheap and unimportant by-product of the brewing mechanism set to work by early modern capitalism. By revealing the moral bankruptcy of the colonizing forces, Lytle seeks to intervene critically in narratives of colonial "discovery" and exploration as material and discursive practices.[14] As a scientific concept, alchemy is the perfect discipline for exploring, in the colonial context of the novella, the dichotomy between materialism and spirituality, matter and soul.

In Lytle's textual archaeology, alchemy refers to the cultural archive of Enlightenment science that attempted to achieve the transformation of matter. Sixteenth-century European alchemists sought to transform base metals into precious metals through the "chemical" use of substances such as salt, sulphur, arsenic, and mercury. Their concern with "matter" is Lytle's metaphor for Europe steeped in materialism and dedicated to the pursuit of gold both in scientific laboratories at home and in colonizing enterprises abroad. As a metaphor that is part of a historical culture concept, alchemy refers to Europe's "science" that served the fetishistic worship of gold and its narcissistic fantasy of riches. The preoccupation with the invention of gold—a rare and most precious commodity in Pizarro's time—and the failed attempts at producing it alchemically so plagued the European imagination that dreams and myths of kingdoms rich in gold gained increasingly wider circularity, fueling the ancient myth of El Dorado and various exploration expeditions to the Americas.[15] Pizarro's conquest of the Incan empire is particularly famous not only because his small band of soldiers slaughtered thousands of Indians in a killing spree that lasted an afternoon but because Pizarro, among all the conquistadores, extracted the largest amount of gold from the Americas, more than Cortés reaped from the Aztecs.[16] The European quest for gold became a conquest of empires rumored to be rich in this most coveted currency.

A careful reading of Lytle's novella proves that there is a subtle shift—a metonymic displacement, perhaps—from the conscious and overt critique of colonialism to the narcissistic self-interrogation of the colonizer's guilt-laden desires. As we will see, the primary goal of the narrative is not to protest the exploitation and colonization of native populations but rather to explore the colonizer's own soul. Although Lytle clearly demonstrates the destructive effects of Western imperialism, he conventionally and disappointingly uses the Native American signifier as a tool for Europeans to probe matters of their own interest. As the central trope of the novella, alchemy expresses both "moves" at once, shuttling between conscious critique and unconscious desire, ultimately revealing the degree to which the European "self" needs the Indian "other" for its own self-definition.

In the cognitive framework of sixteenth-century Spain, the Native American signifier becomes part of a colonialist dichotomy between European civilization and native barbarism. In re-creating these colonialist discourses in order to criticize them, Lytle opens this remote cultural repository to reveal the discursive rules and practices that have shaped the meaning of the Indian other. His ideological critique of imperialism begins with a narrator whose perspective shifts from an unabashedly colonialist viewpoint in the beginning to a humanist moral reflection at the end of the novella. This perspectival shift—we might also call it the narrator's alchemical transformation—initially focuses on the humanity and hardships of the Spaniards (their hunger, weariness, diseases, and struggle with hostile natives) and the corresponding inhumanity of the Indians, whom he compares to beasts. The narrator dehumanizes the Indians, who are simply part of the plague-infested landscape, in order to render the plight of the Spaniards all the more human and their mission more necessary and justified. When the Indians do appear as fellow humans, they are cast in the familiar role of treacherous heathens who harm Christians by ambushing them, murdering them, and tossing them into the sea. The narrator's representation of violence in the "contact zone" is based on clear oppositions between civilized "Christians" and savage "heathens." This flawed colonialist voice of the beginning of the narrative inverts colonial discourses to protect and justify the invasion. For example, the narrator tells us that it is not the Europeans who brought to the New World diseases that nearly extinguished the native populations, but rather the "filthy Indians" who pass on "a new and strange disease [which] consumed us like rotten sheep" so that "for seven months the army lay stricken" (105). This technique of discursive inversion also extends to other topics. The destruction of the city of Tumbes, for example, is primarily attributed to the mortal feud among Indians, not to the violence of Spanish warfare and wreckage. Lytle's purpose is clear: he presents the blatant Eurocentrism of the colonialist cognitive framework in order to reveal the flaws in the arrogant myth of European cultural superiority.

Shortly into the narrative, however, Lytle begins to invert the argument for Spanish cultural superiority with the introduction of material proof of Incan civilization. Drawing on contemporary anthropological knowledge, he uses the manufacture of textiles, for which all Andean cultures are famous, and the Incan road system as recurrent symbols for the presence of a highly advanced Indian civilization. This ethnographic subtext reveals a sophisticated culture that began the manufacture of textiles in ancient Peru long before the establishment of the Incan empire and long before textiles in Europe could muster equally fine cloth.[17] In the narrative, the narrator marvels at the dress of an Indian who "wore a loose flowing robe of cotton stuff, dyed in alternating stripes of brown and gold, of the richest and brightest threads I had ever seen" (109). Cultural sophistication, indicated by superior weaving skills, is balanced against signs confirming the native's primitive status, such as his "sandals of grass" and his heathen status mirrored in the silken sheen of his cloth, "not found in Christendom" (109). Constructed as an ambiguous figure, the Indian is more primitive in his grass sandals than the conquerors in their armor, but also more sophisticated (though perhaps also decadent) in his fine clothes.

The narrative increasingly suggests that "uncivilized" Indians might actually be more civilized than their Spanish invaders. The material accomplishments of Incan civilization continue to impress the narrator. Speaking of the great highway that runs from Quito to Cuzco, the narrator confesses: "The moment I saw its flat stone surface, the shade trees which protected it, and the cool water running in troughs for the comfort of the traveler, I knew that we stood upon the borders of that which we desired, feared, and from which we could never be freed, whether it brought our most extravagant hopes or our ruin" (125). As the Spaniards follow a steep, fortified path up the Andes mountain range toward the Incan emperor's camp, the narrator continues to marvel at Incan architecture and engineering: "I cannot say which was greater, my admiration for the engineer who had fortified this place or my despair" (138). Observing Incan military fortification and social organization, the Spaniards understand that the Indians are an organized society, not a "set of scattered tribes." Their army appears ready and organized; in fact, "they looked much better disciplined than our own foot [soldiers] which, to speak the truth, were a sad lot" (118). Within the historical archive of European colonialism, these allusions to Incan strength set up the magnitude of the Spanish victory over worthy rivals; within Lytle's contemporary archive, however, they serve to criticize the idea of European cultural superiority and to condemn the invasion and destruction of a rich, ancient Native American culture.

Lytle, perhaps more than any other of the southern writers examined in this study, was interested in the moral dimensions of the global colonial imaginary. The brunt of his critique of Western imperialism is therefore reserved for the Roman Catholic Church, an institution that was used to justify the desperate capitalist ventures of sixteenth-century Europe in the New World. As a key player in the exploration and conquest of empires, the church provided not only religious justification for conquest—to Christianize the heathens—but ideological support in the construction of an Indian "otherness" on which such domination rests. The spiritual underpinnings of conquest operate on the level of writing, not only in the narrow sense of obedience to the Holy Scriptures but in the more general sense of the role of literacy. In *Alchemy*, the Incan encounter with the Word forms the climax of the plot, for it provides the "justification" for the Spanish massacre.[18] As the Spaniards are preparing for a surprise military attack on the Incan emperor, Father Vincente de Valverde is sent ahead to spread the word of God and subject the Incan ruler, Atahuallpa, to God's kingdom by handing him the breviary. When Atahuallpa drops the book to the floor, the outraged Spaniards attack.

Did the Incan emperor drop the breviary by accident? Out of ignorance, because the book was meaningless to someone who could not read? Or as a sign of rejection and contempt for those who tried to lecture him? Where historical texts attempt to take a stand,[19] Lytle's novella presents a gap, a silence on the part of the "native," which the conqueror characteristically fills in with his own reading of the scene: "Give him the sword for this sacrilege," Valverde shouts (160). To the Spaniards, the emperor's gesture signals not only the rejection of the Holy Word but his lack of literacy more generally. Unlike the Aztecs, the Incas had not yet developed a writing system and were unfamiliar with the concept of the book at the time of their colonization by Spain.[20] The fact that the holy book cannot "speak" to the great Incan emperor signals more than the absence of literacy; it confirms for the Spaniards the absence of Incan "humanity." Enlightenment-age Europeans privileged writing as the principal measure of a person's "humanity." The absence of writing among those they colonized therefore testified to their inferior status and their lower place on the scale of human evolution. Because the concept of the book in the colonial context primarily functions as "an insignia of colonial authority and a signifier of colonial desire and discipline" (Bhabha 102), Atahuallpa's gesture signals his rejection of Spanish religious and political authority, but it also confirms for the Spaniards the absence of his humanity. The emperor's dismissal of the breviary is a dismissal of the civilizing and Christianizing missions used to justify Spanish dominion, and this marks him as an insulting infidel in the eyes of the colonizers.

Historically, the holy text played a central role in the Spanish claim to the New World: it confirmed the Indians' status as infidels sunk in spiritual darkness as well as the desire of the Roman Catholic Church to convert those "heathens."

This "conversion" is taking place when Father Valverde is talking to Atahuallpa. Patricia Seed argues that what was read to the historical Atahuallpa in his 1532 encounter with Fray Valverde was the "Requirement," a verbal ritual that was part of the Spanish conquest itself and served to invoke the authority of the church (13). So when Lytle's fictional Valverde is "running the Pope's authority from Adam" he is performing the "Requirement," pronouncing the ultimate authority of Christianity's right to rule the people of the Americas. In this crucial and climactic encounter between Atahuallpa, the Incan emperor, and Valverde, the representative of papal authority, Lytle exposes the political use of Christianity to justify the imperial domination on which European empires were built, and for which the Roman Catholic Church, more specifically papal authority, provided the rationale.

Lytle's representation of the historical role of writing, however, produces a double effect that can be characterized as a strategy of disavowal on the level of his own narrative. On the one hand, Lytle protests the arrogance of Western civilization and the complicity of the church in its desire to regulate and domesticate Indians by the imposition of the Word. On the other hand, Lytle is engaged in the very process that he criticizes: his own words reproduce some of the racist assumptions and fantasies of such discourses. Lytle criticizes European colonialism in religious guise, but he leaves unexamined discursive traces of Indians as proud, lazy, and hedonistic idol worshippers. Traces of these stereotypes belong to the contemporary Western discourse of orientalism. By adopting the modernist prose of orientalism, Lytle ironically produces a Native American signifier that corresponds closely with the colonizers' fantasy images of native heathens.

Such orientalism is powerfully evoked in the bath scene, for example. When the Spanish army arrives at the emperor's camp, Atahuallpa is taking a bath surrounded by his women. As military conflict is brewing, the bathhouse with its "lazy vapor" signals the place where Atahuallpa "took his ease and there, out of the indifferent vapors, the fate of Christians blew" (145). As a reference to the Indian's hedonistic pleasures, the bath signals the sexuality, laziness, and vulnerability of the Indian body. The description of the bath scene genders Atahuallpa's body, softening and feminizing him for the colonizer's hard penetration: while the Incan sun king is bathing his "worshipful skins," de Soto is riding up in armor on his prancing horse. When the curtain to Atahuallpa's inner sanctum draws back, we see him seated on a low bench "covered by a delicate mantle" and shielded by two "light-skinned women" (151). Although Atahuallpa is the emperor of an empire of rich textiles, in this crucial first encounter he appears in a state of undress. The "naked Indian" is a stock feature of colonialist texts beginning with Columbus, who commented extensively on the Indians' lack of clothes and for whom their nakedness conjured up a vision of Paradise, a new continent ready for economic and sexual possession.[21] As a standard ideological signal, the naked body of the Incan emperor symbolizes his and his nation's fragility. Even his elaborate ceremonial headdress, representing his status and political power, cannot cover the empire's delicate vulnerability. Instead of power, the headdress connotes the exotic singularity of the orientalized Indian figure. Atahuallpa's headdress, with its "white eagle feathers, [and] two long red plumes taken from the tail of the pillopichiu bird," symbolizes the preciousness of the emperor, who, by way of his plumage, becomes a rare, exotic, fragile, and proud bird. When the Spaniards—and the reader—get their next glimpse of Atahuallpa, he is on his royal litter, gliding "like a lazy bird. But a giant and oriental bird, for the litter was lined with feathered robes and pillows of down, and out of the feathers jewels played with the failing light" (159). As a sign of heathen pride, these parrot feathers, which "curved arrogantly," are too sinful for the priest to even touch for fear of native contamination and pagan corruption (150).

When Lytle, much like his contemporary William Faulkner, orientalizes the Indian as a feathered idol signifying ultimate exotic difference, his text opens up a gap between imperial critique and colonial reinscription. Such a discourse of orientalism has seduced not only fiction writers but literary critics as well, who have argued that the Inca's opulence, pride, and godlike superiority is the result of a "natural vanity" (Bradford, "Dark Shape" 62). The Inca, Bradford argues, "has so completely swallowed his own rhetoric of deification" that it leads to his downfall (62). But to speak of the "natural vanity" of the Indian is to reinscribe and indulge in an ethnic stereotype. Such racist coding of the Native American body as "naturally" lazy and vain belongs to the modernist archive of orientalism and reveals a continuity with those disturbing discourses of Western imperialism that are being challenged.

Ultimately, Lytle is not interested in challenging ethnic stereotypes or exploring Native American life but in the transformation of the European colonizers. In the narrative, the conversion efforts of the colonizers to enlighten and transform a "dark other" end up transforming the colonizers themselves. In this sense, the "alchemical transformation" in the colonial context is specular, reflecting the colonizers' own ideologies, interests, and anxieties. Lytle illustrates this specularity with a geographical metaphor. At the moment when the "West" is conquered, Lytle invokes the spiritual meaning of the "East" both geographically and spiritually in his references to Ethiopia, the Nile, and the "two rivers"—presumably in Mesopotamia, the "cradle of civilization." The drama of the West, Lytle believes, allows no return to the innocence of beginnings.[22] On the contrary, the path of the conquerors leads to destruction and further away from their paradisiacal visions. At the end of the narrative, after the slaughter of thousands of Incas, the narrator realizes that even though "the mighty host of the heathen lord was broken and scattered" (163), the real adversary of the conquerors was death, which "served the unshaken majesty of this Indian lord" (162). As Pizarro and de Soto stand looking at the carnage they have wrought, the narrator notices another companion "in a very different guise": "As they reached out their hands to clasp their desires, that other—the dark thing—stepped forward to receive them" (164). The "dark other" vanquishes the victors in their very triumph. In the process of colonial conquest, colonizer and colonized are transformed as through an alchemical process. In the final analysis, the process of colonization ironically shifts the power balance back to the colonized through the colonizer's knowledge of a defeat larger than his military or monetary victory. For Lytle, colonial transgression emits from the space of otherness to turn the "self" into the "other," forging a moral reversal that changes the meaning of "victory" into defeat.

Lytle believes that colonization, as a psychical strategy much akin to alchemy, alters not just physical and political geographies but also inner mental and moral landscapes. The fantasy of the other—when finally embraced—turns back on itself, splitting the subject and its desires. In the end, however, Lytle's colonialist discourse does not expend much energy in understanding the alterity of the Indian. The narrative is not about understanding Atahuallpa or Incan culture, but about the European mind and soul. And precisely herein lie the drastic limitations of Lytle's critique of empire. While Lytle's novella purports to represent a specific encounter with a racial Indian other, it ends up valorizing the structures of its own Anglo-American mentality through the kind of self-reflexivity that mediates the representation of the other but is really all about the self. Postcolonial critics such as Abdul JanMohamed argue that "such literature is essentially specular: instead of seeing the native as a cultural bridge toward syncretic possibility, it uses him as a mirror that reflects the colonialist's self image" (19). Such colonialist specularity operates in a number of modernist texts, including, most famously, Joseph Conrad's *Heart and Darkness*, and, less famously, Lytle's 1941 novel *At the Moon's Inn.*

Cannibals in the Contact Zone: Conrad's Kurtz and Lytle's de Soto

Both Lytle and Conrad, albeit from different historical moments, activate histories of European colonialism and share a critique of the capitalist motivation of imperialism. Together they show that economic motivations have always driven colonial enterprises, whether of the sixteenth century, the nineteenth century, or our own time. By situating Lytle's virtually unknown novel *At the Moon's Inn* in relation to Conrad's well-known novel *Heart of Darkness* (1902), I want to lift Lytle out of the confines of the southern agrarian context in which he is usually read and into the new neighborhood of classic colonial texts. Like Conrad, Lytle maps onto the route of exploration his concerns with the destructive nature of Western materialism and modern imperialism. This political kinship between Conrad and Lytle, rooted in the critique of imperialism, is expressed in surprisingly similar plots, narrative perspectives, and even metaphors. Both Conrad and Lytle trace the explorers' meandering journeys into remote colonial jungles. Like Conrad's Kurtz in Africa, Lytle's de Soto loses himself in America in the greedy act of searching for wealth and power. After much violent conquest and extortion of native populations, Kurtz and de Soto succumb to their voracious greed in the wilderness, where both die of fever.[23] Like Conrad, Lytle maps exploration as a linear operation that leads into "otherness" and enacts in time and space the longings and the demons of the colonial geographical imaginary. This excursion into "otherness"—a journey into the heart of darkness—which is really a search for the self, is a familiar paradigm of postcolonial literature. Like Conrad, Lytle "takes a dark view of the early European ventures in the New World" (Benson 84) and of the symbolic significance of the Western imperial enterprise more generally. Commenting on the concept of the West, Lytle writes that the West as a geographical space is nothing but a "half-truth," for its symbolic meaning is "death, the grave, the night sea journey; and in spite of the blatant political public assertion that the West is power, underneath we feel the threat of its eternal mythological meaning" (*Hero* 22). Reading the West, particularly Europe and the United States, against the public assertion of its power, Lytle follows in Conrad's footsteps as he reveals modern European exploration as fierce colonial exploitation.

Conrad and Lytle situate their narrators on the fringes of the exploring expeditions in order to gain a vantage point from which to critique the colonial enterprise. Conrad's Marlow and Lytle's Tovar are simultaneously fascinated and repelled by the powerful lie and the "horror" that Kurtz and de Soto represent. With an intertextual reference to Conrad's *Heart of Darkness,* Lytle's third-person narrator introduces the explorer Hernando de Soto, whose "black eyes" seem to sink into his flesh "towards that dark interior where lay the only sustenance able to glut their hunger" (20). Lytle's image of eyes that "rather looked in than out and looked not to see but to devour" powerfully evokes Conrad's Kurtz, whose "fiery longing eyes" are key to the hunger of his soul; his gaze, too, looks inward to a savage, hollow, hungry core at the heart of "civilization." From these descriptions, Conrad's imaginary Kurtz and Lytle's historical de Soto emerge as figures of imperialism best represented as cannibals out to devour the colonial world. In both texts, cannibalism becomes an especially powerful and distinctive feature of the rhetoric of empire: here the cannibals are not the "natives"—although they are certainly associated with this figure in the framework of the colonialist discourse represented—but the colonizers themselves. Both writers seek to invert the metaphor of cannibalism so that the place that is abhorred is finally not the place of the other, but on the contrary, the colonialist self. Through the technique of metaphoric inversion, Lytle, like Conrad, presses a didactic agenda that aims at revealing the destructive power of Europe's voracious imperialism and the materialist motives that drive it. Conrad's "pioneers of progress" become "cannibals incarnate," "slaves to gross appetites, symbolic of the egotistic pleasures of the market gone wildly astray" (Phillips 188). In depicting the voracious greed of European colonialism, Conrad and Lytle share a moral point of view and a literary technique that renders the economics of capitalism in the trope of cannibalism.

Cannibalism as a type of incorporation constitutes a crucial link between a number of different concerns in *At the Moon's Inn.* On a materialist level, there is the Spanish plundering of native food resources and the army's constant hunger, which neither wilderness nor native food stores can ever satisfy. This devouring of food and land is expressive of the overriding desire to rend the world apart in search of gold and material gain. On a sexual level, the materialist greed of the colonizers extends from food to the bodies of the natives, where the "temptation" of the native creates a desire for sexual incorporation and a fantasy of control through enslavement. Indian bodies, male and female, are literally and symbolically devoured as expendable commodities in the process of colonization. As a textual sign of otherness, cannibalism here functions not only metaphorically but also metonymically: it seeks to displace the horror of the "other" by subsuming racial and political anxieties on the level of the body.[24] Such metonymic displacements result in the overdetermination and fragmentation of the native body, as we will see.[25] On a spiritual level, the physical incorporation of the native "other" is sublimated onto a higher plane in the Catholic sacrament of the Eucharist, which can be read as a reciprocal incorporation of Host (God) and believer. As in *Alchemy,* this religious component—the role of Christianity in the process of colonial incorporation—provides the most explicit entry into the moral dimensions of Lytle's critique of empire.

Like Conrad, Lytle emphasizes the colonizing world's voracious hunger for resources and bodies. In his central epiphany, Marlow sees Kurtz with his mouth wide open: "I saw him open his mouth wide—it gave him a weirdly voracious aspect, as though he wanted to swallow all the air, all the earth, all the men before him" (61). Lytle, too, thematizes the voracity of empire. In his opening chapter, "The Feast," de Soto's company is dining, as one guest remarks, as "only the Emperor, the greatest appetite in Christendom, knows how to dine" (52). Comparing the fruits of colonialism to a richly burdened table, Lytle sets the stage for the encounter with the cannibal. Just as the guests are reveling in a feast of delicacies and prospects of colonial power and wealth, Don Alvar Núñez Cabeza de Vaca, one of only four survivors of the earlier, disastrous Narváez expedition, enters the dining room. In a dramatic reversal of de Soto's propaganda promising New World treasures, Cabeza de Vaca illustrates very different kinds of "treasures" that the explorers will find in Florida. He brings all that is left of the Narváez expedition stored in a chest filled with "an ear of maize," a buskin, and "some curious laces of leather." He explains that "the rest of the conquerors, all save their buttocks, were eaten by their companions" for lack of maize (58). Cabeza de Vaca's vivid evocation of the cannibal figure, complete with the shriveled skin of one of his former companions, triggers the Spaniards' momentary recognition of their own cannibal nature and marks a dangerous turning point for de Soto's planned expedition. The colonial discourse is destabilized until de Soto identifies Cabeza de Vaca on the side of savagery as "an Indian" when he welcomes him with the words "You come among Christians, Don Alvar, like an Indian" (54). The temporary deconstruction of "savage" and "civilized" with which Cabeza de Vaca threatens the hegemonic colonialist discourse is resolved when the sign of "savagery" is securely situated on the other side of the social divide and when the "proper" colonial dichotomy is thereby reestablished. In this scene, Lytle illustrates that the symbols of colonialism—feasts versus laces made of human skin—stand not in opposition but in complementary relation to each other. The cultural difference that seemingly splits the field of human relations along the figure of the cannibal and upholds these binaries is in reality part of the same colonial dialectic and tension.

The opening "Feast" of the first chapter of *At the Moon's Inn* stands in stark ironic contrast to the constant lack of food and the wrenching hunger that drives the exploring group from one Indian town to the next on their march through the American wilderness in the rest of the novel. Tormented by hunger, the conquerors—both fictional and historical—swallow everything in their path. Archaeological and ethnographic studies of the de Soto route stress the expedition's disproportionate demand on native food resources. When between 1539 and 1543 roughly six hundred Spaniards combed the American Southeast for treasures, they devoured the food resources of the native chiefdoms like a plague of locusts, robbing them of their means of subsistence and often their winter reserves.[26] De Soto's party, archaeologists agree, must have "continually raided the region for food, devastating the countryside" (Milanich 132). For Lytle, as for Conrad, the hunger of the exploring group operates as a central trope characterizing the voracity of the colonial enterprise as a whole. Tracing the expedition's development from feasting to fasting, Lytle describes their desperate foraging for any roots, plants, and other edible food items. It is not without a touch of irony that he depicts, for example, the enthusiastic way the men greet the corn they find at Urriparacoxit "with the cheer that men show at a feast." Turning in upon the corn, "in half an hour the field had disappeared" (180). Repeated descriptions of such food raids aim at revealing the disproportionate appetites of colonial power for the natural resources of the land. They also show that Cabeza de Vaca's prophecy is fulfilled. As fine daggers with embossed handles are put up against a cup of beans, the "civilized" Spaniards are reduced to primitive "savagery." Lost in the wilderness, they have become cannibals in their need and perverted desire to devour the land.

Lytle and Conrad agree not only on the savage voracity of the colonizers but also on the fact that colonialism is a male imperative. Women of the colonizing culture are important only insofar as they carry the key to the legacy of the imperial heritage; their bodies and sexualities serve the empire. In Conrad's novel, Kurtz's fiancée, the Intended, represents the surviving belief in the validity of the European civilizing mission. She mourns Kurtz's loss and, much like Marlow's aunt, keeps alive the lie of imperialism's Christian and humanitarian goals. Conrad and Lytle both show that women of the colonizing cultures, like Kurtz's Intended and de Soto's Ysabel, are submitted to self-serving patriarchal power and become victims of an aggressive myth of imperial masculinity. In *At the Moon's Inn,* Ysabel falls prey to the prevailing gender hierarchies when de Soto rapes her at the end of "The Feast," an act that foreshadows the destructive power of colonial violence.

Lytle signals the intimate connection between colonialism and sexual domination by prefacing the rape scene with Doña Ysabel's reaction to Cabeza de Vaca's news of cannibalism committed by the survivors of the Narváez expedition. Cabeza de Vaca's story fills Ysabel with horror, the same horror that Marlow encounters in the voice of Kurtz. Ysabel realizes that Florida—a place she imagines to be abandoned by the rules that govern "civilized" society—is not inherently evil but that it is the conquistadores themselves, the rapists of the New World, who are the enemy. Ysabel's epiphany is the result of her ability to imagine the unimaginable cannibal feast: "There could be no more abandoned acceptance of the world than for brother to eat his brother! . . . And then in the instant flash of vision she saw those ghosts of men, forlorn in their desperation . . . she watched the starving Christians fall upon one another, their long teeth tear the dusty flesh and be broken on the bone" (62). Ysabel's sudden understanding of the ferocity of colonial willpower leaves her shaken, and she implores de Soto to refrain from further conquests. But de Soto is unmoved. He defies his wife's request and, taking her to bed, imposes his will onto her body. De Soto's rape of Ysabel at the end of "The Feast" shows his immoderate appetite for the violent incorporation of the "other." After Ysabel's plea—"No, Hernán, no!"—he proceeds to force her and in that act reveals himself as a cannibal, that savage "other" which knows no restraint: "Her arms folded in. Her head whirled as thick and stifling pressed down upon her a sweet and unbearable odor. It was that of corrupting flesh! Cannibal! she opened her mouth, but no sound came; and then she felt herself grow heavy and inert" (68). With de Soto's rape of Ysabel in the Spanish metropole, Lytle foreshadows further acts of brutality in the New World in the name of empire. Abroad de Soto continues to force others, literally eating them up, as in the scene when an Indian woman is thrown to the dogs and de Soto and his men watch unmoved as the animals rip her body to pieces.

The savage voracity of the male colonizing subject is lived out in acts of sexual domination, control, and violence that extend over women of both the colonizing and colonized cultures. Addressing women's role in the process of empire-building, Anne McClintock reminds us that "controlling women's sexuality, exalting maternity and breeding a virile race of empire-builders was widely perceived as the paramount means for controlling the health and wealth of the male imperial body" (*Imperial* 47). As a woman of the colonizing culture, Ysabel is a domesticated and passive figure, like the Intended, who is only important as part of de Soto's imperial will and his patriarchal legacy. Colonizing women like Ysabel and the Intended are swallowed by patriarchal imperatives, but so are native women who become part of a conquered sexual geography. The many nameless native women in Lytle's text and the single "wild woman" in Conrad's are part of an erotic economy of colonial conquest in which they function as objects for sexual consumption that ensures imperial control of the New World. Sexual consumption is an extension of the authors' cannibal metaphor, for it marks political incorporation and imperial domination at the level of the native body. The violence of colonial reality—the rape of the New World and of native women—is usually veiled by a discourse of sexual pleasure that is superimposed onto it. In colonialist discourse, the apparently unbridled sexuality that native women seem to offer and the related symbolic feminization of the landscape itself seek to justify masculine imperial penetration. Both Lytle and Conrad indulge in these sexual fantasies of the colonialist gaze. Conrad stops his narrative for the "wild and gorgeous apparition of a [native] woman" (61) whose mysterious beauty and sexuality lead Marlow to conclude that "she was savage and superb, wild-eyed and magnificent" (62). Her body mirrors the "immense wilderness, the colossal body of the fecund and mysterious life" (62). Lytle, too, presents native women as part of a primitive Edenic world not governed by sexual restraint. He images the female-ruled Indian town of Cutifichiqui as a veritable Eden where unchecked carnal desires govern. It is the myth of America as body offering herself to the invaders: "The world that was flesh was everywhere, its power each man knew in himself, its temptations and its triumphs. But this land was the very body of the world" (324). The colonizer's sexual feast of the native body—Tovar's "Indian marriage" in Lytle's text—signifies both desire and fear, a simultaneous acceptance and rejection of a state of nature that can again be characterized by the cannibal metaphor. From the vantage point of the "civilized" world, Phillips writes, "the state of nature, as a bestial condition of existence, is typically what political economy—as a project of modernity—claims to negate. In this respect, beastliness is the 'primitive' truth of capitalist discipline as 'moral progress'; or, to put it differently, it is the truth of 'Man labouring to transcend nature' " (194). By representing the simultaneous allure and rejection of native "bestiality" in the colonizer's fantasy of sexual conquest, Lytle shows the split in the "civilized" mind that allows for both the fear and the practice of cannibalism. In this larger sense, cannibalism is a metaphor for a political body seeking to consume other human bodies, at least discursively. Slemons writes that in its discursive meaning, "cannibalism enables mobility for the imperial subject and permits the political production of *meaning*" (166). Here he refers to Michel de Certeau's definition of cannibalism as "an economy of speech, in which the body is the price" (qtd. in Slemons 166).

This discourse of cannibalism functions not only on the physical level, as a metaphor for a colonizing body politic whose desire it is to swallow the native "other," but also on the spiritual level. For Conrad and Lytle, Christianity, too, is a textual mechanism for colonial incorporation; it is a metaphor for cannibalism on a "higher" metaphoric level. Conrad's Marlow refers to the explorers with bitter irony as "the Pilgrims," and he vehemently protests his aunt's vision of him as "one of the Workers . . . something like an emissary of light, something like a lower sort of apostle" (12). Lytle shares Conrad's critique of the Christian mission of imperialism, and he carries its complicity in conquest a step further. For the Catholic Spaniards of Lytle's text, the physical incorporation of the other is sublimated onto a higher spiritual plane in the sacrament of the Eucharist: the incorporation of Christ's body by the believers. Maggie Kilgour argues that the Eucharist can be seen as a "paradoxical relation involving the simultaneous identification and differentiation of opposites. It is a banquet at which host and guest can come together without one subsuming the other, as both eat and are eaten" (79). Through Communion and the incorporation of the Host, the believer becomes part of the Corpus Christi, the body and the church of Christ. Lytle dramatizes this idea of social and spiritual incorporation in the "Wilderness" chapter of his novel, where he juxtaposes the celebration of

Catholic mass in the narrative time present with the Indian captivity of Juan Ortiz in the narrative past in order to achieve an ironic contrast. He returns to this idea again in the final, climactic scene of the novel when de Soto publicly affirms his cannibal nature: he renounces the community of Christians by placing his will over that of the highest spiritual power. During the last celebration of mass with the last host that is left after four years of war and wandering through the wilderness, de Soto defiantly renounces the authority of the church. This final rejection of the Host, the holy sacrament of the Roman Catholic Church, signals de Soto's own cannibalistic assertion of the principles of individualism and materialism that give rise to the modern secular individual. Lytle exposes de Soto as a self-interested individual, the prototype of modern man who needs no other legitimation for his actions than his own needs and desires.[27] For Lytle, de Soto's gesture represents a historical rupture that marks the "Fall" of man into modern history and into secular capitalist society. Like Conrad's Kurtz, de Soto is the "will" and the voice of European capitalist imperialism. Lytle may have been thinking of Conrad when he alluded to the "sepulchral" voice of de Soto's ghost: "'Beyond,' he heard the voice, clear and sepulchral, 'beyond lies the abyss'" (395). Like the wraith of Kurtz, de Soto's ghost is conveying a final insight into the colonial situation, but the message is very different: "There is no remedy. For you or me, or for any who come to this land. It is the Moon's Inn for all, heathen and Christian alike. It can never be more than a temporary abode, a stopping place of variable seasons, where the moon is host and the reckoning is counted up in sweat, in hunger, and in blood" (397). The idea that the land can never belong to anyone—that nature is the host—recalls the message of another southern writer: in Faulkner's *Go Down, Moses,* Ike McCaslin renounces the idea of property because he believes that "the earth was no man's but all men's, as light and air and weather were" (4). This understanding of the "land" as a "temporary abode" shared by all is a transparent mask that cannot hide the imperial struggle over land and the conquest, enslavement, and population removals that are its accompanying political realities. The baseline for Lytle and Conrad is that Western history is not a triumphal narrative but one marked by "cannibalism" at the heart of "civilization."

Although both writers unmask Europe as a greedy, colonizing cannibal, Lytle's attitude toward native populations—his celebration of native resistance—differs significantly from Conrad's. The Indians of *At the Moon's Inn* are active agents, and when they drown in a lake rather than surrender to the colonizer's power, or when they choose death by fire rather than being killed by the invaders, we recognize in Lytle's celebration of heroic native resistance his desire to represent the agency and humanity of the colonized. Not so in Conrad. "Conrad's tragic limitation," according to Edward Said, "is that even though he could see clearly that on one level imperialism was essentially pure dominance and land-grabbing, he could not then conclude that imperialism had to end so that 'natives' could lead lives free from European domination" (*Culture* 30). In Conrad's text, the native figure remains silent and passive, a mere element of an exotic background against which European willpower plays itself out, a depiction postcolonial critics have most severely criticized.

Although Lytle does not completely transcend the limitations of Conrad's colonial vision, he seeks to address the power of resistance of the colonized, even if that power remains limited and often confined to reactive strategies. Unfortunately, Lytle's critics have missed this important difference. Benson, for example, has judged *At the Moon's Inn* "a significant work of historical fiction . . . in spite of the burden of repeated confrontations with different groups of Indians" (96). But precisely those "burdensome" encounters with Indians merit a closer look. In sustained and repeated depictions of the opposition to imperial willpower, Lytle recognizes and celebrates the validity of native resistance. The southeastern chiefdoms of *At the Moon's Inn* are active forces that defy European attitudes of superiority, entitlement, and domination. For Lytle, there are two sides to colonial conflict. This acknowledgment of native resistance in *At the Moon's Inn* is a crucial step toward his recognition in literature of the political and cultural menace that imperialism represents and of the malevolence against which native peoples must assert their will.

Unlike in *Alchemy*, in *At the Moon's Inn* the physical, intellectual, and spiritual rebellion of Native Americans in individual and communal acts of defiance impresses upon the imperial culture—and the reader—the independence and integrity of the native culture. Lytle's novel turns upon this reciprocity between intrusion and heroic resistance from the beginning on. Native resistance to conquest begins not long after "contact" in the New World when an Indian ambushes the Spanish exploring group in a suicidal act, and such acts of resistance continue throughout the novel. For example, during a major battle, the narrator-character Tovar, on his horse and armed with a lance, fights Chief Tascaluça's son, whom he drives slowly toward a burning house. At the moment of killing the weaponless Indian, "the Indian raised his head in such arrogance and dignity that he [Tovar] withheld a breath too long the forward thrust" (356). In that moment the Indian chooses to jump into the fire and burn in the flames rather than be killed by Tovar. Lytle's message is clear: the Indians are superior to their European matches not only in terms of physical courage and pride, which repeatedly humble the invaders, but even more so in their spiritual and communal integrity. In another example, the Indians bring the wrath of their gods upon de Soto's men, who have broken into the burial temples of their mound graves to rob the strands of pearls from around the necks of Indian corpses. Tovar realizes why the female chief of Cutifichiqui had pointed their way to the treasures: "Not willingly had she let her sacred places be ravished, and her people brought to shame. Strange it must have seemed to her, this Christian lust for trinkets; and yet, she was quick to use it for her vengeance. Upon Christian heads would she bring down the wrath of the Sun" (316). The violence of imperial invasion does not remain without consequences. For their plundering and raping, de Soto's men fear the wrath not only of Indian gods but more so their own Christian God. When the Spaniards slaughter twenty-five hundred Indians at the battle of Mauvilla, where only twenty-two Spaniards are killed, there is no joy in victory. Much like at the end of *Alchemy*, "the victory, overwhelming as it was, carried for the Christians all the gloom and uncertainty of defeat" (359). This defeat stems from the recognition that the Indians have retained something the Christians have lost: a sense of honor and pride in the cultural and spiritual integrity of a community for which they are ready to die. Lytle's point is clear: whereas the Christians committed bloody massacres, the Indians attempted heroic acts of resistance and self-sacrifice.

Judging by these and many more examples, Lytle represents Indians as doomed warriors in the nineteenth-century tradition: proud and noble, and most of all dying. But in modification of this tradition, Lytle's version of Indian resistance does not support the myth of "progress" in the name of a more advanced and enlightened civilization. On the contrary, Lytle's conquest novels plainly reveal that the tragic destruction of Indian civilizations is proof of the barbarism of Western societies. But in spite of Lytle's depictions of various forms of physical and spiritual resistance to brutal conquest, his text does not approach the postcolonial perspective of Chinua Achebe's *Things Fall Apart*—in many ways the countertext to *Heart of Darkness*—because Lytle's perspective, unlike Achebe's, remains limited to the colonizers and concerned with their actions, motivations, and fears. Even though both authors share the conviction that "natives" would rather commit suicide than surrender to colonial rule, Achebe represents the ideologies of the native culture, not the colonial culture. Only more recent reinterpretations of the colonial experience from the perspective of the colonized in texts by Achebe, Derek Walcott, Salman Rushdie, Franz Fanon, Leslie Marmon Silko, and others have given voice to the native figure, and in doing so they have begun to reclaim colonized territory. Unlike these properly "postcolonial" texts, the narratives of Lytle and Conrad belong to the genre of colonialist literature because, while they are critical of empire, they are unable to represent a perspective other than the European. Like Conrad, Lytle unmasks the true motives of Europe's colonial agenda, but unlike Conrad, he begins to image at least partially and sympathetically what the colonial encounter must have meant to Native Americans, collectively and individually.

Did Lytle in 1940 have a better vantage point than Conrad forty years earlier? Certainly, the periods of literary production were rather different. Whereas Conrad wrote *Heart of Darkness* and *Nostromo* during a period of Europe's "largely uncontested imperialist enthusiasm" (Said, *Culture* xix), Lytle's political moment, characterized by the international crisis leading to World War II, was perhaps less "enthusiastic." Lytle also had more distance to Enlightenment Europe than Conrad had to King Leopold's Congo, but that is not what primarily accounts for their different representations of native populations. Lytle's empathy with the plight of Indians in his novels is the result of a slowly changing understanding of Native Americans in American public life. In this sense, Lytle's text registers an ethnographic change. In the 1930s and 1940s, one hundred years after the Indian removal, Native Americans were no longer perceived as a threat to Anglo-American ideologies; on the contrary, their lifestyles, now seemingly domesticated, were romanticized and celebrated. Public perception was different for blacks and the African world, however, as Said points out. Overall the representation of the non-Western world had not changed much as segregation, apartheid, and colonialism continued through World War II. This does not mean that Lytle's historical vantage point gave him a more "advanced" or progressive understanding of the native other, but rather that the kind of "other"—Indians versus Africans—that Lytle and Conrad are discursively inventing carries significantly different meanings in the Euro-American imagination.

Lytle's and Conrad's geopolitical situatedness also accounts for their different perceptions of the native other. Lytle's location in the American South, a place that was once colonial territory, significantly determines the way he imagines colonialist dynamics. His relationship to the South is fundamentally different from Conrad's relationship to Africa or South America, because unlike Conrad, Lytle is not writing from a remote metropole but from the very place of Native American displacement. This physical proximity—unlike the relationship England had with a remote India, or Belgium with the Congo—marks Lytle's perspective and registers the native presence differently. Although Lytle writes about a time period for which there was and is little ethnographic information available (and what information there is about Native Americans is mostly rendered through Western eyes), he imagines himself "closer" to *native* Americans. The degree to which Conrad and Lytle differ in their representation of "natives" is the degree to which they are able to engage not only their own societies but also the societies, traditions, and histories of the colonized world. And here Lytle makes an arguably better effort than Conrad, because the native tradition Lytle appropriates is historically and mythologically linked with his own national and regional heritage. This heritage was in the process of being exhumed by New Deal archaeology and served the construction of a national narrative that deliberately included the pre-national Native American past. Despite these differences, however, both writers primarily engage a history of domination and victimization, written from the (guilty) consciousness of colonizing societies. In this sense, Lytle and Conrad are part of a continuous discourse of imperialism carried out in literature for which both writers reproduce the imperial ideologies of their own time.

Lytle's return to the discovery period, while inspired by WPA archaeology, stems partially from its apocalyptic significance that eerily echoes the contemporary moment of the Holocaust: What kinds of men could have massacred whole families and tribes? What could they have been thinking as they killed everyone in sight? By dispatching contemporary international anxieties back into a distant historical past, Lytle gives expression to the recurring threat of cultural and physical extermination. The memory of Euro-American imperialism that resulted in Native American genocide and the present reality of fascism and the Holocaust in Europe intersect in Lytle's narratives. Comparing the novelist and the historian, Lytle writes that although both do similar research, the novelist "must become the research." By this he means that the novelist "metamorphoses the pastness of the past into the moving present" so that the reader becomes a witness: "He is there; he sees, he tastes; he smells—if the author succeeds" (*Hero* 8). In 1942, "witnessing" social events past and present, at home and abroad, is a crucial political and moral choice.

Launched from the location of the global South, Lytle's critique of imperialism and colonialism, then and now, (re)defines the cultural and political outlines of the American South. In Lytle's narratives, Native Americans whose homelands are usurped by foreign forces become not only powerful emotional and political figures for southern conservative regionalist struggles but also signifiers in a global political framework of Western colonization. As a writer interested in the international operations of imperialism, colonialism, and capitalism, Lytle transforms our understanding of the southern writer from an insular regional poet into a commentator on global political transformations. Although they are consistent with his lifelong politics hostile to technological innovation and suspicious of modern narratives of progress, *Alchemy* and *At the Moon's Inn* are a long way from those "arguments about farming and family" for which he is best known.[28] Lytle's narratives of conquest wrap the South into a larger international universe of historical and political action, and this, I believe, is the innovative and revisionary aspect of Lytle's work. Although the republication of *Alchemy* in 1984 and *At the Moon's Inn* in 1990 (to mark the 450th anniversary of de Soto's expedition) passed largely unnoticed by the scholarly community, these narratives of "discovery" are of great interest at a time when the United States fights drug wars in Latin America and when the rush for Incan gold is transmuted into the "white gold" rush of the coca trade. Carl Jung, whose theories Lytle studied and admired, writes that "we have often found that a poet who has gone out of fashion is suddenly rediscovered. This happens when our conscious development has reached a higher level from which the poet can tell us something new. It was always present in his work but was hidden in a symbol, and only a renewal of the spirit of the time permits us to read its meaning" (qtd. in Richter 512).

Rereading Lytle from a postcolonial perspective results in an experience of renewal much like the transmutative process of alchemy itself: it is the realization that Lytle's participation in pressing national and international issues transcends the narrow definitions of southern identity and geography customarily associated with his work. In Lytle's moral framework, colonialism and capitalism are expressions of social aggression that continue to threaten the world. Lytle focuses on the world of the conquistadores because he would agree with Tzvetan Todorov that "it is necessary to analyze the weapons of conquest if we ever want to be able to stop it. For conquests do not belong to the past" (254).

3

Gendering the Nation

Caroline Gordon's Cherokee Frontier

> Again, were we to inquire by what law or authority you set up a claim, I answer, none! Your laws extend not into our country, nor ever did. You talk of the law of nature and the law of nations, and they are both against you.
>
> —Corn Tassel, Cherokee, 1785

From Andrew Lytle, Caroline Gordon picks up the European colonial trace leading into the American South during the Revolutionary period.[1] Like Lytle, Gordon was inspired by New Deal archaeology in the South of the 1930s, which brought to the fore the rich archaeological and historical sediments of her home state, Kentucky. Gordon's literary excursions to Kentucky's prehistoric sites were prompted by WPA excavations in progress at the time of her writing and also by archaeological books that brought to the surface the deep strata of history. In 1928, archaeologists William D. Funkhouser and William S. Webb published *Ancient Life in Kentucky*, an important book surveying major archaeological findings in Kentucky, including some of the houses of cliff dwellers ("rock-houses") that feature prominently in Gordon's captivity narrative.[2] Between the 1932 publication of Gordon's little-known narrative "The Captive" and her frontier novel *Green Centuries* (1941), WPA archaeologists undertook major excavations in Kentucky, particularly after 1937 when Webb "organized a major federal archaeological program in Kentucky using WPA support" (Lyon 95). During this time, Webb and other chief archaeologists recovered thousands of artifacts and hundreds of human remains and burials. At Indian Knoll, for example, where in 1915 C. B. Moore recovered 298 skeletons, a much more extensive two-year WPA excavation yielded "more than 55,000 artifacts and 880 burials" (Lyon 99). Many of these excavations occurred at sites that Gordon chose as settings for her fiction, such as the Big Sandy River in eastern Kentucky where

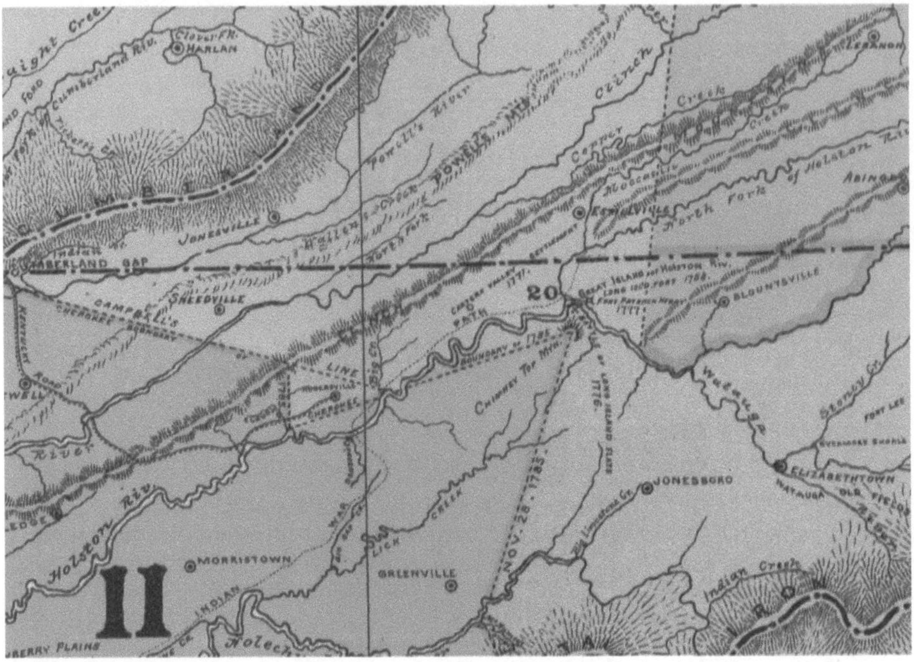

Map 3. "Map of the Former Territorial Limits of the Cherokee Nation of Indians." C. C. Royce. 1884. Published for the Smithsonian Institute, Bureau of Ethnology. Detail showing the Holston and Watauga area. Courtesy of the Alabama Department of Archives and History

"The Captive" takes place and the many salt licks that she describes in *Green Centuries* which furnished much paleontological materials and evidence of the era of the mammoth and the mastodon. In her fiction, Gordon digs into these historically remote sites connected to "prehistoric" Native American life and into the more recent layers of America's colonial and national history. In her multi-layered narratives, which work as palimpsests, Gordon recovers the Native American signifier in three archaeological layers: the distant past of the Mound Builders, the modern colonial era, and the early national period.

Looking back at the colonial conflicts among European and Native American nations, Gordon describes in her narratives the social and legal mechanisms of race and gender differentiation that contributed to the rise of a burgeoning American nation-state. It is no coincidence that during a time of major national inquiry into the cultural and historical resources of the country, Gordon was inspired particularly by questions concerning America's national heritage. WPA archaeology during the Roosevelt administration participated in the political enterprise of American nation-building and contributed to the cultural climate of what Alfred Kazin called an era of "new nationalism." By helping to mine the nation's rich historical materials, New Deal archaeology in the South of the 1930s served to boost the importance of this region to the nation and simultaneously to firm a narrative of American nationalism. Archaeologists readily admit to the long-standing historical relationship between archaeology and nationalism. Kohl and Fawcett, for example, observe that "the nation-building use of archaeological data even occurs in countries, like the United States, that lack an ancient history or a direct link with the prehistoric past; the concept of 'ancient-ness' is relative and 'may lie in the eye of the beholder,' making eighteenth-century Monticello or Mount Vernon for U.S. Americans of European descent or the nineteenth-century Little Bighorn Battlefield for both European and Native Americans as emotionally satisfying and time-honored as much older remains from Europe or Asia" (4). Since archaeology is crucial to the effort of constructing national roots, the recovery of the Native American past becomes particularly important for the narrative of a relatively new country like the United States. Gordon was not unaware of this. In fact, among the writers examined here, she is most interested in the construction of a national narrative and in the ways in which discourses of racial differentiation born during the Enlightenment and transposed to the American frontier intersect with the workings of gender. In her narratives of the Indian frontier, Gordon illuminates the skewed cultural construction of racial and gendered bodies in the American South and in the nation more generally by reading the segregated present back into the past.

The following analysis marks my own archaeological effort to recover Caroline Gordon as an important writer of the American South. Gordon has fallen somewhat out of critical favor despite recent efforts to reexamine her life and work.[3] There are multiple reasons for the critical neglect of Gordon as a talented writer. To begin with, tenacious definitions of the Southern Renaissance as male-centered lasted well into the contemporary period. Recently, however, critics have challenged this paradigm and exposed the imaginary basis for its fabrication; as Susan Donaldson shows in *Haunted Bodies,* early definitions of southern literature were essentially designed to "protect and consolidate the masculinity of the white male southern writer" (505).[4] In Gordon criticism this male-centered paradigm still prevails, as some of her best and most sympathetic critics see her most clearly when she is connected to her husband, Allen Tate.[5] Critics point out that Gordon, married to one of the most influential architects of the Southern Renaissance, frequently struggled with her own self-definition as a writer and often praised her male mentors and her husband's influence on her.[6] Surrounded by literary friends, she was shy about her own work and only hesitatingly sought the advice of close friends such as Ford Maddox Ford and

Andrew Lytle. "Born into a community and culture with complex and rigidly structured gender roles," writes Nancylee Jonza, "Gordon found herself at an early age negotiating the boundaries between expectations and reality, particularly with respect to gender identity" (xi). While on occasion she seems to have deferred to her husband's critical judgment and used his help when corresponding with editors, she also resented her professional denigration to the status of Tate's "wife."[7] Even today as we reexamine her work, Tate's towering influence and intellectual presence often shape what we tend to see in Gordon. What makes a recovery of Gordon difficult for feminist critics is that, according to Anne Boyle, Gordon was adopting a "masculine style" of writing. Personally conflicted about her own gender roles, Gordon struggled with two inconsistent images of herself as a nurturing mother and a writer of serious (male-defined) art. "Complicating her dilemma," Boyle writes, "is the fact that she always lived in close association with powerful and self-absorbed men. Although she established relationships with Sally Wood, Katherine Anne Porter, and later, Flannery O'Connor she . . . had no sister" (41). Reading gender in Gordon's texts is a challenging and complex matter aggravated by the fact that some of her best-known work is male-centered, such as the tangled family narrative *Penhally* (1931) and the fictionalized memoir of her father, James Maury Morris Gordon, whose hedonistic escape from the duties of family life by hunting and fishing Gordon celebrates in *Aleck Maury, Sportsman* (1935).[8] Certainly, Gordon was no feminist who preached sisterhood, but she was a keen observer and a critic of patriarchy who presented the "world of men" for the reader's critical judgment—even if she sometimes withheld her own.

I suggest that by rereading Gordon's work on the American frontier and by tracing her construction of the Native American signifier as part of a postcolonial project, we can uncover new ideological undercurrents in her much-neglected fiction. Steeped in the complex processes of the colonial encounter between settlers and Indians, Gordon was very much concerned with the politics of race and gender in the formation of national and regional identity. Her works about the Indian frontier show that as a writer she was seriously interested in history—not in a fuzzy nostalgic sense of the past, but in the mechanisms of race, gender, and class differentiation. Like Lytle, she did extensive historical research for her frontier fiction, and as a distant descendant of Meriwether Lewis (of the Lewis and Clark expedition) she was interested in the history of American westward expansion and in challenging a variety of borders, cultural and discursive.[9] As such Gordon belongs to a peer group of writers who rethink colonial operations on the (southern) frontier and who are interested in discourses of racial and gendered alterity. As a writer who often felt other—"a freak," as she said—in her own social group of mostly male agrarian intellectuals, she was fascinated by such otherness, and in her Indian narratives she explores in detail the cultural inscriptions of the law of the other. How well she succeeds in challenging these laws and how daringly she trespasses the borders constructed around race and gender is the focus of the following analysis. I argue that although Gordon reveals the ultimate instability of racial identity in her captivity narrative and writes *Green Centuries* in part as a feminist critique of white masculinity and its imperialist agendas, her feminism resides uncomfortably beside her southern conservatism about race. As we will see, Gordon critically investigates but ultimately does not transform hegemonic discourses of Indian assimilation, racial segregation, and the fear of miscegenation.

Indian Captivity in White Southern Culture

Based on a historical incident in the late 1780s, Gordon's "The Captive" (1932) retells the story of Jennie Wiley's captivity as a prisoner of a Shawnee/Cherokee band that held her captive for eleven months.[10] As Gordon transforms this historical material into fiction, she assimilates the colonial inheritance of American life with the contemporary cultural and racial situation of the South.[11] Her interest in the Wiley captivity provides the basis for an inquiry into questions about national and regional identifications, specifically as these are structured by race and gender. In "The Captive," Gordon documents frontier expansion and the formation of the nation at the same time as she sketches a particular regional and racial geography of the South. Looking back at colonial Kentucky from her position in the South of the early 1930s, she centers her narrative around questions of cultural and racial assimilation that were particularly urgent in the segregated South of her time. Much like her southern contemporaries—specifically Lytle, Welty, and Faulkner—Gordon seems to be interested in Native Americans as they participate in the formation of myths about the nation's genesis *and* in the construction of a particular regional identity. But unlike Lytle and Faulkner, she explicitly foregrounds gender and sexuality in her exploration of early contact with Indians. In "The Captive" she explores racial anxieties surrounding discourses of whiteness and sexual anxieties toward the racially coded Indian other.

As in much fiction written by white southerners, this narrative is only covertly about Native American lives and much more overtly—as the title announces—about the white female captive at its center. What lies behind the Indian captivity of the specific social history of Gordon's region is a concern with southern whiteness, a racial marker where regional and national identification neatly intersect. By tracing the captive's journey from "whiteness" to "Indianness," Gordon focuses on the instability of the captive's racial identity and on the anxieties that such shifting racial identifications provoke. The greatest anxiety to the white captive's identity originates in the looming sexual threat of the Indian other, a familiar trope of "Indian intercourse" that Gordon rewrites into a powerful discourse on miscegenation. The narrative's concern with sex, blood, and race opens up suggestive parallels between systems of social power in the American colonial period and in Gordon's contemporary South. As a white woman in the segregated South, Caroline Gordon, much like her character, found herself captive to the strictures of racial and sexual codes that the South shared with many European colonial societies of the time.

Gordon's discovery of the Wiley captivity narrative in the stacks of Vanderbilt's library provided a chance to memorialize the origins of Kentucky, an archaeological enterprise at once regionalist and nationalist.[12] Gordon's fictional captivity narrative relies closely on the historical source by William Elsey Connelley (1855–1930), who published the Wiley captivity in 1910 under the title *The Founding of Harman's Station with an account of The Indian Captivity of Mrs. Jennie Wiley and the Exploration and Settlement of the Big Sandy Valley in the Virginias and Kentucky.*[13] Connelley's history avails itself of fictional tropes, as is abundantly clear in the preface, which is marked by the author's Anglocentric perspective:

> The founding of Harman's Station on the Louisa River was directly caused by a *tragedy* as dark and horrible as any ever perpetrated by the savages upon the exposed and dangerous frontier of Virginia. The destruction of the home of Thomas Wiley in the valley of Walker's Creek, the murder of his children, the captivity of his wife by savages and her miraculous escape were the first incidents in a series of events in the history of Kentucky which properly belong to the annals of the Big Sandy Valley. Over them time has cast a tinge of *romance,* and they have grown in historical importance for more than a century. (47; emphasis added)

Writing frontier history as both tragedy and romance, Connelley freely borrows literary framing devices to elevate the historical events to the level of myth and provide them with a sense of necessity or inevitability. If, on the one hand, the Wiley captivity is a tragedy, then surely Jinny Wiley is the heroine whose pride in her own independence precipitates the tragic loss of her children and home. Following this pattern, Jane Gibson Brown has read "The Captive" as "a narrative of endurance and initiation in which the main character, a spirited and over-assertive woman named Jinny Wiley, learns the code of the wilderness while she is being held captive" (76). Brown argues that Jinny must learn to accept her place as a woman on the frontier and that her captivity teaches her reliance on male protection and guidance which she brashly rejects at the beginning of the narrative. In this reading, the tragic lesson—no irony intended—is that Jinny must learn the "essential helplessness of women without men" (79). If, on the other hand, the Wiley captivity is a frontier romance, then Jinny Wiley's experience of living among Indians is part of a myth of difference that holds out the promise of cultural union by sexual contact or marriage in a New World Eden. This promise is (and must be) constantly frustrated, however, in favor of a hegemonic view of colonization and civilization as a heroic victory over the wilderness and its savage inhabitants. Connelley's history of the foundation and settlement of Kentucky does exactly that. It serves to stabilize the ideological basis of American historical consciousness and posits regional roots—of Kentucky and Virginia—within the framework of a tradition of Indian conflict, or to use Roy Harvey Pearce's more forceful term, "Indian hating." Clearly, history conceived as either tragedy or romance has formal limitations and specific ideological goals.

Connelley readily admits to his goals in presenting regional history as part of a larger national discourse of colonization. Consistent with the myth of the frontier as "a deep, dark, dangerous, unexplored, unknown, but with a fascination wholly irresistible" and populated by "mongrel hordes of painted savages" (59), he presents a list of male explorers who helped to tame the wilderness, "a land having the inherent capacity for the development and maintenance of an empire unpeopled and wrapped in the unbroken silence of perpetual solitude" (59). But in order to obtain "the land of plenty," settlers like Tom and Jennie Wiley have to suffer the dangers of frontier life, which means returning to "blazing cabin homes in the red glare of which lay murdered and scalped families, captive wives and daughters led away into the wilderness to degradation worse than death, fathers and sons tortured at the stake," all of which were "common occurrences all along the western borders of the English settlements until the peace of Greenville in 1795" (58). This is not the language of history but the myth of the frontier per se, or in Richard Slotkin's words, the "myth of regeneration through violence [which] became the structuring metaphor of the American experience" (*Regeneration* 5).

Fascinated with this myth, both Connelley and Gordon structure their captivity narratives around the importance of "race" and "blood" in a frontier community where Indians function not only as imaginary obstacles to Anglo-American domination but as perceived sexual threats to racial "purity." When Connelley wrote in 1910 that "the blood of the mountaineer is the purest on the continent," it is impossible not to be reminded of the racial logic of the "one drop rule" South or to hear a note ominously foreshadowing Nazi rhetoric. Connelley's text initiates a discourse of heritage and genealogy based on biological criteria such as "pure blood" aimed at remaking the region into a "white territory" of undiluted racial origins. If this strikes us as crassly racist and nativist, it is important to remember that Connelley and Gordon wrote their captivity narratives against the background of the segregated South of the early twentieth century. Grace Elizabeth Hale explains that

> as culture, southern segregation made a new collective white identity across lines of gender and class and a new regional distinctiveness. Yet paradoxically, the southern whiteness that segregation created provided a cultural foundation for the very "natural" racial differences white southerners had hoped to protect and a route back into the nation. Grounding the modern whiteness that in turn grounded national reconciliation, the specifically southern culture of segregation became doubly important for the nation, as racial narratives and spectacles utilized southern settings and reworked southern history and as southern blacks in growing numbers began to migrate out of the region. (9)

And, we might add, as Native Americans who had already been removed from the Southeast one hundred years earlier (1830) continued to be understood as a non-presence, no matter what the number of actual Native Americans remaining in the South.[14] When Gordon read Connelley in 1931, his introduction must have struck her as odd, perhaps even portentous. In rewriting the Wiley captivity, she therefore purposefully foregrounded precisely those questions about race, blood, and sex central not only to the suspense and meaning of a narrative about captivity but also to a society that was struggling with problems of racial assimilation and miscegenation.

In order to address these problems explicitly, Gordon makes four significant changes to the historical source. First, unlike Connelley's text, written in the "objective" third-person voice of the historian, "The Captive" is a first-person narrative featuring the voice of "Jinny Wiley" herself. By centering her text around a woman's perspective as opposed to that of a male historian who relies on the memory of other men (specifically Wiley's son Adam), Gordon creates a convincing portrait of the cultural psyche of white female America. Second, unlike Connelley, who embeds the experiences of Jennie Wiley in a larger framework of American settlement and the courageous actions of "heroic men," Gordon focuses exclusively on the experiences of the female captive from the traumatic moment of her capture to her safe return. By moving Jinny to the center of the narrative, Gordon can more conveniently and poignantly address the anxieties surrounding the white female body in the American colonial situation. Because sexual control and reproduction affect the very nature of colonial relations, the captivity of a white woman endangers the hierarchies of authority and potentially contests the very power structure of colonial society itself. The captivity of a woman is crucial because it reveals through the threat of sexual contact and control how colonial authority and racial distinctions are fundamentally structured in terms of gender. Third, unlike in the historical source where Jennie Wiley's sexual relations with her Indian captors are silenced and relegated to a footnote (albeit a lengthy one), the fictional narrative highlights those repressed anxieties about sexual violation, possession, and desire. Precisely by increasing sexual tension surrounding the white female captive, Gordon dramatizes not only her character's personal vulnerability and the danger to the integrity of her body but also the potential vulnerability of American colonial space and the political body more generally. Sexual tension, and more importantly the white woman's sexual resistance, is crucial because it shows that her body, although vulnerable, must remain strong and impermeable. Such impermeability is doubly significant in the context of southern literature, as it serves to reflect not only on the defensible borders of the American nation in the colonial context but also on the firm borders of contemporary southern racial spaces marked by the taboos of miscegenation. Finally, Gordon reworks Connelley's concerns with the purity of racial genealogy by suggesting the potential for miscegenation. The assertion of American supremacy, which is expressed in the historical source in terms of the patriotic manhood of all those frontier men who were famous Indian fighters for the Republic, returns in the fictional narrative in the form of a question about racial virility and sexual access—white and Indian. By alluding to the possibility of a sexual union between white women and racial others, such as Jinny and the Cherokee chief Mad Dog, Gordon's text dips deeply into the nation's sexual and racial anxieties. Opposing racially codified Indians to the "white blood" of an imaginary frontier community, Gordon's captivity narrative ponders the dangerous prospects of cultural and racial assimilation of both the female captive, who is threatened with the loss of her "whiteness," and of Native Americans, who fear the loss of their culture and lives as whites increasingly advance into Indian living space.

White Dreams/Dreaming White

Gordon's story not only endorses a clear separation of race into "white" and "Indian" by drawing secure boundaries around these racial identities, but it also undercuts this crucial distinction necessary to the formal operation of captivity by revealing the ultimate instability of racial identity. As a captivity narrative, Gordon's story reveals a certain set of ideologies in both content and form.

Whereas the content of Gordon's story—the exploration of a racial contact zone—might itself be ideological, it is its form, the genre of the captivity narrative, that permits this ideology to be read. In both form and content this genre fetishizes a particular model of cultural confrontation: the act of being taken captive, the endurance and dangers of captivity, and the return. This formal pattern predetermines to a large part the ideological work captivity narratives can perform even if they should contain subversive elements or views that seem radically opposed to a hegemonic reading of captivity. Like many other American captivity narratives, beginning with Mary Rowlandson's, Gordon's narrative adopts such a hegemonic form particularly in its representation of race. Gordon dramatizes her concern with racial markings of colonized spaces by dividing the setting into "white" and "Indian" territory, separated by a natural boundary, the Ohio River. As the captive moves from the safety and stability of white space into Indian space, and as assimilation pressures increase, so do the pressures and anxieties around her own racial identification. With shifting territory, therefore, Gordon probes the shifting nature of racial identity. By centering her narrative on the body of the white female captive, she can investigate at a safe historical distance those discourses of race that were circulating in the South of her own time.

Gordon's use of the Ohio River as a geographical and symbolical divide is apparent from the beginning of the narrative. After Jinny Wiley is brutally captured, she travels with her Indian captors, a group of Cherokees, under the leadership of Mad Dog, and Shawnees, under the leadership of Crowmoker, into Indian country.[15] Pursued by "Tice" (Matthias) Harman, the famous Indian fighter, the group travels north to safety across the river. When Jinny asks Crowmoker if "the white people were still following us," the chief "laughed and said no white men could get across that river." Jinny fears that "the Indians would probably take me so far away that I'd never again see a white face" (228). This is the first note sounding anxiety around the disappearance of whiteness. According to captivity narrative conventions, in Indian country—this space beyond the reach of whiteness—Jinny makes many cultural adjustments and becomes increasingly integrated into the native economy. She works at collecting firewood and smelting bullets made out of lead from nearby mines, and she learns how to flesh and cure pelts, split a deer sinew for thread, make a deer whistle, and sew skins to make clothes. She is even promised a better status in the tribe when the group will return to the main camp in the spring. Meanwhile, Jinny answers to Crowmoker, the old Shawnee chief whose captive she is, and he tells her "to do all the work around the camp from now on, the way the Indian women did" (229). Jinny's wilderness savvy earns her respect from Crowmoker, who says in his best stereotypical Hollywood Indian-speak: "White woman know. . . .

White woman teach Indian women" (220). In Crowmoker's view, the white woman's knowledge needs to be assimilated into his culture, and therefore he teaches her not only the drudgery work of the camp but also something about the traditions and wisdom of his people, including knowledge of "yarbs and roots," the secrets of tribal medicine. Ultimately, the chief's plan is the full adoption of Jinny into the Shawnee nation in lieu of the daughter he had lost.

Although Gordon's text contains references to Indian women, it excludes them entirely from the plot. One reason for this may be historical: among the Cherokee nation, for example, only women could decide the fate of captives. As Paula Gunn Allen writes, these decisions "were made by vote of the Women's Council and relayed to the district at large by the War Woman or Pretty Woman. The decisions had to be made by female clan heads because a captive who was to live would be adopted into one of the families whose affairs were directed by the clan-mothers" (*Hoop* 36). It would make sense, therefore, that in this raiding war-party camp run by men, the captive's fate remains undecided and full adoption is indeed deferred until the company returns to the main camp. But I think in addition to historical accuracy, Gordon had another reason: she excluded Indian women from the plot because Jinny's status in a matriarchal environment in which women hold power may have skewed the traditional sexual and political dynamics of the genre in which the white woman's fate is in the hands of Indian men. Writing from her own position in a patriarchy, Gordon imposes the mainstream Anglo-American view of gender dynamics onto Native American history and culture. In doing this she is part of a long tradition of writers who rewrite Native American cultural traditions largely by reducing the status held by Indian women. This tradition began in the colonial context when "the British worked hard to lessen the power of women in Cherokee affairs. They took Cherokee men to England and educated them in European ways" (Jaimes and Halsey 307). This cultural assimilation into a model of male leadership was disastrous for Cherokee society; it "greatly weakened the Cherokee Nation, creating sharp divisions within it that have not completely healed even to the present day" (307).

Crossing the borders once more between fact and fiction, Gordon's captivity narrative remains trapped by its own hegemonic form and by its mainstream cultural assumptions, which center on the sexual attraction Indian men supposedly feel for white women. In this scenario, there is no place for the Indian woman except as an imaginary other. With Indian women conveniently excluded, the narrative centers instead on Jinny's body as a site for exploring anxieties surrounding whiteness and the traumatic expression of its perceived disappearance. With increasing assimilation pressures, Jinny worries about the loss of her identity: "I asked him [Crowmoker] wouldn't I still be a white woman after I was adopted into the tribe but he said no, the white blood would go out of me and the Spirit would send Indian blood to take its place, and then I would feel like an Indian" (238). The chief believes that Jinny's "white blood" will be transformed into "red blood" with the cultural initiation of the captive into the tribe. Gordon opposes this Native American concept of racial identity based on cultural practice to the captive's Euro-American understanding of racial identity based on blood, an inherent physical quality that is essentialized. As such, blood functions as an ontological category of identity, a fixed racial subjectivity that operates independently of any historical or cultural circumstances.

Gordon takes care to introduce the discussion of whiteness, not as the raceless or unmarked subjectivity that it often appears to be, but as an ideologically contested category.[16] Jinny's blood lineage—her whiteness—is threatened by the Shawnees' plans of integration, and although she is no longer afraid of the "dark" bodies that surround her during the day, her anxieties surface at night: "I thought nothing of seeing dark faces around me all the time, but in the night sometimes I would dream of white faces. White faces coming towards me through the trees. Or sometimes I would be in the house again and look up all of a sudden and all the faces in the room would be white" (239). The captive's unconscious reveals what her conscious awareness denies: a deep-seated anxiety around the instability of racial categories such as "whiteness." This sense of racial instability fuels Jinny's nightmares of racial assimilation and her dreams of white rescue. The "white face" of Tice Harman which haunts Jinny's dreams signifies both rescue and a deep-seated race hatred responsible for Jinny's capture in the first place. As such, Jinny desires and detests Harman as much as the Indians do. Her critical daytime view of Harman's unprovoked aggressions changes into admiration of his strength at night, and in an act of subconscious substitution, the nameless "white boy" who is brought to the camp as a prisoner leads Jinny to freedom in her dream. This short dream segment, in which the white boy shows Jinny the way to the settlements, mentions the word *white* seven times and the word *light* sixteen times, and in classical captivity narrative symbolism, white and light, qualities associated with the captive, are opposed to the darkness of the forest and the Indians. Jinny's internal journey is toward whiteness, the whiteness of her house—"white all over and the walls so thin you could see the light from the lamp shining through the logs" (244)—and the whiteness of her people, whose hair is "light" like the white boy's and Harman's.

By exposing the largely unconscious roots of whiteness in Jinny's dreams, Gordon clearly reveals the structure of racial identification that is threatened. Judith Butler argues that "identifications are never fully and finally made; they are incessantly reconstituted and, as such, are subject to the volatile logic of iterability. They are that which is constantly marshaled, consolidated, retrenched, contested, and, on occasion, compelled to give way" (105). The production of whiteness in the colonial context hinges on the successful reiteration of white identity, because interracial contact is both a precondition to its successful production (the racial other makes whiteness possible) and a reminder that it is also always subject to failure (Seshadri-Crooks 358).[17] The reproduction of whiteness as depicted in Gordon's narrative therefore depends not only on such reiteration of identity but also on the production of a racially coded other. In the story, Jinny's need to delineate her whiteness becomes stronger with increasing pressure to assimilate and more possibilities for an imaginary identification with the Indians. Although Jinny acknowledges such alternate racial identifications, she regards them with a mixture of anxiety and desire. Her dreams are a confirmation of the unstable status of her racial identification, the fact that whiteness needs to be produced again and again.

A sudden, drastic step toward Jinny's assimilation into the native culture occurs when Crowmoker asks her to dye her skin "red" so that she looks more like a Shawnee woman. This change in skin color, the surface structure of racial identity, affects Jinny deeply. She is asked to abandon the external signs of whiteness, a procedure that subjects her to a phantasmatic identification with the other that the body's surface seems to literalize. Commenting on this racial transformation, Jinny says, "[he] fixed me up some of the red root mixed with bear's grease, and after I'd been putting it on my face for a while you couldn't told me from an Indian woman, except for my light eyes" (237). As an essentialized racial marker, Jinny's "light eyes" are the last reminder of her whiteness.[18] But the clear dividing lines between self and other become slippery when Jinny blends in so well with her captors that the white male prisoner who is brought to camp does not recognize her as "white." This failure of recognition by someone of the same racial group causes Jinny much pain and anxiety. When her positive semblances of herself as "white" are effaced, Jinny calls out to the boy in a deep expression of racial fear and guilt: "'I'm a white woman, but I can't do nothing. Christ!' I said, 'there ain't nothing I can do'" (240). Her self-identification as a white woman is endangered here not only because she is stripped of the power to rescue the captured boy but, and more fundamentally, because she is no longer even recognized as being "white." This loss of whiteness destabilizes her racial core self and results in an experience of frustration and guilt, a trauma that impresses itself unconsciously on her psyche and is relived and repeated in her dreams.

That borderlines between self and other are more porous than they appear to be is evident in the narrative's pressure to collapse the separate spheres of "whiteness" and "Indianness" in the bodily entities that represent them. Indian otherness represents a threat to the captive's racial *and* sexual integrity. This is particularly so because the female captive's body is especially vulnerable to penetration by an other. As assimilation pressure steadily increases and finally culminates in Crowmoker's sale of Jinny to Mad Dog, and as her sexual status in the community changes from daughter to wife, Jinny must recross the river into white territory in order to preserve her sexual and racial integrity.

Gordon places sexual fear and desire at the center of her narrative. The sexual strain of the narrative, however, has less to do with the relationship of body and spirit (as in Rowlandson's classic Puritan captivity, e.g.) than it does with a racialized narrative of miscegenation. Slotkin argues that the captivity narrative is defined from the beginning as the temptation of the Indian marriage, and in the Puritan context specifically as a fear of the "marriage" of English and "American" cultures (*Regeneration* 125). Moreover, "for the women captives," Slotkin explains, "there was the immediate threat of a literal forced marriage to an Indian brave"—as there is for Jinny Wiley—and such "marriage symbolized this process of acculturation in terms of merging of the races" (125).

Whereas Gordon's narrative also contains the horror implicit in the idea of sexual intercourse with the "savage," the primary anxiety expressed and symbolically addressed in her narrative is the traumatic experience of miscegenation, the mixing of blood. Writing in the 1930s, Gordon sees the captivity narrative as an especially effective means of addressing cross-racial experiences that allows her to assimilate America's colonial inheritance with the specific racial situation of the South.

As in many other captivity narratives, in "The Captive" the white woman's sexual integrity assumes a central importance because it is intimately connected with the purity of the blood lineage it represents—in this case, the Scotch-Irish genealogy.[19] In Connelley's history, whose goal is to sketch the European heritage of the Kentucky settlers, Jennie Wiley's potential sexual promiscuity is relegated to a footnote. Among all sorts of speculations about her sexual purity, Connelley trusts her son, Adam, his principal informant, who insists on his mother's sexual integrity and on the fact that "his mother was to be the *daughter* of the Shawnee chief" (89). Connelley adds, however, that "it was natural, of course, for Mr. Wiley to believe that his mother escaped violation" (89). Although Connelley carefully judges the source of this information and the personal interests of his informant, he dismisses the following alternate accounts as "mere conjecture": an Indian daughter was born to Mrs. Wiley; Adam Wiley is the son of the Shawnee; Mrs. Wiley was the wife of the Cherokee. Connelley states that even though "there was never any uniformity in these versions," he considers it his duty to "state all the facts in his possession" (89). Although marginalized in a footnote, the question of sexual contact is crucial in Connelley's genealogical record of the first settlers of the Big Sandy Valley. Blood relations constitute a fundamental value, because to be of the same "blood" means to be part of the same family, and this extended family forms the blood of a new society.[20]

In Gordon's narrative, by contrast, such anxiety about the "blood" of the settlers is speculatively foregrounded as sexual tension between the characters steadily increases. In the colonial context as well as in the contemporary context of the segregated South, Gordon's story illustrates Foucault's insight that discourses about sex and blood work together to form a system of power.[21] While Foucault specifically points to the second half of the nineteenth century as a time when "blood was sometimes called on to lend its entire historical weight toward revitalizing the type of political power that was exercised through the devices of sexuality" (149), this was particularly so in the South, where racial and sexual laws were regulated by the "one drop rule." According to this rule, one drop of "black blood" was enough to make a person black. It was when the one-drop rule was most sharply enforced in the second half of the nineteenth century that the kind of "modern" biological racism took shape which culminated in the European holocaust of the 1930s. As Foucault writes, "it was then [in the late nineteenth century] that a whole politics of settlement . . . accompanied by a long series of permanent interventions at the level of the body, conduct, health, and everyday life, received their color and their justification from the mythical concern with protecting the purity of blood and ensuring the triumph of the race" (*History* 149). It is no accident that the nineteenth-century American Indian genocide, supported by discourses about a "vanishing race," coincides with biological blood rules for African Americans. These events precipitated and participated in an awareness of the meaning of "whiteness" and caused whites to become increasingly self-conscious about their "race" (Hale 23).[22]

Gordon's ear seems finely tuned to these discourses of race, blood, and sex and their relation to the maintenance of social power. In "The Captive" Gordon uses the sexual tension surrounding Jinny's white body not only symbolically, to illustrate the threat to the power of American colonial rule, but pragmatically as well, to allude to the social politics of her own segregated society in which gender and race are implicated in a wider set of power relations. A pressing issue in Gordon's narrative is the relationship between gender prescriptions and racial boundaries, and more specifically how sexual control figures in the construction of those boundaries. Gordon changes the historical record again in order to increase the sexual tension between the white prisoner and her Indian captors. In Connelley's text the danger to the white woman's sexual integrity is diminished by the age of the chiefs who lay claim on her. The Shawnee chief who adopts Jennie as his daughter is "an old man" of "a more kindly disposition than the other Indians." And although the Cherokee chief is described as "fierce and irascible," "stern and hard of countenance, resourceful, full of energy and quick of mind and body for an Indian," he is "more than fifty years of age, possibly sixty" (80). The historical narrative also locates the Cherokee chief's sexual power mostly in his past: "Mrs. Wiley stood much in fear of him from the first. He had carried away a white woman from some Kanawha settlement a few years previous to this raid" (80). By contrast, Gordon imagines the Cherokee chief younger, handsome, vigorous, and sexually potent. Mad Dog, as his name implies, threatens Jinny from the beginning on. When the Indian raiding party realizes they are burning down the wrong person's house, Mad Dog suggests killing Jinny along with her children. But for the protection of the older Shawnee chief who claims her as his prisoner, Jinny narrowly escapes with her life. But Mad Dog has his eyes set on her. Powerful, impulsive, and potent, Mad Dog remains a threat to Jinny's safety throughout the story. In the brute violence he shows toward Jinny, Gordon captures the mounting sexual tension between the "red man" and the "white woman" (225). In the early scenes of her narrative, Gordon establishes Mad Dog's power to physically control and dominate Jinny. Unlike the old Shawnee chief, Mad Dog is interested in Jinny not as a daughter but as a wife and, as we are led to believe, as an attractive sexual partner. According to this familiar sexual myth, Indian men—and men of color more generally—consider white women desirable and seductive. Gordon's narrative plays with this latent sexual threat not only as a manifestation of the structure of the captivity genre itself but also as a historical and ideological particularity of her own society.

Gordon heightens the sexual tension surrounding Jinny's body every time Mad Dog appears in the story in order to show that the sexual fear surrounding the white woman's body is closely related to racial anxiety. Commenting on the linkage between sexual control and racial tension, Ann Laura Stoler writes: "While sexual fear may at base be a racial anxiety, we are still left to understand why such anxieties are expressed through sexuality. . . . If, as Sander Gilman (1985) claims, sexuality is the most salient marker of otherness, organically representing racial difference, then we should not be surprised that colonial agents and colonized subjects expressed their contests—and vulnerabilities—in these terms" (346). But sexuality in Gordon's imagination is double-edged: it symbolizes not only a racial threat and a political vulnerability but also a deep-seated (though largely repressed) desire for the Indian other. Although Mad Dog acts violently and sullenly toward Jinny, he is sexually provocative and attractive to her. When we follow Jinny's gaze, we see a stereotypical good-looking "bad Indian": "The fire shone in his black eyes and on his long beak of a nose. When he moved, you could see his muscles moving, too, in his big chest and up and down his naked legs. An Indian woman would have thought him a fine-looking man, tall, and well formed in every way, but it frightened me to look at him. I was glad it was the old chief and not him that had taken me prisoner" (220–21). Carefully distinguishing between her own desire and the projected desire of an Indian woman, a woman ostensibly unlike her, Jinny hides her own sexual attraction to, but simultaneous fear and repulsion of, Mad Dog. Behind her assertion that Mad Dog would have been attractive to an Indian woman, Jinny is betraying her own fascination with the eroticized body of the Indian other—the naked legs, the moving muscles, the big chest.

This desire for the other is ultimately canceled out by racial fear when the possibility for the consummation of that sexual attraction actually threatens. Although Jinny has several escape fantasies in which she sees herself slipping away from her Indian captors to the safety of a settler's cabin (231), she never tries to escape until her status in the tribe changes from daughter to wife. When Jinny is sold to Mad Dog for "five hundred brooches," she fights the decision, desperately pleading with the Shawnee chief who is selling her out. The last step to total racial assimilation is to become the wife or concubine of Mad Dog, a sexual union that Jinny feels she must prevent at all cost. Gordon shows the degree to which Jinny fears this step by introducing traditional religious imagery representing Mad Dog as a devil: "His eyes were black in the circles of paint. His tongue showed bright red between his painted lips. The red lines ran from his forehead down the sides of his cheeks to make gouts of blood on his chin. . . . A devil. A devil come straight from hell to burn and murder" (242). Attempting to underscore the dramatic and dangerous otherness of the Indian, Gordon resorts to the most traditional and canonical representation of racial difference. To assure his "prize," Mad Dog ties Jinny up "tight with the thongs that he cut from buffalo hide," and Jinny waits late into the night for his dreaded return that would complete the bargain. But sexual contact is delayed indefinitely; in fact, as in the historical narrative, it never occurs: "I laid there on the floor, listening to the Indians and thinking about how it would be when Mad Dog came down to take me for his wife. I laid there, expecting him to come any minute, but the singing and dancing went on and he didn't come, and after a while I went to sleep" (243). Jinny's fear of sexual contact with the devilish Indian leads directly to the imaginary escape in her dream in which the white boy shows her the way to freedom, and to her actual escape after she wakes up unharmed and finds the Indians are gone. The dreaded consummation never takes place.

Perhaps Gordon avoids the sexual union to which her narrative builds up because she clings closely to the historical source she trusted most, and according to Connelley, Jennie Wiley probably "escaped sexual violation." But Gordon's own comments on her story suggest another reason. When Gordon was working on "The Captive" she wanted it to be the first in a sequence of stories about early Tennessee that would center on the pioneers as "heroes" of the new nation. In a 1966 interview she emphasizes the heroic qualities of her female character: "I would have been dead nuts by this time, and I think most modern women. She [Jinny] is of heroic stature but still she is a human being. . . . I think she's got about forty times as much moral fibre as almost any woman I know" (qtd. in Makowsky 107). While celebrating the moral and physical strength of the pioneer woman, Gordon simultaneously extols the strength of the new (white American) nation. In the contest of cultures for cultural and political dominance, avoiding sexual contact with the "native" then means avoiding implication in the pattern of Manifest Destiny and ensuring racial and cultural survival.[23] Gordon's narrative makes this abundantly clear both explicitly (in references to racial extinction) and implicitly (in the story's setting). In terms of time, assimilation into Indian culture means abandoning the Anglo-American narrative of progress and reverting to a premodern native past. In terms of place, assimilation means dwelling among the graveyards of ancestors and the bones of prehistoric beasts.

Gordon's Indian country is littered with the bones of prehistoric animals and various remains from the Mound Builders period.[24] These archaeological remains form a stable pre-colonial setting against which modern American national life develops. Indians in Gordon's narrative are trapped in the past; the settlers, by contrast, live in the present and signify the future. Gordon sets up the captive's modern history against an imaginary ethnohistory of Native Americans by referring to three archaeological locations in particular: the cliff paintings, which had already faded when Connelley was retracing Jennie Wiley's steps in 1910; the Indian mounds that were marking the graves of native peoples during the Mound Builders era; and the salt licks that were littered with the enormous bones of prehistoric animals "bigger than buffalo." All of these sites point to a past of flourishing Indian populations long before the advent of the Europeans. What is left in the 1780s are mostly fragments of these archaeological layers—those remnants of bones, artifacts, and cave art that were excavated during the 1930s, when Gordon was writing her captivity narrative.

In much American fiction, entry into Indian life signals not only the halt of time and progress but a return to a premodern, even "prehistoric," era. In Gordon's narrative this entry is symbolically marked by Jinny's loss of her sense of time and place. "I knew it was some time in October that the Indians come and burned our house," she says, "but I didn't know how long we'd been on the trail and I didn't have any idea what country we were in" (228). Gordon sketches more than just the loss of orientation here; she creates a timeless Indian environment ruled by ancient native traditions. The rock houses where the Cherokees and Shawnees make camp are decorated with "deer and buffalo and turtles as big as a man painted in red and black on the rock" (229). These cliff paintings represent, as the old chief explains, "the Indian's fathers" and form part of an ancestral environment to which tribal members respond with awe and curiosity (230). The rock houses symbolize a timeless Indian space where the cliff dwellers' lifestyle has apparently not changed much since the Paleolithic period several thousand years ago and where modern southeastern nations such as Cherokees and Shawnees supposedly continue the ancient traditions. Of the fading cliff paintings that decorate the rock houses, Connelley writes in 1910:

> On the face of the cliff overhanging the waters of the larger creek were formerly found many Indian hieroglyphics and strange pictures. These pictures were usually skeleton drawings of animals native to the country, such as the buffalo, bear, deer, panther, wolf, turkey, and a few of turtles and rattlesnakes. These figures were put on the cliffs with black or red paint. . . . Time, thoughtlessness and mischievous vandalism, and the weather have destroyed them all. In 1850, it is said, some of the groups were faintly visible, and as late as 1880 one group of deer in black, on the cliff over the larger creek, was yet very distinct. (109–10)

For Connelley, the erased traces of Native American art are symbolic of their own fading existence. The meaning of those "hieroglyphics" and "strange pictures" depicted on the walls is left to the speculation of the white historian behind whose descriptive prose lurks the familiar ideology of the vanishing Indians.

This discourse of Manifest Destiny still haunted American historians of the early twentieth century. The same year Connelley published his captivity history (1910), James Mooney, a fellow historian with the Mississippi Valley Historical Association, presented his case study about "The Passing of the Delaware Nation." As Brian Dippie points out, Mooney's title echoes James Fenimore Cooper's *The Last of the Mohicans* and "all the sunset imagery of the Vanishing American tradition" (239). Mooney supported his thesis of the "vanishing Indian syndrome" by counting only full-bloods in his aboriginal populations study. "Mooney dismissed as 'untenable' the contention that Indian numbers had been more or less stable throughout history," writes Dippie, "given 'the patent fact that the aboriginal population of whole regions has completely disappeared.' Some well-meaning individuals had even been fooled into assuming an increase in Indian population by including in their estimates mixed bloods, who for all practical purposes were white. Once mixed bloods were excluded, the

'Indians of the discovery period,' the true full blood, were seen to have suffered a drastic numerical decrease" (238). Based on census evidence, Mooney's thesis on the vanishing Indian syndrome influenced historians and anthropologists of the early twentieth century, and as Dippie says, "heresy became orthodoxy, and the Vanishing Indian, in its most literal sense, an accepted historical fact" (241). In a scientific climate in which biological blood rules for African Americans decided color and "race," it is not surprising that Mooney counted only full-bloods in his study and that such a concern with the purity of "blood" is a popular topic in southern literature of the time.

In both fiction and history of the 1930s, the discourse of the "vanishing Indian" was supported by a renewed interest in ethnographic and archaeological research in the South that concentrated on populations that had long "vanished." Many of the WPA-sponsored projects in Kentucky and Tennessee undertook major archeological mound excavations. When Gordon, too, integrates references to the Mound Builders into her captivity narrative, she attempts to situate native life in the past. Jinny recalls when the old chief points out the mound graves to her for the first time: "He said that he and his people always stopped when they come this way to visit the graves of their fathers that was all over the valley" (230). And the historian remarks in a footnote: "It is known that the Shawnees, Delawares, Wyandots, Toteros, Cherokees, and Iroquois, regarded the Big Sandy Valley with peculiar and lasting veneration. They clung to it with tenacity, and it was the last stream in Kentucky to be surrendered by them. It was a favorite valley of the Mound Builders, as evidenced by many remains of their occupation" (Connelley 110). It is no accident that in telling the late-eighteenth-century story of Jennie Wiley's captivity, the historian gets sidetracked into the Mound Builders period. In both fiction and history, this association of modern Indian nations with the ancient Paleolithic, Archaic, or mound-building peoples constructs a historical continuity among all Native Americans across thousands of years, an alignment that has the effect of associating living people with vanished "prehistoric" peoples and creating a historical trajectory that points to their own cultural extinction as well.

This is true for Gordon's story, in which the danger to modern Native American survival is classically underscored by the chief's remark that swarming bees at the end of summer signal the arrival of whites and a lot of Indian "bloodshed" and death. In the chief's words: "When the bees swarmed out of season they were running away from the white people who had scared all the game out of the country and made it so that even bees couldn't live in it" (230). Jinny traumatically relives this experience of racial genocide in a dream in which she sees the old chief talking to the moon: "The white people. . . . The white people are all over the land. The beaver makes no more dams and the buffalo does not come to the lick. And the bees swarm here in the ancient village. Bees swarm on the graves of our fathers" (246). These explicit admissions of cultural extinction by the Indians themselves—also a tradition in American literature—are complemented by descriptions of Indian country as a dying and stagnant environment. Gordon underscores the past glory of Native American culture by littering the setting with bleached bones, frightening reminders of time and mortality. While in captivity, Jinny repeatedly returns to the graveyard of bones at the salt lick, where she spends her days retracing the evidence of a distant past like an archaeologist who sorts through bones trying to reconstruct past life by the fragments and remains left over from a bygone era. In this graveyard, time assumes different proportions; it seemingly stands still, as it often does in Indian cultures depicted by Anglo-Americans.

It is clear now why Jinny must avoid sexual intercourse with the Indian other: it would signal the mixing of her own Scotch-Irish blood with native blood and its apparently degenerative inheritance. With increasing pressures of cultural assimilation and physical (sexual) incorporation into a culture of "vanishing Indians," Gordon's captive develops conscious and unconscious strategies of resistance. Jinny not only literally dreams of whiteness but also escapes into "white space" in memories of her life before capture, particularly when she is surrounded by bones at the salt lick. These memories, which are inserted as a flashback into Jinny's life in the narrative present, preserve a sense of her Anglo-American cultural heritage and her racial self-identification as white. When these identifications are further threatened by her impending sexual contact with Mad Dog, she does not wait any longer for a better chance to escape—as she had for eleven months—but leaves immediately.

The captive's successful reentry into the settlers' culture demands, however, another dangerous river crossing in which Jinny again barely escapes with her life. As we saw earlier with Jinny's entry into Indian country, Gordon characterizes racial crossings by the use of spatial metaphors that underscore the shifting and porous frontier lines in terms of both territory and body. When Jinny returns to her community, the spatial coordinates of territory change as well as those physical and psychological determinants of her own body. This return is predicated upon her final self-identification as "white"; that is, only after certifying Jinny's whiteness does the settler community attempt to bring her into the safety of the fort's high stockade fence. Jinny's striking act of self-identification—"I'm Jinny Wiley . . . Jinny Wiley that the Indians stole"—is followed up by her racial identification: "God's sakes, man, you going to let me die right here before your eyes? I'm white! White I tell you!" (255). Gordon's protagonist does not chance another experience of racial misrecognition, and with Mad Dog hot on her heels she takes charge of rowing the makeshift raft across the river and bringing herself into the safety of the fort.

Told from the historical perspective of a woman whose physical and emotional hardiness Gordon celebrates, "The Captive" reveals the complex intersections of race and gender in the captivity context. The relationship between gender prescriptions and racial boundaries—and more specifically how sexual control figures in the construction of those racial boundaries—is a pressing issue not only in the narrative's colonial context but also in the segregated social environment from which Gordon rethinks colonial history. As she was rewriting captivity in the early 1930s, Gordon seemed to have been held captive by the racial boundaries of her narrative; in a strikingly symbolic passage, she admits that she, too, was trapped in the wilderness of her imagination and left with dreams of whiteness: "I do remember this—that I suffered more writing it than any story I ever wrote—than any short story. . . . [W]hen I got through with it, I got some white satin and embroidered pink roses on it . . . because I felt as if I had been living in the wilderness for weeks from jerky. . . . And I really was exhausted, and I felt I needed to coddle myself" (qtd. in Baum 449). Returning from the "contact zone," Gordon—like her female character—emerges heroic but exhausted and fully aware that it was the wilderness of her own imagination that was entangling her and holding her captive for six weeks. Captured by the spell of writing this captivity narrative, Gordon suffered with her protagonist, and in order to celebrate her own return to "civilization" she sets about a feminine domestic task of embroidering in pink and white, standard symbols of feminine innocence and purity.

Captive white women both, Gordon and her fictional protagonist test the ideological boundaries drawn around white womanhood, a racial and sexual identity that was used to structure social control in the segregated South. As a white woman in the South, Gordon had a personal investment in "captivity," a genre that allows her to probe the meanings of white subjectivity. "Due to their capture," writes Christopher Castiglia, "white women found themselves in contexts that necessitated a revision of discourses of knowledge and identity policed at/as the borders of white society. Crossing cultures forces white women to question the constitutive binaries of civilized and savage, free and captured, Christian and pagan, race and nation, on which their identities were based" (6). The degree to which Gordon crosses those borders of gender and race in her narrative is left open for discussion. I think she does venture across the traditional borderlines drawn around gender by celebrating the physical and emotional strength of a frontier woman. In this sense, her narrative is clearly part of a tradition of fictional captivity narratives written by women who loosen the constraints on gender and genre.[25] But underlying Gordon's progressive attitude toward female heroism and liberation—some might even call it her feminist agenda—there is the racial grain of the story, particularly a discourse about whiteness, assimilation, segregation, and miscegenation that takes on a decidedly southern conservative flavor. Very much a product of the segregated South, the story *investigates* the borders—geographical, physical, mental, and psychical—drawn around race, but it does not really *transgress* or *transform* them.

Gordon's story is valuable, however, because it illustrates the colonial anxieties around sexual and racial definitions of the body, many of which were still circulating in the South of the 1930s. Written from a cultural context marked by fears of racial and sexual difference—such as the danger of sexual contamination and social ostracism—Gordon's Indian story reveals striking similarities between the South's contemporary moment and America's colonial past. But more: if we expand the geographical framework around the narrative to look at the South in a global context, we notice that anxieties around white female bodies are not specific to this region but are echoed in pre–World War II colonial contexts all over the world. European colonies in Africa and Asia, for example, were structured by similar anxieties built around such racial hierarchies. Referring to twentieth-century European colonization of Africa, Stoler asserts that "the presence and protection of European women [in the colonies] were repeatedly invoked to clarify racial lines" (352). Much like in the early-twentieth-century South, where the "protection" of white women was predicated on heavily racist assumptions about the virile bodies of colored men, in the modern colonial context, equally racist evaluations "pivoted on the heightened sexuality of colonized men" (352). This imagined sexual threat to a white woman's purity links the American South with colonies in southern Rhodesia and Kenya of the 1920s and 1930s, where preoccupations with black male virility led to the creation of citizens militias and ladies riflery clubs, and with the European presence in New Guinea, where the White Women's Protection Ordinance of 1926 signaled death to any colored person *attempting* to rape a European woman (353). If this sounds like a racial scenario from southern fiction or if it is reminiscent of KKK protocol in the American South, it is because pre–World War II southern society retained a strongly colonialist structure of clear social and racial hierarchies predicated upon gender and sexual control. As a white woman in and of the South, Gordon herself is part of a system in which white male power is affirmed by the vulnerability of white women. In this sense, her preoccupation with the captivity of a white woman by racially coded others reflects on her own status as a "captive" of southern culture, which drastically prescribed and limited her sexual and racial liberties. Against this global background of European colonialism and domestic segregation, it is much less surprising that

Caroline Gordon found narratives of captivity "fascinating" and that the imaginary encounter with the Native American past—a marvelously exotic world of bleached white bones—leads us straight back to the contemporary sociopolitical moment and to the New Deal excavations of her home state.

Indians and Outlaws: Going Native in *Green Centuries*

When Gordon returns to the Indian frontier in her novel *Green Centuries* (1941), she shifts from her female-centered captivity narrative to a male-centered text that examines the rise of American nationalism and the legal construction of the white male body as a citizen. By setting her novel during the years of the American Revolution (between 1769 and 1779), she captures the political climate on the southern frontier at a time when settlers fought for their freedom from the British Crown and when American Indians fought increasingly against their colonial neighbors who threatened their freedom in turn. In order to sketch these colonial complexities, Gordon double-codes the Native American signifier: because the Cherokees are siding with the British imperial forces, they become the political enemies of the new American nation for which they are an obstacle both to westward expansion and to the fulfillment of the American creed of independence based on the "Laws of Nature." By depicting America as both a colonized and a colonizing space, Gordon's novel centers on the resulting tensions and complications that such a double "occupation" involves. On the one hand, Gordon rejects British imperialism from a hegemonic U.S. perspective that celebrates the settlers' growing resistance to British governance. The novel's hero—significantly named Rion Outlaw—is a prototypical American who fights English colonialism by refusing to pay taxes to the king, organizing attacks on royal forces, and attempting to make land deals with the Indians outside the Crown's reach. In this sense, the novel provides a hegemonic nationalist approach celebrating American resistance to the European imperial metropolis. On the other hand, Gordon criticizes the Americans' own colonizing behavior and the settlers' violence toward the Indians whose space they come to occupy by increasingly aggressive means. The American "Outlaws," it seems, are indeed outside the bounds of political and moral law. Much like their predatory English counterparts, they have imperialist goals and become embroiled in wars over territory and political dominance that are ultimately destructive.

Green Centuries is the story of two brothers, Rion and Archy Outlaw, who flee west because Rion, the older brother, had joined in an armed uprising against British colonial forces. On the way there, Archy is captured by Cherokees and the brothers get separated. After unsuccessfully searching for his brother, Rion and his household move on, leaving Archy behind for dead. But the fifteen-year-old Archy lives and grows up in the Cherokee nation, where he is adopted by the peace chief's clan. There he joins a new brother, the Owl, who initiates him into the Cherokee rituals of manhood. Archy and the Owl both become warriors, important young men in the Cherokee nation. Meanwhile, Rion settles on the Holston River with his family, which consists of his wife, Cassy, his brother-in-law, Frank, and their neighbors. When Rion and Archy meet again, years after their separation, in a Cherokee town, Rion wants Archy to come back with him. But Archy, who started a family of his own among the Cherokees, resists the pull of white fraternity because he identifies increasingly with the cultural and political life of the Cherokee nation. Although he is riddled by occasional identity crises, especially when the war breaks out—after all, he is a "white man"—he remains loyal to the Cherokees. The brothers then find themselves on opposing sides of the battle for land and political independence as a result of their moral and political convictions. Fighting for American independence, Rion comes into conflict not only with the British imperial government, the "Red coats," but with the Cherokee nation and his own brother. Fighting for Cherokee independence, Archy and the Indians battle settlers like Rion who intrude upon their lands and kill their long-standing political allies, the British. In an increasingly complex frontier situation of political alliances during the Revolutionary War, Rion and Archy meet during a surprise attack on a Cherokee settlement during which Rion's men kill Archy, his family, and most members of his clan. Reminiscent of the biblical story of Cain and Abel, Archy is slain by his brother, who survives and carries on the American legacy.

In this drama of national brotherhood, Gordon splendidly characterizes the rise of the American nation as a choice of political identification. The fraternal bonds between men such as Rion and Archy, forged by "blood" and "family," are put to the test of a political ideology based on racial and cultural identification. The origin of the American nation, Gordon seems to say, is bound up with the crucial choice of white American manhood—the identification that Rion chooses and Archy rejects—which leads to the successful survival not only of individuals but of a whole political system. The construction of this political system is paradoxically based on the "Laws of Nature," the seemingly timeless and universal principles that act as a mechanism for disguising the social and racial basis of the very "natural" laws that become the foundation of American civil law.[26]

From her location in the South and against the background of southern laws of segregation, Gordon examines those laws on which the American nation was based at its inception, and she traces the interpretation of law as it applies to African Americans, women, and Native Americans to show how the cultural politics of the early national environment resulted in a definition of citizenship as white and male. Gordon, I argue, traces the origins of modern southern whiteness back to the beginnings of the nation, thus locating the roots of southern racial identity and white supremacy in America's *national* heritage. Her central focus on the Outlaws leads into a discussion of different but interconnected notions of law at work in the construction of race, gender, and nationhood.

With respect to race, she illuminates those laws in America that led to the establishment of white male citizenship during the Revolutionary period. As written law, the Declaration of Independence and the Constitution provide the ideological foundations for the principles of "life, liberty, and happiness" and establish the egalitarian basis of American democracy. At the same time, however, those "laws" were in practice clearly raced and gendered and ruled out those to whom they did not apply. This can be seen most famously in Jefferson's *Notes on the State of Virginia,* particularly in his chapter on "Laws," which bases intellectual and artistic differences between blacks and whites on what Jefferson believed were scientifically verifiable biological differences. He does this, Dana Nelson argues, in order to "enable a legal construction of a white body clearly separated from the 'black' body" (54), a move that contributes to the "consolidation of national manhood through the production of the racial Other" (52). But whereas Jefferson excludes "blacks" from the protection and promise offered by America's legal body on the basis of a seemingly certifiable racial difference, he includes Native Americans in a gesture of political incorporation. Native American inclusion and African-American exclusion are political strategies "not contradictory, but mutually confirmative" in writing into being the white body of male citizenship (Nelson 55). Picking up on the contrary impulses of Enlightenment discourses about race, Gordon illustrates this exclusion of African Americans from the national promise of freedom and the right to property in a story tracing the aggressive territorial expansion of white settlers and the colonization of Native Americans. Both slavery and colonization become historical signposts that signify an expansive white body: a body that is simultaneously within and outside the rule of law.

With respect to gender, this lawlessness also extends to the formation of the American "family," characterized by an ambiguity that surrounds the status of the father and the role of patriarchy. Read through the Lacanian concept of "the law of the father," the name of Gordon's characters, the Outlaws, is ironically symbolic because the father, instead of being an authority figure who represents law and order, is positioned outside the law. Not surprisingly, the American sons take over as fathers both politically, by rejecting the father figure of the King of England, and libidinally, by enacting the oedipal paradigm. *Green Centuries* offers a complicated structure of masculinity based on the blatant rejection of the social and legal significance of the paternal metaphor as articulated in "the law of the father." This does not mean, however, that patriarchy is abandoned. In revealing the masculine desire for power, Gordon challenges the operations of patriarchy by revealing the limits of the oedipal fantasy, criticizing the misogynist discourses of her male characters, and opposing the system of Anglo-American patriarchy to Cherokee matrilineal laws.

And finally, with respect to nationhood, Gordon uses the family metaphor to mark shifting political alliances during the Revolution. Moving from an oedipal paradigm to a new fraternal paradigm, she centers the plot of her novel on the relationship between two brothers. This fraternal model requires a shift from patricide to fratricide, evoking the primal curse of Cain and Abel. Using the moral "laws" of this myth to characterize the beginnings of American nationhood, Gordon sketches the Revolutionary War as a war of division between white and Indian brothers. Unlike the French Revolution, which was guided by the motto "liberté, egalité, fraternité," the American Revolution ultimately rejects "fraternité" (brotherhood) for selfhood and individualism. Rion must sacrifice his "native" brother for the sake of American political unity. Gordon offers Indian brotherhood as an imagined necessity to the identity of the new American nation at the same time that she shows how the fantasy of brotherhood results in the trauma of Indian violence. The slaying of the "Indian br/other" is the traumatic act that calls forth the creation of the modern American citizen.

The Laws of Race and the Making of Whiteness

When Gordon rewrites early colonial history from her location in the South, she is precisely interested in how the concepts of race, nation, and gender based in discourses of "naturalization" support a hierarchy of power with the American white male on top. Although Europeans in the mid-eighteenth century did not yet identify themselves collectively as "white," Enlightenment Europeans often characterized themselves as superior to Africans or Native Americans.[27] And although their various experiences of colonial life in America, or their experience of the Revolution, did not work to draw them into "a seamless, common sense of identity," it was not long before the concepts of "whiteness" and "Americanness" came into being and were inextricably linked (Nelson 5). Both identities grew out the Revolutionary period, as Nelson argues: "Indeed, historians, sociologists, and philosophers concerned with historical manifestations of race/racism have similarly isolated the Revolution and its aftermath as the period when racial consciousness, and specifically whiteness, became more generally important as an identity category" (6). Scholars point particularly to "the late 1780s, in the Constitutional era," as the originating moment for the creation of the concept of "free white persons," a concept that implied white manhood.

"White *manhood* was thereby specified as the legal criteria of civic entitlement, attaching the 'manly confidence' idealized by defenders of the Constitution to the abstractly unifying category of 'whiteness'" (6). This concept of white manhood "worked symbolically and legally to bring men together in an abstract but increasingly functional community that diverted their attention from differences between them" (6). It may be that white men lacked a unified identity either as "white" or as "American" in colonial America prior to independence, but for Gordon, of course, these concepts existed as indelible realities in the South of her time. Thus, in her portrait of the early colonial South the concepts of "whiteness," "brotherhood," and "Americanness" emerge as closely linked theoretical and political articulations. Centering her story of the nation around two brothers—a younger, Indian-identified brother and an older, American brother—Gordon examines the historical confluence of "Americanness" as a new *racial* identity and "whiteness" as a *national* identity.

Gordon's depiction of the rise of a concept of the "white male" as a national and political agent gains particular significance in a political climate influenced once again by theories of racial superiority both in America prior to desegregation and abroad in Europe's colonial world. In Gordon's narrative, national identifications are bound up with race and gender in such a way that the political agency of the white male emerges in its difference from African Americans, women, and Native Americans. Nelson argues that such a recognizing and managing of "difference" marked "Democracy's Others" and at the same time "promised white men a unifying standpoint for national identity" and "an experience of citizenship as fraternity in the abstracted space of universalizing authority over others" (11). Precisely because Gordon seems interested in such an articulation of American citizenship as fraternity and in an exploration of the myth of white male superiority, she carefully sketches those scenes of racial difference.

African-American characters in Gordon's novel perform a racial identity against which the white man can become a "white" citizen, and they serve as symbolic reminders of what American nationhood promised but ultimately failed to achieve. Being black means being outside the American legal discourse of liberty and freedom. In chapter 4 of *Green Centuries* the reader encounters a group of unnamed African Americans who are being taken to the West. This scene provides a backdrop for Gordon's white characters to remark upon the symbolic freedom that the West offers exclusively to white men. Although Rion agrees that "it ain't right to put chains on a man," he believes that "a nigger ain't hardly a man" (42). Gordon could not have spelled it out more clearly: American manhood applies only to those who are white and therefore "free" to go west; or, putting it differently, Rion's sense of manhood and agency is dependent on his race. The novel's images of African Americans—both as chattel and entertainers—suggest that the rejection of British imperialism in the Revolutionary War and the promises of the Declaration of Independence will change nothing in the social psychology of racism and the hierarchies of white American imperial power. By depicting American colonialism not only in terms of westward expansion but also in terms of slave-trading practices, Gordon wants her readers to see how each of these attempts at subjugation—via colonialism and slavery—seems to provide a secure national identity for white men. As Rion muses on the fact that black men were going west "chained, packed in straw, like hogs to market, he swelled with a sense of his own freedom" (42). Gordon's strategy of voicing imperial rhetoric through Rion's racist imagination reveals the racial hierarchies on which white American manhood depends and on which the concept of American nationhood at its inception is based. The irony is that a rhetoric of freedom based on the violence of colonialism and slavery will not ensure true freedom even for white men like Rion, whose naive belief in individualism will be disappointed in the course of the novel.

Looking "west" from her position as a southern writer, Gordon recognizes what critics of American imperialism like John Carlos Rowe have recently pointed out: the close connection between the cultural histories of southern slavery and westward expansion.[28] In a revealing episode of "black-face" masquerade, Gordon illustrates how identities of "others" can be (and have historically been) appropriated by whites in order to achieve American national goals. After Rion joins the Regulators, a group of men who decide to take justice into their own hands in order to stop excessive taxation by Britain, he joins in a raid on an ammunition transport from Charleston. The men blacken their faces with soot to get ready for the rebellious uprising: "The soot worked alright. You couldn't see anything of their faces except the whites of the eyes and the teeth. It was like being out with a bunch of negroes. He wanted to laugh. Suppose word got out that a whole gang of negroes was loose and suppose everybody turned out to hunt them . . . " (120). The revolutionary potential of blackness as a racial identity is appropriated here to further American nationalist goals. The American anti-imperialist gang turned "black" is clearly outside the "law," and only from this rebellious position as "outlaws" can they achieve a new national identity. In this conflation of "Regulators" with African Americans, Gordon creates an identification that oscillates between a biologically anchored view of race as located in the (black) body and a cultural understanding of Americans as a new "race." As this "black-face" episode shows, American cultural self-construction is dependent on its difference from other "races," but it also relies on them and appropriates them. Although the whites in Gordon's novel feel comfortable adopting the black form in order to break the law—also a sign of racial ownership—the racial masquerade supports a different political goal: the construction of a new American race.

As a southern writer, Gordon brings the dangers of this masquerade clearly into perspective. Her suggestion of capture and her omission of the terrifying consequences in the ellipsis that ends the sentence recalls southern social law—specifically the lynching of blacks. Superimposed on this story of national liberation from British imperialism is the shadow of the South's own imperialism as practiced in the form of slavery, segregation, and racial terror. Gordon skillfully maneuvers this racial field full of double entendres and ironic political overtones by highlighting the new role "whiteness" plays in America. In her description of the raid, she foregrounds the tension "black-face" produces by introducing the White brothers as important characters in this scene. The blackened White brothers signal not only the racial base for the construction of a new political identity but also an important generational shift, as the following conversation shows: "Pa ain't going to like that," John White says, referring to their plans of stealing horses from Old Man White for the raid. "He ain't going to know who you are, blacked up as you be," answers a member of the group. The sons become unrecognizable to their "fathers" as they assume new identities as Americans. Linking national identification with racial masquerade, the White boys have to become "black"; that is, they have to assume a racial and political position on the fringes of "the law" in order to gain freedom and independence. Their blackness, however, only serves to secure rather than to destabilize their sense of themselves as white American men and future citizens. American national identity is therefore based on a central paradox: on the one hand, the emerging citizen needs racial "others" to define himself *against* so that a new ideal of American nationality intricately tied up with white masculinity can emerge; on the other hand, the new American adopts strategies of racial masking that allow him to define himself *with* the "other" precisely in order to achieve those very goals of white male citizenship and national self-definition. These strategies of racial masking and (mis)identification, however, involve a risk (such as castration, dismemberment, or death) and are therefore accompanied by anxieties about the loss of masculinity.

The Laws of Gender and Its Libidinal Outlaws

Gordon's novel often evokes this threat to American masculinity. It is sometimes explicitly expressed, as in the scene when a white man (Fred Mouncy), captured by Cherokees, announces that he "ain't had his manhood since" (230). But more consistently, the fear of emasculation is implicitly expressed in the misogynist attitudes of Gordon's male characters. Early in the novel, one is struck by a comment the legendary John Findley, the famous explorer who "discovered" the Cumberland Gap, makes to the Outlaw boys as he picks up one of their mother's caps: " 'Women's gear,' he said, 'I got some in my pack. Ought to have more, I reckon, but I hate to fool with the stuff.' '*Master Findley,*' his voice suddenly went high and mincing, 'I *ain't plumb sure I want the pink ribbons. Maybe I better take the blue.*' He spat on the floor as if to clear his mouth of the sound. 'I'd rather trade with the Indians any day' " (8). Findley's sexist comment signals the need to establish a version of masculinity clearly opposed to femininity. This difference from the female—American masculinity—is both likened to and opposed to a homogenized Indian identity. Although Indians are preferred over women—because they are men!—both Indians and women occupy places of otherness. Gordon signals this early on: women, though central to the novel's action, are absent from chapter 1, where the reader is introduced to the Outlaw brothers and where John Findley gives the young men these lessons in patriarchy and misogyny. With this quick sketch, Gordon characterizes the frontier as an early national environment of white men who seek fraternity by bonding over their perceived differences from women, blacks, and Indians. In this scheme of nationhood as imagined brotherhood there is little space for white women, who hover on the edges of the wilderness, relegated to a domestic existence of housekeeping and childbearing. Gordon seems to say that as a consolidating agent in American history, the frontier is explicitly patriarchal: American frontier men both historical, like Findley and Boone, and fictional, like Rion, seek to flee the civilized domestic environment.

Gordon's technique for representing the novel's gender hierarchies is to leave the patriarchal metanarrative mostly unchallenged but to present it in such a way that power is constantly thematized by a narrator conscious of flaws in the myth of the American frontier man. A case in point is Gordon's early comparison of Rion with the mythical hunter Orion and with the constellation for which he is named. By conflating Rion with Orion, reality with myth, and human with god, Gordon creates a slightly ironic distance from her main character. Like the classic mythical hunter, Orion, and the great American explorer Daniel Boone, Rion is a powerful imperialist figure who at once fears domestication and desires patriarchal control. Rion thinks of the "womenfolks" as mentally and physically weaker than men, a belief in keeping with eighteenth-century treatises of gender that characterize women as naturally more delicate and "fair." By addressing such male prejudices through the limited consciousness of her characters, Gordon builds into her novel a critique of the western enterprise as masculinist and patriarchal. Pulled forward by the frontier, which provides an outlet for masculine aggression and promises landownership and financial rewards, and pulled backward by domestic responsibilities, white men find themselves torn between two seemingly rivaling imperatives. Yet the imperialist impulse that leads away from the family also contributes to its wealth and that of the nation. Masculine individualism is therefore compatible with rather than contrary to civic or family duty.

Gordon's most explicit critique of masculine individualism is articulated in the social and libidinal laws that govern the male characters of the Outlaw family. Beginning with the father, Malcolm Outlaw, the family name points to a crisis in American political and psychological identity. To Rion, the Outlaw name represents a mystery around paternity and origin; it represents a "lack." This mystery around "the name of the father" complicates the relationship between father and son because the name of the father is supposed to symbolically position the son as a subject. According to Lacanian theory, "In introjecting the name-of-the-father, the child (or rather the boy) is positioned with reference to the father's name. He is now bound to the law, in so far as he is implicated in the symbolic 'debt,' given a name, and a authorized speaking position" (Grosz 71). But what if the formula is flawed? What if the father is not "law" but "outlaw"? With this ironically symbolic name, Gordon positions her colonists both literally and libidinally outside the law. In her novel it is precisely the symbolic father—the authority figure instilling a sense of lawfulness into the child—who is outside the law and lacks the power to work the oedipal prohibition articulated by Freud, by which the father regulates the child's sexual access to the mother. "The boy perceives his father as a potential castrator, an (unbeatable) rival for the mother's affections. . . . In exchange for sacrificing his relation to the mother, whom he now recognizes as 'castrated,' the boy identifies with the authority invested in the father" (Grosz 68). The resulting metaphorical relation of the son with the father produces a tension: the son must be sexually like his father but also unlike him in the sense that he cannot desire the mother. For Rion, the law of the father functions symbolically as the phallus (although even that is in question, as Malcolm Outlaw "married late in life"), but the oedipal prohibition that the law of the father spells out is disregarded: Rion lives a common-law marriage with a woman named for Oedipus's mother and wife: Jocasta, or "Cassy." Symbolically reliving the oedipal incest taboo, Rion honors the name of his father—he is an outlaw, indeed. And yet, Rion's status as an outlaw is uncertain because the name of his father, which supplants Rion's connection to his mother, is quite possibly not his real name and therefore begs the question of the father's authority over him. On a more general level, this deeply ironic move leads the reader to question the status and the role of patriarchy in Gordon's novel.

Although the law of the father is questioned and perhaps even ironically rejected in Gordon's novel, this does not mean that patriarchy has no power. It means that male power has shifted away from the father's control to the son's through the enactment of the oedipal paradigm. Let's look first at Rion's attempts to escape from the law of the father. Rion rejects the love object he could legally have—Kate Lovelatty—for a fantasy of displacing the father by "taking" Jocasta: "he could have this girl if he wanted her" (71). He refuses societal rules when he enters the wilderness of desire with Jocasta, who has neither father to protect her (he is dead) nor access to social laws that would enforce marriage customs. Cassy's brother, Frank, does not oppose the informal union between his sister and Rion. Rion transgresses social law when he takes Cassy to be his wife in the forest, a place rather fittingly outside all social sanctions. Like Hamlet's Ophelia in the Lacanian reading, Cassy is an object of desire that gets "taken" outside the bounds of law. With Cassy, Rion institutes himself in the place of the father and breaks—at least in the perverse fantasy of his desire—the incest taboo.

Leaning on this oedipal structure, Gordon accomplishes a number of goals: she dramatizes the absence of fathers and the resulting anxieties around masculinity and phallic power in the New World; she emphasizes the pathological underpinnings of the American family and the female characters' problematic role in it; and finally, she relates incestuous sexual desire with desire for Indian lands. Rion, the white American imperialist, wants to "take" Cassy the same way he wants to take the land—off the public record. He is unwilling to pay for land that seems for the taking, because "the Indians ain't using it. They ain't got a right to keep people from settling on it" (183). The popular land-use argument articulated here was based on the belief that Indians who did not farm their land were not properly using it. Colonists felt that they were right to take "unused land" from the Indians in order to cultivate it, because agricultural labor was part of the gospel of progress and blessed by God. But contrary to Rion's naive belief in free agency on the frontier, he cannot escape from the King's law prohibiting private purchases of Cherokee land in the British colonies.[29] Instead, he finds himself in the midst of a complex political situation governed by the financial power of the imperial metropolis. Even out in the wilderness, Rion is advised to stay within the letter of the law by his neighbor, who counsels Rion to strike a legal land deal with the Cherokees because they are reasonable, "that is, for Indians" (183). Although Rion Outlaw tries to flee from the law, it catches up with him, and his dream of masculine autonomy ultimately turns out to be a self-destructive myth. Rion's desire for living outside the law—his illegal pursuit of land, his violation of the King's law, and his incestuous pursuit of "Jocasta"—spells disaster and untimely death.

Gordon teases her characters with the idea of America as an Edenic paradise, but she complicates this metaphor in such a way as to foreclose this fantasy. Rion's desire for Jocasta, the mother/wife figure, is an account not only of the American male's incestuous desire for the New World maternal garden but also of his position in the socio-symbolic structure of a society in which fathers are absent. Rion's enactment of the law of the father reveals that he is literally accepting the name of the father (Outlaw) but also that he is actually rejecting the legal and libidinal prohibition of the paternal metaphor. Together with his brother-out-law Frank, he displaces the father, a move that results in the economic exchange of woman and land between "sons." This indicates that patriarchy continues, but as a new fraternal paradigm characterized by the father's libidinal and political displacement. Without fathers, America provides a space for the sons' rebellious and unlawful actions, actions aimed at establishing a new national identity through the negotiation and management of racial and sexual difference. As Jay Fliegelman shows, in America of the Revolutionary period the familial metaphor that was activated was one of colonial children angry with the leadership of the "father" of the British empire, King George III. This rejection of the father/king resulted in ideological and political modifications of manhood that took practical expression within family structures that shifted from fatherhood to brotherhood. Fliegelman writes that "a call for filial autonomy" and the emergence from what Kant called "man's self-incurred tutelage" echoes throughout the rhetoric of the American Revolution (3). As Nelson argues, both freedom and fear resulted from this rejection of the authoritative father figure: "this replacement of Father with Brothers seemed symbolically to evoke anxiety and weakness, not confidence and strength," because "breaking with the King/Father necessitated a reconfiguration not only of political power, but also—analogically and practically—of the ideals of manhood" (35). Because of these anxieties, the formation and maintenance of white male American subjectivity was dependent on a definition of femininity that served as its clear opposite.

The social philosophy of the Enlightenment that Gordon rehearses in her novel espoused a belief in the betterment of society through women's crucial roles as mothers and wives but also in the subordination and control of the female body for the sake of achieving the full potential of national manhood and fraternity. Gordon obviously does not agree with this antiquated view of women, and her protagonist has to learn a lesson at the end of the novel. Only after Cassy dies does Rion understand that the principles of male individualism that undergird the ideals of white American manhood lead to isolation and destruction. In a final didactic passage, he muses on the sacrifices of westward expansion: "he looked up and saw Orion fixed upon his burning wheel, always pursuing the bull but never making the kill. Did Orion will any longer the westward chase? No more than himself. Like the mighty hunter he had lost himself in the turning" (469). Born out of a politics of expansion and conquest, the American ideal of masculinity—the hunter pursuing his kill—demands the sacrifice of the very family that men desire for their own progeny. By ending her novel with Cassy's death, Gordon shows that the myth of American masculinity based on competitive white manhood eventually leads to self-destruction. Undergirding this traditional definition of manhood with classical myth, she points to those gender binaries that have been persistent in Western traditions and are systemic to the theories and practices of domination of women and all those constituted as others.

The Law of the Mother and the Fantasy of Indian Brothers

In a final move to question the values of white imperial patriarchy upon which American nationhood rests, Gordon opposes patriarchy to the gender dynamics in Native American culture. In chapters alternating between the settler culture and the Cherokee culture, she carefully sketches the Cherokee laws of matrilineal descent and creates a narrative structure that compares women's relative powerlessness in white patriarchy to women's power in Cherokee culture. By thus alternating the perspectives on colonization, Gordon distances her reader from the masculinist narrative of the settler culture. But she also shows that colonialism and the introduction of patriarchy into Cherokee society weakens the power traditionally held by women as the power balance tips in favor of men whose business is warfare. In subtle steps, Gordon traces the rapid transformation of Cherokee culture in the late eighteenth century from the "law of the mother" into the "law of the father" in order to underscore the cultural damage done by patriarchy and westward expansion. The new laws of patriarchy effect not only a cultural change from maternal to paternal society but a political change as well; they ensure that the rise of the American nation is linked to the decline of the Cherokee nation. American political unity then comes at the cost of genocide based on divisions between men and women, self and other, American and Indian. Gordon underscores this negative dialectic again through the trope of captivity, which problematizes these divisions.

In *Green Centuries,* the Cherokee laws of matrilineal descent, kinship, and citizenship serve as alternative models for regulating gender and genealogy. By shifting the narrative perspective to Native American culture, Gordon produces a temporary reversal of cultural margin and center. She presents the marginal perspective of the doubly other—not only Indian, but also woman—in order to invoke what I would like to call the "law of the mother." Through the Dark Lanthorn, a fictional Cherokee woman, Gordon comments on the cultural and political life of the Cherokee nation and the events leading to the war with the settlers on the frontier. Indians in Gordon's novel do not embody a critique of Europe, as they often do in American literature of the nineteenth century, by marking the boundary lines of an emerging national identity in opposition to European colonization; on the contrary, the Indians depicted here—the Cherokees—were actually allies of the British. This means that no such romantic critique of Europe or England is possible in *Green Centuries.* However, what is critiqued through the Cherokee perspective is white manhood and the deficiencies of the Anglo-American patriarchal system. To put it bluntly, Gordon uses those portions of the novel told from the Indian perspective for her feminist critique of white masculinity and its imperialist agendas.

Gordon was well read about Cherokee society—in a footnote to *Green Centuries* she mentions that "the Cherokees had a maternal organization and succession was through the female line" (390)—and her extensive historical and ethnographic research allowed her to situate Cherokee women in their proper economic, spiritual, and political environment.[30] Cherokee women tended crops and were responsible for ensuring a rich harvest. This means they were also in charge of protecting crops, for which they built large scaffolds in the fields from which they could watch invaders, animal and human alike. Here, in a passage very much in keeping with ethnographic sources, is Gordon's depiction of this responsibility of Cherokee women: "Over in the middle of the field was a scaffold built of hickory poles. Sitting on top of it, holding long leafy switches in their hands, were two old women" (271). Although the characters speculate that "They're out here to scare the deer off" (271), the women's job was often more dangerous than that because of their relative isolation in the middle of summer, which was the season of war (Perdue, *Cherokee Women* 20). Ethnographer James Adair, who appears briefly as a historical character in Gordon's novel, describes their vigilance: protecting the crop "usually is the duty of the old women, who fret at the very shadow of a crow, when he chances to pass his wide survey of the fields; but if pinching hunger should excite him to descend, they soon frighten him away with their screeches" (qtd. in Perdue 20). Women guarded the corn because they were spiritually and ceremonially associated with it, and this connection to the most important Cherokee community ritual, the Green Corn Dance, gave them "considerable status and economic power" (Perdue 25).

Gordon also provides ethnographically correct information about other tasks that Cherokee women performed. They kept house, cooked, made baskets and gourds, and manufactured items from deerskin. They also made clothing and pouches from buffalo hair, and wove cane mats and hemp carpets painted with bright colors. When the reader first encounters the Dark Lanthorn, she surveys her vegetable garden, and with her house in order, she sets to painting a carpet that she had woven. Into the Lanthorn's design, Gordon weaves much information about Cherokee society, such as the clan structure (Cherokee society was divided into seven different kinship clans), the artistry of women, and their place in the political life of the Cherokee nation. Gordon also depicts the power and prestige Cherokee women held in their society. Particularly older post-menopausal women, like the Dark Lanthorn, were held in high esteem. One of the most powerful Cherokee women of the time was Nancy Ward, also called the Ghigau, or the beloved woman, a woman who fought as if she were a warrior, spoke in council, and was listened to.[31]

On the whole, women's political power did not rest on fighting but rather on "their position as mothers in a matrilineal society that equated kinship and citizenship. In such a society, mothers and, by extension women, enjoyed a great deal of honor and prestige, and references to motherhood evoked power rather than sentimentality" (Perdue, *Cherokee Women* 101). As mothers, Cherokee women had considerable influence on political debates in the nation: they discouraged or encouraged warriors and adopted or condemned captives to torture and death. Most importantly, "mothers also conveyed a Cherokee identity; no one could be a Cherokee unless he or she had a Cherokee mother" (Perdue, *Cherokee Women* 55). Women's participation in Cherokee government was not only possible but crucial. Perdue cites Chief Attakullakulla's surprise at the absence of women in South Carolina's Governor's Council: "he demanded to know why no women were in attendance" and pointed out to the governor that "White Men as well as the Red were born of Women" (55). It is clear that, compared to their white sisters, Cherokee women enjoyed relatively greater agency both in communal life and as individuals.

Gordon also validates this distinction by drawing a sharp contrast between white women's limited sexual agency in patriarchal frontier society and their relative latitude in Cherokee society. Gordon opposes the timidity of the white woman Cassy, who had "never tried to image what it would be like to be taken by a man" (99), to the assertive approach of the Indian woman Monon, Archy's wife, who "didn't wait for him to make the first move, took it away from him as they said," and who forces him to admit that "this Cherokee girl was hotter than he was" (250). Perdue writes that "autonomy translated into sexual freedom for Cherokee women because no one controlled their sexuality. Unmarried women engaged in sex with whomever they wished as long as they did not violate incest taboos against intercourse with members of their own clans or the clans of their fathers. Married women also enjoyed considerable latitude" (*Cherokee Women* 56). Male infidelity, however, caused "considerable disharmony in the community" (57). The relative power and freedom that women enjoyed in traditional Cherokee society, however, soon came to an end with increasing colonial conflict. Gordon astutely traces this shift of power from Cherokee women to men to the late 1800s, when European invasion and colonization changed the traditional gender structure of Cherokee society. As Perdue notes, "incessant warfare brought men to center stage . . . because war was the occupation of men. . . . Cherokees increasingly equated political power with military might and associated individual and national welfare with warriors" (*Cherokee Women* 86).

Although Gordon's narrative captures the waning power of the Cherokees, its plot structure alternates between matriarchal Indian and patriarchal Western societies. *Green Centuries* presents a kind of Indian/Anglo dialectic in which the Outlaw brothers function as representatives of opposite ends of a relationship with Native Americans. Rion and Archy Outlaw signal variants of American history, including denied possibilities and missed opportunities: Rion stands for Anglo-American individualism, racial purity, and modern imperialism, whereas Archy, the brother "gone native," symbolizes pastoralism, racial hybridity, and communal politics. Both ideologies, as detrimentally opposed as they seem, are equally important parts of America's political and cultural self-imagination. By immersing Archy into matrilineal Cherokee society, Gordon destabilizes the narrative of white manhood and dramatizes the failed production of white male citizenship. She demonstrates that white male citizenship is achieved through the subordination of Indian or Indian-identified others, but Indians are rehabilitated—unlike blacks or women—through their annihilation and imaginary reconstitution as the white man's "brothers." The historical and political dimensions of such a "brotherhood" between white men and Indians serve two intersecting purposes: Indian brotherhood calls into being emerging racial identities and self-perceptions of American manhood as implicitly "white," and it simultaneously helps to establish an American national identity in the imagined difference to the white man's Indian (br)others. As Shari Huhndorf argues, the politics of cultural and racial assimilation (what she calls "going native") are rather complex: in the cultural imagination of the twentieth century, "going native has served as an essential means of defining and regenerating racial whiteness and a racially inflected vision of Americanness. It also reflects on the national history by providing self-justifying fantasies that conceal the violence marking European America's origins" (5).

"Going native" is often an integral part of the captivity myth that is reshaped into a story of successful assimilation, albeit with a tragic ending in *Green Centuries.* The captured white man, Archy, becomes absorbed into the Cherokee nation both legally and culturally; he becomes subject to the kinship laws that regulate Cherokee culture, and within this social system he finds a family, gains a new brother, marries a Cherokee woman, and becomes a warrior who fights for Cherokee independence. He moves swiftly from "captive" to white man "gone native," shedding his white masculinity and choosing his side in the brewing political conflict.[32] As his name implies, Archy fulfills a bridging function—building an arch to another culture—which symbolizes the young nation's desire for brotherhood with Indians. As the Indian-identified brother, Archy is the shadowy duplication of Rion, a reminder, perhaps, of what could have been in American history but was never allowed to happen: cultural negotiation instead of extermination, merging instead of murder. Archy's cultural assimilation into the Cherokee nation is a racial crossing not unlike the one Gordon described in "The Captive" ten years earlier: here, too, the formal adoption ceremony promises to drain the "white blood" out of Archy. However, Archy's essential whiteness is confirmed by other characters both white and Indian. When Rion encounters Archy in the Cherokee town of Chota, years after their separation, he describes him as "all fixed up like a raree show" (278). To Rion, Archy has remained white under his Indian exterior, which is merely a mask or disguise. To the Dark Lanthorn, the Cherokee mother who adopted him, Archy also remains essentially white. Measured by the Dark Lanthorn's cultural standards of masculinity and beauty, Archy appears initially as "a thin, grayish, wormlike creature, his head covered with matted brown hair, his arse tied up like a woman's in strips of filthy cloth" (236). Even after he is culturally integrated into the clan, his skin "would never have any of the reddish lights that so delight the eye when a man is walking past and the sun plays on his naked limbs. Even when he wore the warrior's white crown of swan's feathers he would still be ugly" (237). Through the critical voice of the Dark Lanthorn, Gordon reverses Anglo-American racial and sexual hierarchies: from the Native American perspective, the white man emerges as feminized and sexually inferior. The subject of a rumor circulating among Indians—and between the textual strands of Gordon's narrative—is the belief that "White men were all eunuchs" (247). Conversely, white male characters project their fears of feminization onto Indian men, who are seen as womanish and sexualized accordingly. Rion notices that their greeting is like an embrace, a "gesture that was strangely like the caress one might give a woman" (198), and his gaze eroticizes the Indian peace chief: "As Rion watched, the chief's nostrils flickered. His black eyes opened wide. They looked enormous in the yellow face and they glistened as Rion had once seen the petals of a lily glisten under the vigorous strokes of a bumblebee's legs. 'Robertson knows how to tickle him, all right,' he thought" (200). Any political threat to white expansion that the peace chief Attakullakulla may have represented at one point is removed by his feminization and his projected desire for (sexual) stimulation by the white man. Even his fierce warrior son Dragging Canoe is feminized in the gaze of the colonizer: "He was over six feet tall and broad for an Indian, but he stepped light as a woman. No, he moved like a 'coon" (200). Oscillating between comparisons to women and African Americans as indicated in the double-edged "coon" reference, American perceptions of Indians project onto them an otherness that is at once rejected and desired: "Rion gazed at the naked back [of Dragging Canoe], finding a fascination in contemplating flesh so unlike his own" (201). The sexy subaltern is a familiar stereotype of colonial literature. But whereas Gordon reveals and to some extent perhaps even indulges in such a stereotype, she identifies this discourse specifically as her character's. By displaying Rion's ignorance of Indian cultures and his racist attitudes (as we have seen earlier), she creates an ironic distance from her white male protagonist, whose naïveté about Native American cultures the reader easily perceives. Through Rion, Gordon creates a flawed narrative trajectory that simultaneously feminizes, infantilizes, demonizes, and eroticizes the Indians while masculinizing and elevating the white settler culture.

These gender dynamics are also readily apparent in Rion's attitude toward Archy, who has rejected the laws of American manhood: Archy is the other, weaker, "female" part of the brotherhood, a man who joins and flourishes in a matrilineal society. Archy's ultimate rejection of white masculinity by social and political assimilation into the Cherokee nation points toward an alternative model of gendered behavior. And yet the pattern is familiar with respect to the white male captive's status: Archy's hybrid identity is feminized, domesticized, and subordinated to Rion's white manhood. Rion notices "how long the lashes were that fringed his brown eyes. And the eyes themselves might have belonged to one of the heifers out there in the pasture, so large they were and with that same liquid sheen" (6). And he thinks, "Archy was too thin for a boy of fifteen" (6). Neither white man nor Indian, Archy is the hybrid fantasy of whatever reconciliation between Indian and settlers might be possible, a fantasy crucial to America's cultural imagination.

Unlike in "The Captive," where racial integration meant the forbidden "tainting" of the white female body, in *Green Centuries* the racial integration of the white male body is permitted, but at the cost of the loss of masculinity. So it is not primarily race but gender that transforms Archy into a political nonentity in patriarchal society. Moreover, it is not "blood" but an act of political identification that dissociates Archy from white brotherhood and makes him unfit for American nation-building. There are two crucial scenes in which Archy chooses sides. The first true identification with the Cherokee nation happens when Archy and Rion meet again years after their separation. When Rion asks Archy, "you want to stay here the rest of your life?" Archy does not answer, and when Rion makes a racist remark about white men married to Indian women—he calls them squaw men—Archy falls silent, and they part ways for the rest of their lives. Archy's refusal to come "home" with Rion is as much a validation of Cherokee culture as it is a rejection of white supremacy and racism. In Rion's racial hierarchy, neither blacks nor Indians are human. "An Indian ain't hardly a man," he says, and echoing his earlier statement "a nigger ain't hardly a man," he goes on, "He's sort of like a nigger. . . . Naw, he's worse'n a nigger. I ain't got nothing against a nigger, long as he behaves himself but I can't even look at one of them red bastards without having my gorge rise" (398). As sovereign subjects of their own nation who do not "behave" according to the white man's law, Indians—and Archy's Indian identification—represent an ultimate threat to white agency and power. By interspersing the narrative with the racist rhetoric of Rion and by subordinating Archy's experiences to the masculinist master narrative, Gordon does not let us forget that the American nation originates in white supremacy supported by violent conquest and war against Indian "brothers." The second time Archy chooses sides, war with the Cherokee nation is impending and he is offered a chance to leave; instead he decides to remain and serve as a messenger for Chief Dragging Canoe on a mission to British General Hamilton. At this point Archy fully identifies with the political body of the Cherokees, and when the general recognizes him as a "white man," Archy, affirming his loyalty to the Cherokee nation, identifies himself as a "blood brother to the chief" (426).

Far from "natural," brotherhood in Revolutionary America is essentially political. The cultural and ideological dualism Gordon creates in the novel reveals that from the start the unity of the American nation proves to be illusory and elusive. Although Archy and Rion are brothers—part of the same family union—they are different. What splits them apart and leads to the apocalyptic ending is precisely the impulse toward a homogenized racial and national identity, a concept of totalized nationhood. Addressing the fundamental division in America's origin, Gordon creates a national drama of rupture. Rion must kill his brother for the sake of American political unity. But in killing his brother, Rion loses part of himself, and by extension, the American nation loses that which paradoxically identifies it, distinguishes it, and gives it access to the myth of national "origins." In this sense, Archy signifies a greater possibility for which the nation mourns and for which it develops nostalgia. Gordon evokes such nostalgia in deft strokes as she describes the scene of Archy's murder in the peaceful domestic environment of his own village as he is embracing his Cherokee wife, Monon, outside their cabin. Just before the fatal shots are fired, "their laughter floated thinly across the meadow" (463); then they are struck down. At the end of the massacre, when Rion and his friend walk over to inspect the bodies, Rion recognizes his brother:

> "You know the feller?"
>
> "I knew him once," Rion said. He leaned over and pulled the arm out from under the body and straightened it at the side. "I knew him a long time ago." (465)

In Rion's final recognition that he has killed his brother, Gordon connotes the wider implications of her character's loss: Archy symbolizes that portion of the national self that is abandoned, lost, sundered, and murdered. It is that portion of himself which the white male citizen must "sacrifice" in order to pursue his imperialist dreams. Gordon signifies this sundering in the two-tier structure of the novel that follows each brother separately so that the torn brotherhood develops as the underlying psychological and social relationship in the novel. Brotherhood is paradoxically that which already "is" but never comes to pass as Archy is from the beginning rejected by Rion until Archy, too, rejects his brother. Much like the story of Cain and Abel, *Green Centuries* is a story of division and differentiation.[33] But unlike in the story of Cain and Abel, the preference of Cain over Abel or Rion over Archy is not arbitrary but deeply ideological: the ideal of a free and democratic nation is based on the slaying of the Indian brother. The murder of Archy and his family metonymically represents the dispossession and slaughter of millions of Native Americans. This "blood sacrifice," beyond all human dignity, is the essential foundation of the American nation.

Locating the origins of the nation in a failed fraternal paradigm, Gordon uses the brothers as a powerful metaphor for the internal divisions that emerge prominently at the boundaries of a nation engaged in colonial struggle. The brothers symbolize a contest of values—Indian and American—that is, as Slotkin says, endemic to literature about Indians: "the Indian is the representative of a culture and a social order that offers a radical alternative to the established order of Euro-American society. His very existence, even as a symbol, poses the fundamental question: why should we order our lives in this way, since there is clearly an alternative?" (*Regeneration* 558). But beyond such an Indian/Anglo dialectic, the fraternal paradigm symbolizes the violence of self-division that characterizes the modern self and the nation. The fantasy of a national brotherhood with Indians never even begins to involve "real Indians," as Gordon shows, but only their surrogates, in this case a white brother "gone native." Such brotherhood, even in its inception, is a romance not with the image of the other but with the white colonizer's own image imagined as other. Identification with the native other turns out to be a variation of self-identification. Therefore it is not the Indian figure who serves American patriotism in this early national environment but rather the imagined brotherhood with Indians, who are actually mirror images for the Euro-American self. So the opposition here is not just between other and self but between self and self-as-other. This self-as-other occupies a space characterized by a deep ambivalence about white masculinity and modernity.[34] Gordon articulates such ambivalence about American cultural modernity: on the one hand, she represents the consolidation of white masculinity and American citizenship around principles of individualism; on the other hand, she represents a nostalgic longing for an earlier, premodern time of racial undifferentiation and communal unity. By twinning the fates of the brothers, Gordon depicts these contradictory desires in the violent birth of America as a modern nation through the myth of American masculinity based on the "clashing imperatives of fraternity and competition, brotherhood and self-interest" (Nelson 16).

Andrew Lytle defined Gordon's literary vision as "traditional and historic," not in the narrow sense of a "historic[al] novel," "that is, the costume piece or the arbitrary use of certain historic periods dramatized through crucial events" (*Hero* 155), but rather as an essentially contemporary and ironic vision. In *Green Centuries,* the irony results from a superimposition of two seemingly disparate historical layers: the contemporary moment, characterized by a rising nationalism that led to the Holocaust and America's intervention in World War II, and the historical moment of America's national formation during the Revolutionary years, which—in the name of freedom and democracy—led to slavery and Native American genocide. In a climate of international crisis, Gordon returns to America's early national history and reworks the past moment from the present situation of rising national tensions. Deeply disturbed by imperial expansion in Europe and by the entry of the United States in the war across the Atlantic, she wrote to a friend: "I feel as if some horrible Grendel were lurking in the marshes, bellowing for a sacrifice of young men, and that all our business, nowadays will be to pack them up and ship them off to him properly" (qtd. in Makowsky 158). And she was particularly irritated by the rhetoric surrounding the war—as she says, by the "asininity, the hypocrisy that accompanies it" (158).

Green Centuries addresses such hypocrisy in the founding rhetoric of the American nation and in the reification of its history. When Gordon mines the historical archive, she represents the specificity of the past—its racial and gender laws—in such a way as to disclose an underlying solidarity of its passionate polemics with those of her present day. By inserting herself literally into history—when she suggests in the novel that father Outlaw's real name may have been "Gordon"—she signifies ironically on her own implication in the history of imperialism and its continuing presence. As a southern writer, Gordon relocates and translates cultural history and local memory not necessarily faithfully—

most obviously she takes the liberty of changing dates—but as a critique of the failed promises of the nation. When she turns to the American Enlightenment and its specific vision of progress and imperial expansion, she comments critically and ironically on the coming into being of the modern self and the modern nation. For Gordon, the modern nation-state, based on processes of racial and gendered individuation, turns the ideal of brotherhood into a nostalgic fantasy. In her novel, the deaths of African Americans, Indians, and women lead to a point of apocalyptic closure that discloses the limits of the ideological formation of white male citizenship. Although Gordon's text does not explicitly link the past to the present, its "political unconscious" points to a crisis in modernity: the binary structure of her novel both reifies eighteenth-century colonial history as Western progress *and* revolts against its domination and dehumanization of women, blacks, and Indians by showing that white masculine autonomy is ultimately an illusion. In *Green Centuries* and "The Captive," Gordon's political and ethnographic imagination, fired by WPA excavations into the deep structure of Native American history, is linked to an inescapably Western discourse about race and gender. Gordon's writing explores a cultural archive that brings us ethnographically to the borders of the Indian other but stops short of transgressing those borders. What Gordon brings back from this borderland are Native American shards and fragments from which she presumed a world of Indian contact very much anchored in the politics of segregation and patriarchal domination of her own time.

4
Native Americans and Nationalism

Eudora Welty's Natchez Trace Fiction

> We should have to study together, genetically and structurally, the history of the road and the history of writing. We are thinking here of . . . the *itinerant* work of the trace producing and following its route, the trace which traces, the trace which breaks open its own path.
>
> —Jacques Derrida, "Freud"

From her location in Natchez, Mississippi, Eudora Welty participates in the literary construction of the nation's Native American heritage. Like her southern contemporaries Andrew Lytle, Caroline Gordon, and William Faulkner, Welty uses the Native American signifier in her fiction in order to imagine the South as a region whose history has an impact on the discourse of American nationalism. Welty's narratives of the early 1940s, particularly her novella, *The Robber Bridegroom* (1942), and her short-story collection *The Wide Net* (1943) yield the shadowy outlines of an Indian presence not only in the geographical signifier of the Natchez Trace itself but also in the historical time periods—particularly the colonial and early national past—to which it points. Focusing on Mississippi Territory, Welty explores colonial history as it is sedimented in this specific region. In "Some Notes on River Country" (1944) she defines the outlines of her location as "a string of abandoned and overgrown frontier towns between Vicksburg and Natchez" that serve as an entry point into the fossilized history of a specific time and place. Welty's literary excavations of civilizations now buried "under the cloak of vegetation" (*Eye* 295) expose the cultural sediments of this location now abandoned. Here Welty excavates the remains of British and French colonialism, European immigration, frontier history and mythology, plantation culture (symbolized by the grand ruin of Windsor), the Revolutionary period, African-American communities, nineteenth-century minstrel shows,

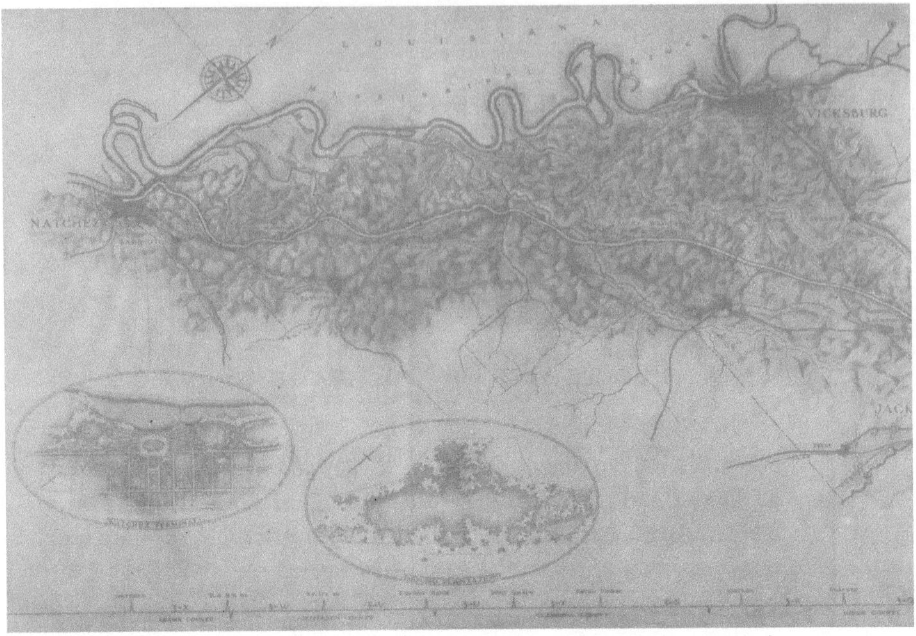

Map 4. Detail of "Master Development Plan of the Natchez Trace Parkway." National Park Service. U.S. Department of Interior. 1940. Courtesy of the Mississippi Department of Archives and History

and, of course, those Native Americans who gave Natchez its name. Here in River Country, where "the Old Natchez Trace has sunk out of use" and the river has retreated, Welty hears the music of antebellum mansions and the drums of Indians as she imagines the cultural substructures buried in the landscape. In "the loess country" into which history has sunk like the Trace itself, which, "made by buffalos, then used by man, [is] trodden lower and lower, a few inches every hundred years" (287), Welty digs into the strata of "solid blue clay, embalming the fossil horse and the fossil ox and the great mastodon" to reach the layers of Native American history so intricately connected with this region. Her archaeological allusions reveal that for her place becomes the entrance into the deep structure of history; it is both witness (like the old live oaks that remain) and archaeological archive. Welty reads place like a "text" that bears the traces of the irrecoverable past that can only be imaginatively and partially recovered through language. As she follows the Natchez Trace in her fiction, her writing, too, etches deep traces into the landscape and the Native American history underneath it.

I would like to highlight in Welty's celebrated definition of place as the most crucial factor defining the writer's point of view this archaeological deep structure that points to the Indian signifier in her fiction. As we will see, Indians play a crucial part in Welty's self-fashioning as a beginning writer, because they contribute directly to her own imaginary positioning of herself in the frontier South. Welty's excavation of the substrata of a rich Native American heritage in her home state provides her with a very special sense of "roots" of a fascinating "place" that she is setting out to explore in her fiction and to explain to those outside her region. In a 1940 letter to her New York agent Diarmuid Russell and in her 1944 review of *The Western Journals of Washington Irving,* Welty claims special access to knowledge about local Indian populations on the southern frontier. In both documents she situates herself on the side of "the wild country," the Old Southwest, a geographical position opposite to that of her East Coast agent and Washington Irving's New York. When she first writes to Russell about her ideas for a book that would later become *The Robber Bridegroom,* she emphasizes the "folk quality" of the frontier and the directness and simplicity—what she calls the "dignity" and "the feeling of the legendary"—that has historically characterized life in Mississippi. For Welty, Mississippi has retained this frontier character; she speculates that it is a place that "would be so relatively raw and recent to you, with all that is in your country, that it might seem not so powerful . . . but to make up for the sketchiness of what we know is all the long vast mysterious history of the Indians who lived there. Have you ever heard or read about the Natchez Indians?" (qtd. in Kreyling, *Author* 43). Welty claims the rich cultural and historical heritage of the Natchez Indians for her own "country" and for her special understanding of herself in relation to the world. Historical and imaginative proximity to Indians becomes a source of her cultural authority as a beginning writer in the late 1930s and early 1940s. This claim to authority over "Indian land" on the Mississippi frontier—imaginary or real—is of course not unproblematic, as the white writer's sense of "discovery" of a particular place is rather resonant with the colonialist project itself. Welty's famous pronouncement that "location . . . is not simply to be used by the writer—it is to be discovered" (*Eye* 129) applies both to the "discovery" of place itself and, more importantly for Welty, to the imaginative and ethnographic discoveries of writing about it. In one way, Welty's desire to "discover" the Indian signifier in the substrata of her Mississippi landscape implicates her in a familiar colonialist discourse that seeks to lay claim to Indian territories and identities; but in another way, Welty writes Indians back into the textual landscape of the colonial South. In this sense she participates in the project of modernist ethnographic invention, not "discovery," of the Native American signifier.

This textual, imaginary construction of Indian land is part of Welty's strategy of positioning herself securely in the frontier South. It bolsters her authority as a geographical insider to a culture that remains exotic and distant to critics and writers from the Northeast. In her review of Irving's *Western Journals,* Welty praises his sketches for the unselfconscious elegance with which they capture his journey through what was in 1832 the western frontier. Irving, she writes, met "the excitements and pleasures of a strange life with an emotion somewhere justly between intoxication and amusement, between curiosity and pleasant objectivity" (*Eye* 178). His writing reflects an artistic enthusiasm for the Indian frontier not unlike Welty's own. However, Welty's review also emphasizes an important difference between her own understanding of the frontier and Irving's. Irving, who was "breaking thro a country hitherto untrodden by white man" (177), retains very much an outsider's perspective on the "West." Welty's stylistic positioning of Irving's "delicate" prose, for example, brands him as a mere visitor from the "East." "Such delicacy seldom went West," writes Welty, and she explains that "Irving's work is unique in Western annals because it is not robust nor rambunctious nor raw" (179). By contrast, Welty styles herself rhetorically as a native insider to the frontier environment when she complains that "there is a marked absence of any of *our* own Western tall tales in this book, samples of *our* wild humor or ways of talking" (180, emphasis added). Welty exposes Irving's linguistic, ethnographic, and cultural distance from the Indians he encounters on his travels in a particularly colorful passage from his journal that she quotes in her review: "Pass several Creeks—one with scarlet turban and plume of black feathers like a cock's tail—one with white turban with red feathers—Oriental look—like Sultans on the stage—some have raquet [*sic*] with which they have been playing ball—some with jackets and shirts but legs and thighs bare—middle sized, well made and vigorous. Yesterday one had a brilliant bunch of sumach. They look like fine birds on the Prarie [*sic*]" (*Eye* 180). Although Welty does not comment on this heavily orientalized image of Native Americans, she does point out the contrived "stage directions" of Irving's observations. The New Yorker remains "ever the detached gentleman" who, she assures us, did not "consciously condescend—and is a great defender, of course, of the Indians." But, she adds, "he does refer to the guides and such in the party as 'servants' and the Frenchman Antoine as 'the half-breed.'" She concludes by noting that overall Irving must have enjoyed himself in the West; "he never did learn to spell 'prairie,' though" (*Eye* 180–81). In Irving's consistent spelling mistake of the word "prairie," Welty measures his vast cultural distance from his subjects (the frontier and the Indians), finding therein proof of his ultimate urban outsider's perspective.

When Welty wrote this review of Irving's *Journals,* she had been thinking about Indians for a while and they had become an integral part of her Natchez Trace fiction. The Indian signifier in her texts can be traced to some of her earliest stories, such as "Keela, the Outcast Indian Maiden" and "First Love," both of which were first circulated in 1941 and later published in the short-story collections *A Curtain of Green* (1941) and *The Wide Net* (1943), respectively, as well as to her novella, *The Robber Bridegroom* (1942). Welty casually referred to the stories of *The Wide Net* as her "Natchez stories" or simply the "Natchez book," and she called *The Robber Bridegroom* her "Mississippi book."[1] Her definitions reveal the importance of local geography and frontier history to her early fictional universe. Strung together by the famous historical pathway named for local Indian populations, these texts also contain some of her most interesting meditations on the complex relationship between fiction and history.

Welty's interest in local history began with her work as a publicity agent for the WPA in 1933, for which she traveled all over Mississippi collecting information, conducting interviews, and taking photographs on the side.[2] When the Federal Writers Project was published in 1938 as *Mississippi: A Guide to the Magnolia State,* three of her photographs were included. The *Guide,* a volume of impressive length, would have familiarized Welty with the history of her hometown and state, the Indian tribes in Mississippi, territorial acquisitions and Indian treaties, and the historical significance of the Natchez Trace and its famous travelers. Considering her interest in and use of local history, it seems all the more startling that she cautions us against reading her fiction historically. In a 1980 interview she declared: "I don't write historically or anything. Most of the things that I write about can be translated into personal relationships. I've never gone into such things as guilt over the Indians or—it just hasn't been my subject" (qtd. in Prenshaw, *Conversations* 299). And yet the Natchez Trace, with its historical encounters and its origin in Indian history, is at the center of her early work.

Welty's denial of history is especially interesting in conjunction with Mississippi's Indian heritage. When prompted about Faulkner's sense of "blood guilt about the Indians" by an interviewer who suggested that her own work lacks that aspect, Welty simply replies: "Well, it's not my theme" (qtd. in Prenshaw, *Conversations* 299). Why does she claim that "blood guilt" about the Indians is not her "theme"? Why should it be Faulkner's but not hers? For Welty, Faulkner's Indians are an integral part of the entire Yoknapatawpha saga: "Faulkner created an entire world: all the history of Mississippi and the Indians and everything. Mine was just an appropriate location" (qtd. in Prenshaw, *Conversations* 333). Although Welty does not see her own writing as an attempt to write toward a panoramic view of history, her modesty should not mislead us into believing that her own fiction was not also rooted in the history of Mississippi and that the Indian characters she creates have no significance in her stories. On the contrary, as we will see, her Indian characters are central to the history she sketches, particularly in her early fiction.

Perhaps as a result of Welty's conviction that her writing shrinks away from the larger issues of southern history and politics, historical traces in her fiction have been generally minimized. Michael Kreyling, for example, argued that "even though the stories [of *The Wide Net*] are grounded in the history and geography of the Natchez Trace, they take place—as fiction—in a state of heightened imaginative possibilities" (*Eudora* 17). Reviewing *The Wide Net* in 1944, Robert Penn Warren also concluded that Welty has shifted her emphasis away from history and "very far in the direction of idea" (qtd. in Turner 50). Because Welty is said to foreground "ideas," the "actual world" of politics and history appears to recede into the background. This understanding of Welty remains prevalent even with recent critics like Alexander Ritter, who argues that in order to foreground her thematic concerns with identity and individuality, Welty "withdraws to the back-country of the state of Mississippi in the 1920s and 30s" (25) and to Natchez as "a region altered to a provincial, narrowed, regressive locality. . . . [where] the world appears as if foreshortened because world history and global possibilities of the place are indiscernible" (26). Welty's apparent flight from history and world politics is itself a political gesture in which Ritter perceives an essentially conservative "agrarian conception of society" (26). But the fact that Welty often does not *explicitly* deal with social and political reality does not mean that she is not representing such a reality in her stories or that she is not "historicizing" her fictional materials. In a recent "historical approach" to Welty's novels, Kreyling now suggests that "Welty's personal predisposition to steer away from the politics of literature might serve as a paradoxical indicator that, on the level of imagination, she knows full well that literature is political" ("Welty as Novelist" 7). The contributors to the collection *Eudora Welty and Politics: Did the Writer Crusade?* also highlight Welty's "politics," both in her fiction and in the social context of regional and national racial strife that surrounded and influenced Welty's creative work. Some critics have usefully suggested that Welty might approach "History" differently than her male colleagues in southern literature. Welty, Patricia Yaeger argues, catalogs histories that are "subsemantic, unspoken, out of use," and much like other southern women writers, she weaves her politics into domestic scenes and female bodies (157). Following these critics, I want to historicize and politicize Welty's fiction against traditional claims (Welty's own included) that her fiction shrinks away from the larger issues of regional history and national politics.

A close look at her Natchez Trace fiction reveals that Welty engages not so much in a conservative rejection of local ethnographic and political materials as in an artistic transformation of those materials. The fact that the larger political and historical meanings of the Natchez Trace are not immediately visible on the textual surfaces of her narratives does not mean they are not there. I would like to suggest that what is "there" in Welty's Natchez Trace fiction is historical meaning precisely as a "trace." Borrowing Jacques Derrida's concept of the linguistic trace, we might see how Welty uses the history of the Natchez Trace to address questions that are, like Derrida's, profoundly philosophical and historical. Derrida argues that "sense"—historical, philosophical, or literary—is never simply present; "it is always engaged in the 'movement' of the 'trace,' that is in the order of signification" (Kamuf 27). Applied to Welty, this means that the meaning of her narratives is never simply present; rather it is available only in the traces that the text might leave. This process of presencing (and absencing) is itself addressed in Welty's fictional method, particularly in her way of sketching various historical moments in the history of the Natchez Trace that famously obscure as much as they seem to reveal.

My project in this chapter, then, is to trace a return journey into the kind of historical "truth" that Welty weaves into the opening story of *The Wide Net* and into *The Robber Bridegroom.* I will argue that the Natchez Trace functions in these narratives as an Indian signifier with three different but related meanings: linguistic, historical, and political. Welty, like Derrida, uses the linguistic concept of the "trace" to probe the manifestations of speech and truth in a philosophical and phenomenological context. If we understand her concern with the language used to make sense of an event—any event—we recognize more readily that her choice of a deaf narrator in "First Love" and a pathologically lying heroine in *The Robber Bridegroom* is not aimed at concealing or distorting the truth about a historical incident, or at simply romanticizing it, but rather at reflecting on the difficulties of telling the "truth" about any (historical) event. When Welty writes her Natchez Trace collection in the early 1940s, gone is the illusion that we can accurately describe political and social reality; gone is the illusion that literature is mimetic and that ethnographic and political details can be "correctly" described. Consistent reflection from the Western viewpoint is precisely what modernism begins to critique and what postmodernism more openly and radically attacks. If we take seriously Welty's concern with problems of representation and "linguistic traces," we might recognize that Welty is a modernist writer with a postmodern sensibility.[3] She uses this sensibility to question American expansionist history at a time when the country is faced with difficult decisions about engaging in the international war theater of World War II. Traveling the Natchez Trace back in time to early days of the nation, Welty reflects upon a topic of timely and continuing interest in the early 1940s: imperialist expansion and American nation-building.

As a historical signifier, the "Trace" is used by Welty as an important symbol for nineteenth-century national history when the famous Natchez Trace was a vital link from the nation's capital to the Mississippi river town of Natchez and into the "territories." It was the Natchez Trace that made expansion and travel into the "Southwest" possible, after General James Wilkinson gained permission from the Chickasaws and Choctaws to transform the path into a wagon road in 1801. The *Guide* describes its stream of travelers: "Mail carriers, traders, boatmen, and supercargoes from New Orleans followed it north; an increasing stream of settlers afoot and on horseback traveled on it south to the new Eldorado of the lower Mississippi Valley" (*Mississippi* 84). As one of the most important north-south routes, the Natchez Trace grounds the lives of many characters traveling though American history and through Welty's fiction.[4] Read carefully for the textual traces of the Native American presence, Welty's Natchez Trace fiction takes on a decidedly sociohistorical theme. By anchoring this theme in the specific location of the Natchez Trace, Welty chooses a historical place that perfectly embodies the epistemological struggle for historical truth. In 1934 the Department of the Interior made a national park out of the Natchez Trace by paving it over and opening it to car travel. Along the route are marked sites where historical incidents occurred, many of them remnants of pre-colonial days, such as Indian mounds, the foundations of Chickasaw villages, and sites of former council houses, as well as more recent territorial markers, travel stops, and camps that dot the parkway. As the Trace was reconstructed, history was not just "preserved," it was *rewritten:* the paved road that is the "Trace" today is not at all identical with the historical pathway. So the Natchez Trace of 1934 captures a historical moment that never was and can never be repeated; only new, non-identical traces can be created. As a historical location whose modern construction dates from Welty's time as a WPA agent, the Natchez Trace itself reveals the very constructedness of time and place, history and location.

As a political signifier, the "Trace" points backward to the era of American westward expansion and the Indian wars and forward to Welty's own era, which was marked by national anxieties that gathered increasingly around domestic and foreign politics. As Barbara Ladd suggests, in the early 1940s Welty was "deeply engaged with some of the most pressing political issues of the twentieth century, most notably with questions of the nature and impact of nationalism in the modern world and related questions concerning the impact of the State on private life" ("Writing" 156). Welty's awareness of questions concerning a new kind of literary nationalism can be seen in her attempts at reworking national history, a project for which she used "heroes"—both of the mythical legendary kind, like Mike Fink in *The Robber Bridegroom,* and the historical kind, like Aaron Burr in "First Love"—that belong to a distinctively American cultural archive. I suggest that Welty's turn to national culture rooted in regional mythology and history seeks to accomplish two goals: it engages a kind of patriotic nationalism that was fostered in part by the surveying and cataloging activities of the WPA, and it counters the threat of fascism abroad. Alfred Kazin observes that "Hitler made nationalists out of many American writers" who turned the literature of the 1930s and early 1940s into an experience of national self-discovery (487). Although I am not suggesting that Welty is an overtly nationalist writer, in the politicized climate of 1941 she was worried about the political impact of her fiction. She communicated these worries to Russell when she feared that her story "First Love" might be misunderstood as making a pro-fascist statement (Kreyling, *Author* 76), and she did turn to an examination of American mythology and history as subjects for her fiction.

In *The Robber Bridegroom,* Welty anchors national history in local places such as the Natchez Trace in order to reveal America's rich cultural heritage, which appropriates, transforms, and even parodies the European literary traditions. The source of *The Robber Bridegroom* is a German fairy tale of the same name by the Brothers Grimm, which, being relocated in the American wilderness, gains a distinctly national agenda and purpose. While Welty's American rendition of this fairy tale participates in what Kazin has characterized as the celebratory experience of national self-discovery during the 1930s, it also remains critical of national history. Welty's focus on the history of imperialist expansion and Native American genocide in *The Robber Bridegroom* conveys both national pride and shame. Here Welty's comments about Indians in a September 1940 letter to Russell might prove helpful again: "The French never could stand the Indians, and the Spanish were always very good to them, I don't know why. Of course they both stamped them off the face of the earth. We have a few poor Indians now, up in a reservation, and let them marry Negroes, and ride their ponies in a little annual fair" (qtd. in Kreyling, *Author* 43). In Welty's characterization of the genocide of the Natchez Indians—here inaccurately attributed to French and Spanish colonial efforts only—the United States emerges as fortunate inheritor of the "long vast mysterious history of the Indians" and their rich cultural legacy. And not without local pride, Welty points out that the Natchez Indians "were supposed to be the most intricately cultured of all of the U.S. tribes" (43). Native American history and cultural heritage have always been important for national(ist) identification, but particularly so at times of international political uncertainty and crisis.[5] As a source of national identification, however, the Indian signifier is always double-edged: although American Indians are used to boost national pride, they are also a reminder of shame and guilt, as Welty's reference to a "few poor Indians" reveals. The present condition of Native Americans—and here Welty sarcastically alludes to their confinement on the Choctaw Reservation in Philadelphia, Mississippi—is a blemish on the face of American democracy and a continuous source of national anxieties.

In the following analysis I trace the appearance of the Native American signifier in two of Welty's texts in order to reveal their participation in American history and politics. In her short story "First Love," set in Natchez in 1807, Indian signifiers are subtly integrated into the story of Aaron Burr, a historical character who serves as a symbol of national expansionism, and a young deaf boy, who represents the nation's inability to listen to Native American interests and needs. In her novella, *The Robber Bridegroom,* an imperial romance that merrily mixes myth, fairy tale, and history, Welty leads us back to the traumatic beginnings of the nation. In her version of colonial history, Indian violence puts a "mark" on white settlers in their succession from pioneer to planter to merchant. Linking the rise of the southern plantation economy with the discourse of Manifest Destiny, Welty's narrative mocks the national promise of free agency and the capitalist desires that serve as the driving force for westward expansion. Welty's playful celebration of historical pastiche sharply contrasts with Lytle's and Gordon's earnest desire to turn history into historical fiction, and her irreverent attitude toward "violent Indians" contrasts with their elegiac mood.

Tracing the "Trace" in "First Love"

In "First Love," the Natchez Trace leads us back to Thomas Jefferson's contemporary Aaron Burr, whose alleged plot was to secede from the Union and establish himself as the new leader of a Southwestern Republic. The historical Burr was traveling down the Natchez Trace into the Old Southwest in order to pursue his dreams of empire; the fictional Burr of Welty's story becomes a historical symbol for national expansion and U.S. colonial politics. While the Natchez Trace in Welty's story points to the contest for territories and the American political and military presence in the wilderness, it also signifies an absence. Originally brought into being and used by Indian tribes, the Natchez Trace in "First Love" signifies the absence of Native Americans from the political events of 1807 that centered around nation-building and the expansionist politics of the United States at the cost of native lands and lives. Reading the "Trace" as a political signifier in Welty's story will lead us back to the country's historical origins, origins grounded in acts of political exclusion and physical extermination that culminate a few years later in the traumatic removal of Native Americans from the American Southeast. By exploring these related meanings of the figuration "trace," we will see that "tracing" is a method for Welty that simultaneously presences and absences history, a method that allows her to reflect on the fragility of language as the medium for the transmission of historical "truth."

Welty weaves the historical episode of Burr's alleged conspiracy into a story centered around a young deaf boy's encounter with Burr. Joel Mayes, who is a bootboy at an inn along the foot of the Natchez Trace, encounters Burr and his friend Harman Blennerhassett one evening as they search for shelter and privacy in Joel's room. Seemingly unaware of Joel's presence, they talk until morning and meet for many nights thereafter to discuss their plans. Joel, who is deaf and therefore does not understand the meaning of their words, is nevertheless fascinated by the men and their nightly visits. Waiting for them to return every night, he imagines that his room and his silent companionship might provide the safety and hospitality they are looking for, and from this new sense of self-importance he gains positive self-awareness. It is only after a few days that Joel learns from a public notice that Burr is wanted for treason and that his trial will be held in Washington, capital of Mississippi Territory. Alerted to the true circumstances of Burr's nightly visits, Joel closely watches his friend and the town's reactions to his presence. He sneaks off to the river to see for himself the indicting evidence, the remains of Burr's flotilla; he watches as Burr and Blennerhassett gather in celebration on the last evening before the trial; he witnesses Burr's splendid performance at the trial; and he stands in the shadows as Burr makes his escape on horseback, followed by a posse.

Whether or not Burr was guilty of treason remains unclear not only in Welty's fictional account but in history books as well. As an ambitious young man seeking the office of the president of the United States, Burr ran for office against Jefferson in a tied election that was decided by the House of Representatives, which chose Jefferson as president and Burr as vice president. After his four-year term ended in 1804, Burr failed to be renominated as vice president, and he also failed to win the governorship of New York State because of the forceful opposition of Alexander Hamilton, a sharp Federalist critic of Burr. After he killed Hamilton in the famous duel, Burr became involved in a scheme that made his political recovery hopeless. Scholars have not been able to determine the exact outlines of the so-called Burr conspiracy. Alexander DeConde summarizes three different scenarios: "Some contemporaries, as well as historians, believed that . . . Burr planned to detach Louisiana and states along the Mississippi from the Union and create a separate nation. His defenders said no; he merely wished to live in peace on lands he owned in the Territory of Orleans. Others . . . thought he wanted to raise an army to invade Texas and Mexico, an idea that appealed to the anti-Hispanic prejudices of Westerners" (237). The precise nature of Burr's political intentions remains shrouded in mystery, but his desire for conquest, whatever shape it took, was shared by many of his contemporaries. When Burr came to Natchez in 1807 to seek refuge and to launch his new adventure into the "territories," he had already been arrested twice on the charge of treason for seeking western secession from the Union. Both times he was triumphantly released, and evidently "his popularity mounted with what seemed to be persecution of him" (Daniels 164). Welty focuses on this glamorous side of Burr while keeping his true political intentions veiled.

By making a deaf observer privy to Burr's nightly discussions with his confidant, Welty uses an effective method for perpetuating Burr's aura of mystique and avoiding disclosure. Almost all critics have commented on Joel as a narrative consciousness, and most agree that the deaf narrator's limited perspective on the historical incidents in Natchez unfortunately reduces the story's social and political impact. The result of this narrative technique is that Welty appears to shrink the "political factum Aaron Burr to a romantic myth of subconscious self-experience of man" and that "reality becomes an integrated part of a visionary view of the world, which is experienced as mystery" by the adolescent narrator (Ritter 24). This narrative strategy has been characterized as "unsettling" and as an outright "problem of narration" created by the fact that the reader encounters two views of Burr simultaneously: Joel's private view and history's public view (Thompson, "Burr" 77). But while Victor Thompson believes that Welty assigns private meaning to public history through Joel's limited consciousness, I think the opposite might be true. Welty's concern with Joel's perception draws attention not to a private world of symbols but to the very constructedness of public meaning. In other words, Welty's choice of a marginal character to report on the events of Burr's trial is not a romantic flight from historical reality but rather a shrewd reflection on the ever-elusive nature of past events. Her concern with the construction of historical meaning expressed through Joel's communication handicap leads Welty to phenomenological speculations about how language makes meaning, speculations intricately linked with her message and revisionary view of "History." Looking at a particular historical moment through the eyes of a marginal adolescent observer who is detached from the world of speech estranges the events surrounding Burr's visit to Natchez and calls into question the very nature of historical reality as a construction of the past that is never fully available for knowledge. In the story's opening, Welty provides a comment on time and the elusive nature of the past: "Whatever happened, it happened in extraordinary times, in a season of dreams, and in Natchez it was the bitterest winter of them all. The north wind struck one January night in 1807 with an insistent penetration, as if it followed the settlers down by their own course, screaming down the river bends to drive them further still. Afterwards there was the strange drugged fall of snow" (*Wide Net* 3).

"Whatever happened." This opening qualifier questions accepted certainties about knowledge and truth, and by casting its doubt over history it marks a crisis in both epistemology (the study of the nature and limits of human knowledge) and ontology (the study of the nature of being).[6] As if to counteract the stormy thrust of epistemological uncertainty, Welty anchors the location of her story securely in a specific narrative moment, a living present literally frozen. And yet, despite the freezing of time and space, neither the historical moment nor its meaning is ever simply present other than as a "trace" of something else. Welty's representation of history as a net of elusive traces can be illuminated by Derrida's idea of the "trace." The concept of the trace, for Derrida, is central to a theory of meaning as located in difference. Commenting on his choice of the term "trace," Derrida writes: "If words and concepts receive meaning only in sequences of differences, one can justify one's language, and one's choice of terms, only within a topic [an orientation in space] and an historical strategy" (Kamuf 41). Looking back at the history of philosophy, Derrida critiques the understanding of meaning as presence and substitutes in its stead the idea of the "trace."[7] As a concept, the trace is neither an entity, nor an origin, nor the signified itself. "The trace is nothing, it is not an entity, it exceeds the question *What is?* and contingently makes it possible" (47). The trace defies our search for origins as well, as Gayatri Spivak explains: "In our effort to define things, we look for origins. Every origin that we seem to locate refers us back to something anterior and contains the possibility of something posterior. There is, in other words, a trace of something else in seemingly self-contained origins" (194). When Derrida introduces the concept of the "trace," he refers to an idea of temporality that implicates the past and the future in the present moment: "the living present springs forth out of its nonidentity with itself and from the possibility of a retentional trace. It is always already a trace. This trace cannot be thought out on the basis of a simple present whose life would be within itself; the self of the living present is primordially a trace" (Kamuf 26). Signification is always engaged in the "movement" of the trace, as Welty's own comments on time show: "time tells us nothing about itself except by the signals that it is passing" (*Eye* 163). Fiction writers can tamper with time by freezing or accelerating action, but they are incapable of capturing the present—in other words, of presenting the present to itself. Welty's comments about the ephemeral quality of the present again evoke the Derridean understanding of time: "It is by the ephemeral that our feeling is so strongly aroused for what endures, or strives to endure. One time compellingly calls up the other. Thus, the ephemeral, being alive only in the present moment, must be made to live in the novel as *now,* while it transpires, in the transpiring" (*Eye* 168).

What exactly transpires in the frozen historical moment of "First Love"? By freezing the setting, Welty prepares the reader for a transformed understanding of reality and history characterized by a loss of proportion and a new narrative perspective: "Bands of travelers moved closer together with intenser caution, through the glassy tunnels of the Trace, for all proportion went away" (4). As she is negotiating the tunnels of her own textual "traces," Welty prepares the reader for the seemingly disproportionate perspective of the twelve-year-old deaf boy. His deafness is crucial because it allows Welty to link the character's existential isolation (and her own interest in the mysteries of language, signification, and speech) with problems of historical transmission, trauma, and "truth." Thus composed of numerous interrelated layers of interest, the fabric of Welty's story is woven of interior and exterior realms of experience in which history, phenomenology, and psychology intersect to form a rich texture. Welty says, "Maybe that was the trouble with the story, everything (for me) carried the burden of being so many things at once" (qtd. in Kreyling, *Author* 58). But this multitude of meanings merges successfully in the figure of the "trace," which relates Welty's exploration of signification (the linguistic trace) to the historical location (the Natchez Trace) and to questions of political representation. It is for this reason that Welty renders Joel's speech visible. As a deaf boy, Joel cannot hear himself or others except under the special circumstances of this winter when the icy air makes invisible speech visible: "He saw the breaths coming out of people's mouths, and his dark face, losing just now a little of its softness, showed its secret desire. It was marvelous to him when the infinite designs of speech became visible in formations on the air, and he watched with awe that changed to tenderness whenever people met and passed in the road with an exchange of words" (5). This physical and visible manifestation of speech becomes a central concern in this story. When Joel walked out in the cold, he "let his own breath out through his lips, pushed it into the air, and whatever word it was it took the shape of a tower. He was as pleased as if he had had a little conversation with someone" (5). By seeing himself speak, Joel is able to represent himself in language to himself. The phallic "tower" of his breath signifies self-presence in language made visible; his silent phonemes literally present themselves to his gaze and in the process transform his understanding of his position in the world.

Joel learns what speech and silence mean to the world of hearing. When the settlers are hiding from the Indians in the canebrake off the Natchez Trace, Joel cries and makes a sound. The frontier guide, old man McCaleb, threatens to kill him with an ax in "a kind of ecstasy of protecting the silence they were keeping" (7). In an instinctive reflex, Joel presses his mouth against the earth, comprehending for the first time "what silence means to other people" and feeling in this "speechless embrace" a "powerful, crushing unity" (7). His learning experience here is not just of private importance, as critics often assume. Joel's story is not simply about his overcoming "the numbing effects of his private psychological and spiritual tragedies," as St. George Tucker Arnold writes (97).

Nor is Joel a handicapped observer who simplifies the political and historical dimensions of the events to a "childish level of experience" (Ritter 24). Far from providing us with a naive perspective, Joel's silent observations highlight the presence of other silent characters, the anonymous Indians, with whom his life is inextricably linked. Joel's experience of the "powerful crushing unity" therefore extends not only to the speaking settler community of Natchez, and later on specifically to Aaron Burr, but also to the silent Indians who seem to be responsible for making him an orphan in the first place.

Joel's story, much like Burr's own, is about the American experience of settlement. As settlers who came from Virginia looking for new land and a new life, Joel and his parents are part of the American national epic of westward expansion marked by the violence of the encounter with Native American populations. Like his counterpart Aaron Burr, Joel represents the flotsam of this pioneer spirit and the promise of the American dream. Welty zooms in on the dreamlike quality of the frontier experience; she focuses on the dreams of the men who sleep in the little inn on their journey into the wilderness, on Joel's own difficulty of distinguishing between his dreams of Burr and the reality of his visit, and finally on Burr's own dreams. Recast as a dream of expansion and conquest, and symbolized by the boots of the westward travelers and pioneers, this American dream is rooted in personal trauma for Joel. On his way to Natchez, Joel lost his parents as they became separated from the group of travelers on the Trace and "vanished in the forest, were cut off from him, and in spite of his last backward look, dropped behind" (6). The trauma of his loss and separation, deeply ingrained in Joel's memory, is repressed. Welty captures such repressed violence and terror in an appropriately western image: "His memory could work like the slinging of a noose to catch a wild pony. It reached back and hung trembling over the very moment of terror in which he had become separated from his parents, and then it turned and started in the opposite direction, and it would have discerned some shape, but he would not let it, of the future" (13). Dreams of the future, the "arms bent on destination" that dragged him forward and away from the scene of loss and death, are necessary for the young nation's destiny and development. But conquest also involves leaving loved ones behind—for Joel as well as for Burr—and the dream of conquest is never far from being a nightmare according to a historical logic by which colonial cultures succeed each other.

Welty carefully sketches such a colonial environment. When Burr enters Joel's room, "everything in the room was conquest, all was a dream of delights and powers beyond its walls" (15). Burr and Blennerhassett convene at Joel's table, carved with Spanish words of love, "for anyone to read who came knowing the language" (9). Languages of colonial conquest, Spanish and English, mark Joel's room, signaling the West as a continuous process of colonial domination and as an ongoing contest for property, profit, and cultural dominance. In this climate of national expansionism, Burr's "dream" becomes Joel's dream in the famous gesture Burr makes during his first visit to Joel's room, a gesture "like the signal to open some heavy gate or paddock" that opens Joel's mind and heart to larger panoramas of historical and personal significance. Burr's dream is also passed on through the pressure of his burning hand, which transmits his "wisdom" to Joel at the climax of the story and before Burr disappears from Joel's life. The fierce, possessive grip of Burr's hand is nevertheless that of a sleeper who is wildly dreaming and threatens to reveal himself in his dangerous dreams of conquest. When Joel grasps Burr's hand, he shares the same cultural dream that uproots him and his parents in the first place and brings them to a violent confrontation with Indians. This memory of violence has to be repressed in order for America's ideology of progress and expansion to succeed, and therefore Joel does not allow himself to remember or grieve for his parents until he stands on Liberty Road at the end of the story. Having lost Burr, the person who most fiercely embodies this dream, "Joel would never know now the true course, or the true outcome of any dream" (33). With the dream of expansion cast in such uncertainty and eluding Joel's grasp as Burr is riding off on Liberty Road, a shadow is cast as well over the American credo of "life, liberty and happiness." And it is only then, in the catharsis brought about by the recognition of loss, that Joel falls to the ground and weeps for his parents.[8]

In fact, a careful reading reveals that Joel's perspective on the political events of 1807 is haunted by Indians, who are voiceless like himself, who live in a world deaf to their presence, and whose ghostly traces are deeply rooted in his unconscious. Indian traces appear five times in the story and in the signifier of the Natchez Trace itself. As a spatial signifier, the Natchez Trace is a meeting ground for colonizer and colonized, a place that ultimately points to the disenfranchisement of Native American nations and toward white westward expansion and nation-building, whether in the form of Lewis and Clark's expedition or in the form of Burr's treasonous "plot." The Indians first appear when Welty describes the time and setting of the story: "The Indians could be heard from greater distances and in greater numbers than had been guessed, sending up placating but proud messages to the sun in continual ceremonies of dancing. The red percussion of their fires could be seen night and day by those waiting in the dark trace of the frozen town" (4). We encounter Native Americans here as a typically proud, fierce, dangerous but anonymous force. The description of drumming and dancing Indians serves the purpose of othering them, with the "red" of their fires marking their racial difference.

Welty's failure to identify the Indians by tribe or affiliation indicates that they function merely as traces of an American past, as a group of people who seem marginal to the current political events. By depicting the Indians as sun worshippers, Welty most likely alludes to the Natchez, who were famous for their sun worship and the fires they burned perpetually in their temples. As historical signifiers, the Natchez Indians do not point to the narrative present, however, but are a historical trace that takes us back to the French/Choctaw massacre of the Natchez in 1729, which left the tribe nearly extinct. Natchez survivors joined the Creek, Cherokee, and Chickasaw tribes and became assimilated, or they were sold into slavery by the French. Therefore, it is historically highly unlikely that Joel's parents were killed by "a band of Natchez," as Kreyling assumes (*Understanding* 52). The Natchez were believed to be practically extinct by this time, and at the time of the composition of this story they were already listed as an extinct native tribe. Welty's allusion to the Natchez therefore registers their sudden ghostly presence, which takes us backward *and* forward in time to scenes of Indian slaughter. In the narrative present of 1807, when the settlers in Mississippi Territory were, after all, on Indian lands, U.S. territorial conquest involved not only negotiation with other European powers—a conflict foregrounded by the Burr case—but also negotiation with Native Americans, who were systematically dispossessed of their homes, languages, cultures, and lives. This historical reality manifests itself as a trace in Welty's text that points backward to attempts at their extinction in the past and forward to their removal from Mississippi in the 1830s. Accordingly, Indians file through Welty's text in metaphorical fashion: "The Indians had gone by, followed by an old woman—in solemn, single file, careless of the inflaming arrows they carried in their quivers, dangling in their hands a few strings of catfish. They passed in the length of an old woman's yawn" (7). The Indians are solemn figures followed by an old woman who symbolizes the nearness of death, connoting their own extinction. This passage seems to be Welty's elegy for the "noble savages" who live by their arrows, work with simple tools, and eat from the rivers and forests. By recording the passing of a subsistence society to the advances of the settlers, Welty's text evokes nineteenth-century discourses of social Darwinism that were often used to justify colonialist enterprises. The Indians themselves are marked by "single files," "arrows," and "strings," all of which signify the linearity of their passing (through and away). Their brief appearance—in the length of a yawn—and immediate disappearance, both from the settler's and the reader's view, emphasize their temporality, immateriality, and ghostliness.

It is therefore not surprising that the next trace marking Indian presence in the text links them with the disembodied presence of ghosts. After Burr's first mysterious nightly visit to Joel's room, Joel wakes up and "his first thought was of Indians, his next of ghosts, and then the vision of what had happened came back into his head" (12). Joel is haunted by Indian ghosts who have found their way into his dreams and his unconscious. But this presencing of the repressed is not just Joel's individual nightmare; the ghostly return of Indian slaughter and dispossession is shared by the settlers of Natchez and the United States at large. If "haunting belongs to the structure of every hegemony," as Derrida asserts, the haunting in Welty's text expresses a drama of national guilt (*Specters* 37). Because such guilt about conquest and extermination is repressed, it returns in the textual traces of an Indian presence whose absence the settlers so desire.

The Indian traces may also manifest guilt and doubt in Welty's own unconscious, returning us to her earlier insistence that she does not go "into such things as guilt over the Indians." But for the writer who occupies a space in the South that is marked by the traumatic removal of Chickasaws and Choctaws to Indian Territory just one hundred years earlier, it is precisely such a denial that points to an important presence in the traces of her own fiction. Renee Bergland argues that "when ghostly Indian figures haunt the white American imagination, they serve as constant reminders of the fragility of national identity" (5). In writing about Burr's conspiracy, Welty presents a well-known public debate about national unity and identity, one so familiar that its plot threatens to erase the underlying traces of Native American history. By alluding to the Indian presence in the story, however, Welty does more than create a historical backdrop; she presents the plot of American history in the local traces that remain. Welty was interested in local history and place-names. In her review of George Stewart's book *Names on the Land,* published just three years after *The Wide Net,* Welty remarks that "the record of our place-names is of course the skeleton of our nation; in that array the intrinsic and underlying structure shows" (*Eye* 182). She was particularly interested in the structures that pointed to Indian names: "the book deals constantly with Indians, of course, and manages to correct many an error about Indian names" (187). In this discussion of Indian signifiers in the American landscape, Welty highlights the history of colonization that led to the obliteration of origins, and she explains that place-names are often untraceable: "Transference, translation and false etymology are the three ways in which a place name can be passed from language to language. . . . So the Indian names enduring as such are not the actual, original Indian names—they are what the French priests wrote down, what the Spanish thought they sounded like, what the English thought they undoubtedly meant, what the Dutch made sound as nearly Dutch as they could" (187). For Welty, Native American names are signifiers of a colonial history that opens up "panoramas of the nation at a given time" (185). The linguistic displacement of Indian names in the mapping of American geography corresponds both to the physical removal of

Indians (from the Southeast) and perhaps also to the psychic displacement of the Native American presence in Welty's imagination. In both external and internal landscapes, Native Americans function as traces—repressed, displaced, and silenced—that threaten the rationalist hegemony of the United States and hence the successful construction of national identity.

American national identity was still very young in 1807 (it was less than thirty years earlier that amid calls for a revolutionary war with Great Britain the Declaration of Independence was adopted), and the boundaries of the new nation were ever changing and often ambiguous. Because national identity centered around issues of expansion and conquest, Welty uses Burr primarily as a symbol of American expansionism. In researching the Burr conspiracy, Welty may have encountered the historical study by Walter Flavius McCaleb (1903), who conspicuously shares his name with one of Welty's frontier characters. McCaleb, the historian, argues that "the conspiracy of Aaron Burr was preeminently a revolutionary product, receiving its inspiration from that unprecedented period of upheaval which began with the Revolution of 1776, its compelling force from the character of the American pioneer, its license from the disturbed condition of affairs existing in the New World" (1). In short, Burr's expansionist schemes were a product of American nationalist ideology and perhaps only one symptom in the drama of American expansionism, which was officially pursued by Jefferson in the Louisiana Purchase of 1803 and in the Lewis and Clark expeditions from 1803 to 1806.[9] President Jefferson himself instructed his Indian agent to convince native tribes "of the justice and liberality we are determined to use towards them, and to attach them to us indissolubly" (qtd. in McCaleb 12). Clearly, Burr is not the only expansionist who favored growth at the expense of other nations. During this time, armed intrusions into countries then at peace with the United States—so-called filibustering expeditions—were rather common (although most were unsuccessful).[10] Similar to earlier border skirmishes of English, French, and Spanish colonists, such private forays into neighboring countries, particularly popular in the United States in the early nineteenth century, grew out of the ideology of expansionism. Encouraged by the prerogative of Manifest Destiny, American filibusters like Burr had an interest in the acquisition of territory for political and personal financial gains. McCaleb argues that the mind of the settlers in the territories has to be taken into consideration when looking at the conspiracy. Emphasizing the West's fervent nationalism and its revolutionist disposition, McCaleb reminds us that "for years the West harbored the most devoted adherents for the Constitution *and* the most unscrupulous filibusters" (13, emphasis added).

Put into this sociohistorical context, Burr's paradoxical activities (both for and against his own country) appear more representative of a general political climate and less the sign of a greedy man's personal character flaw, and this may be why Burr is not depicted as a villain but as an ironically romanticized hero in Welty's story. Charles Nolan's study of Aaron Burr in the American literary imagination singles out Welty's depiction of Burr as an unusual portrait because "Welty is able to depict Burr as an object of adoration and a seducer at the same time, harmonizing these apparently antipodal poles by making the Colonel's seductiveness lie in what he is, a character of dazzling brilliance whose personal charm makes people cherish and want to support him" (112). But despite his popularity, Burr and Harman Blennerhassett failed in their filibustering enterprise.

Welty's depiction of Burr's failure centers around the arrival of his diminished flotilla in Natchez, which Joel witnesses.[11] And not surprisingly, Indians appear also in the context of this event: "Where Joel stood looking down upon them, the boats floated in clusters of three, as small as water-lilies on a still bayou. A canoe filled with crazily wrapped-up Indians passed at a little distance, and with severe open mouths the Indians all laughed" (22). Why are they laughing? At whom are they laughing? The Indian laughter here might be a comment on Burr's miserable failure to dispossess native inhabitants of their lands. Their "severe" laughter signifies amusement and triumph but perhaps also anxiety and even terror. It is this laughter that haunts the American national consciousness and ultimately pollutes American attempts to seriously justify rightful possession of the land. Bergland argues that "land ownership may be the source of the nation's deepest guilt" (8), and I think it may also explain why traces of Indian presence undermine the official drama of Burr's "transgressions" in Welty's story.

In a final, brilliant stroke, Welty even links Burr himself with the Native American signifier. As a fugitive traveler on the Trace, Burr disguises himself as an Indian to escape the posse sent after him. Welty here changes the historical record, which claims that Burr was disguised as a riverboatman, although historians disagree on this aspect of Burr's adventure as well.[12] Dressed as an Indian, Burr represents a double figure of the nation in crisis: he is a "native son," first because of his famous American ancestry and his role in shaping the political destiny of the nation, and second because of his feathery disguise, which symbolizes original native ownership of America and alliance with Native Americans. Articulating this paradoxical double bind, Burr's disguise—his dirty and ragged clothes, the "little cap of turkey feathers on his head," and his face darkened with boot polish—is part of a persistent tradition of Indian masking in American culture. Philip Deloria reminds us that Indian disguise symbolizes the age-old American desire to "feel a natural affinity with the continent" (5). Indians, he argues, could best teach settlers such "aboriginal closeness." The tragic irony, however, is that in order to possess themselves of the land they called their own, the settlers tried to destroy the native inhabitants, their source of native identification. By destroying the Indians but preserving and adopting the very images that served for national identification, Indian masking was (and is) an important means for creating an American national identity. Reading Welty in this context, it seems that she uses Burr's Indian disguise to articulate a crisis in American identity by drawing attention to the ironic gap between the "rightful" possession of land—Jefferson's and not Burr's—which is always at the same time the wrongful dispossession of the native populations. Such a historical scenario, which centers around the political silencing of Native American voices in the national drama, is also symbolically reflected in Joel's deafness (the young settler's deafness), which represents the nation's inability to hear and listen to Native American interests and needs.

Read carefully for the textual traces of the Native American presence, "First Love" reveals the anxieties underlying America's history of westward expansion. The historical trace takes us back to the conflict over political power in the young nation, a national drama of conquest that erases the presence of Native Americans and silences their political voices. However, these Indian voices come back to haunt the national narrative; they enter into historical discourses with clearly audible "signs": the "red percussion of their fires" and a mocking "laugh" that echoes eerily. The Indian signifier in Welty's short story marks linguistic, historical, and political traces that render "present" their absences from dominant political discourse.

The Robber Bridegroom: Postcolonial Parody and Manifest Destiny

Welty examines the ideology of expansionism as part of America's national narrative not only in her short story "First Love" but also in her 1942 novella, *The Robber Bridegroom.* In the latter, Welty asks, with Homi Bhabha: "How do we plot the narrative of the nation that must mediate between the teleology of progress tipping over into the timeless discourse of irrationality?" (Bhabha 142). *The Robber Bridegroom* is a narrative in which the conventions of history—the claims of chronology, teleology, cause and effect—are suspended and brought into a relationship of dialectical tension with the timeless irrationality of the fairy tale. As such, this novella can be read as Welty's response to Bhabha's question.[13] History, derailed from its chronological track, leaves a trace into the cultural unconscious where the ambivalence about the nation's modernity is reflected most prominently in Welty's Indian characters. Unlike in "First Love," where Indians remain ghostly traces in the drama of national expansion, in *The*

Robber Bridegroom they step into the foreground as characters who frame the narrative and influence its course. Accordingly, the Indians in *The Robber Bridegroom* have received some critical attention beginning with the reviews published in 1942. John Peale Bishop opens his review for the *New Republic* with a quotation from the novella that emphasizes the violence of the frontier; writing for the *Nation,* Lionel Trilling notes that in the fairy-tale cast of the story, "its spirits of air are Indians"; and in a review for *New York Herald Tribune Books,* Alfred Kazin comments on the Indians as agents of disenchantment: Indian captivity and violence break with the dream of an "enchanted world."[14] Taking his critical cue from Kazin, Michael Kreyling has pioneered a reading of the novella that focuses on the role of the Indians as part of a serious thematic concern in Welty's otherwise "light-hearted tale." The historical and the pastoral elements of the novella, he argues, form a "perpetually unresolved rivalry" ("Clement" 25). In this rivaling opposition between these two different modes of representation, the Indians, Kreyling suggests, "spark something other than laughter" (29); they "furnish a certain gravity"; they "are created with a depth and quality of sympathy sometimes found in Cooper. . . . They have nobility, mystery, beauty, and pride. They are the spirit of the country" ("*The Robber*" 136). In short, for Kreyling the Indians are part of the narrative's serious consideration of history.

Welty's Indians, I agree, do represent a serious historical trajectory, but only as signifiers in a discourse that mocks precisely the traditions of representation that Kreyling alludes to: the romantic, primitivist, and Darwinian notions that have traditionally been used to explain the "vanishing Indian." In *The Robber Bridegroom,* Welty takes delight in parodying the kind of historical continuity based on nature, nobility, and evolution that spells "doom" for the Indians. By collapsing the distinctions between history and fiction, she critically intervenes in America's historical discourses of Manifest Destiny and capitalist progress, and by weaving history and fiction into a tight web that reveals the limits of their logic through multiple ironies, she questions their status as useful metanarratives or serious master narratives. History, in Welty's novella, is not separate from but an inextricable part of local legend, fairy tale, and fiction. By blending all of these genres, Welty creates a postcolonial parody that functions not in a historical but a "historicist" manner, that is, as a text that raises critical questions about the writing and the narrating of the nation's "History."

Given Welty's experimental mixing of genres in *The Robber Bridegroom,* it is understandable that critics have attempted to identify and separate different formal elements of her text in order to see how they might work together.[15] However, in order to clarify the question of genre it might be useful to listen to Welty's own explanation of her narrative: "I made our local history . . . legend and fairy tale into working equivalents. It was my firm intention to bind them together" (*Eye* 305). Like the knotted sleeves of the robber bridegroom's coat, history, legend, and fairly tale form a tight knot in Welty's novella (and there may even be a little dirk hidden in it). By linking these different discourses and setting them into a relationship of "equivalence," Welty brings them all onto the same discursive level; in the process of leveling them, she denies the demand of "History" for superiority and "seriousness" over the other two discourses. By drawing attention to the textuality of history and the (distorting) web of language, Welty not only blurs genre distinctions between "literary fantasy" and "serious history" but also radically dissolves the discursive boundaries between them, thereby invalidating any such disciplinary and discursive distinctions or hierarchies. By firmly knotting these discourses together—one a historical "reality" with a truth claim, the other a fictional fantasy with no such claim—Welty breaks down both disciplinary discourses, exposes the laws of their operations, and mocks their logic. It is this act of deconstruction that constitutes the joy and the avant-garde brilliance of *The Robber Bridegroom.*

Welty is not interested in straight fairy tales any more than she is in accurate historical representation; instead, she enjoys the parodic subversion of both. The reason we laugh at the jokes in *The Robber Bridegroom* is that we seem to recognize first and most easily the parody of the fairy-tale genre. Because the rules of this genre as it operates in Welty's text can clearly be dismantled as unsuitable, we enjoy the obvious discrepancy between the rules proper to the fairly-tale discourse and the text's subversion of them. What provides narrative unity and logic of explanation are the fairy-tale characters (the bad stepmother, the cave of robbers, the speaking raven), the romance plot (after much confusion, Jamie and Rosamond find each other), the names from mythology (most obviously Salome and Orion), allusions to other plots (Hansel and Gretel, Rapunzel), and the tall tale (Mike Fink, the Harp brothers). In addition, the story is stocked with binary oppositions that provide the illusion of order and meaning. For example, Rosamond, the young heroine, is "beautiful as the day," whereas Salome, her stepmother, is "ugly as the night." These clear-cut linguistic and moral binaries, which belong to the conventions of the fairy-tale genre, are mocked and deconstructed on all narrative levels of the text, from the sentence level to the overall plot.

The novella's fairy-tale plot is based on the Grimms' original tale of the same name, but with a distinctly local flavor. In Welty's version, a rich planter (Clement Musgrove), a famous bandit (Jamie Lockhart), and the legendary flatboat man (Mike Fink) meet one night when they are forced to share sleeping quarters at an inn on the Natchez Trace. Jamie saves Clement's life from a murderous attack by Mike Fink during the night and he is invited to the planter's house for dinner and to meet his beautiful daughter Rosamond and Clement's second wife, Salome. As a robber, Jamie is very interested in the planter's wealth and eagerly accepts the invitation. But Jamie and Rosamond meet earlier than planned as she is gathering herbs in the woods along the Natchez Trace one morning. When Jamie in his berry-stained disguise discovers the beautiful Rosamond, he robs her of all her clothing. But when he, without his robber's rags, comes for dinner the next day, he and Rosamond do not recognize each other. When they meet again the following day alone in the woods, Jamie robs her of more than her clothing. As a result of their (sexual) encounter, Rosamond falls in love with Jamie and follows him to his robber's lair. When she does not return home, Clement believes that his daughter has been kidnapped and hires Jamie to help him find her. Jamie—who wants the reward money—agrees to the job, not knowing that the girl with whom he now lives in the forest is the lost Rosamond whom he needs to find. When one night Rosamond recognizes Jamie's true identity by wiping the berry-juice stains off his face while he is sleeping, and he subsequently recognizes her as Clement's daughter, Jamie flees. The now-pregnant Rosamond goes in search of her lover and finds him in New Orleans, where they get married, settle down, and are reunited with Clement.

Although she is seemingly playing by the rules of the fairy tale, Welty parodies the genre by introducing the rules and expectations of this discourse only in order to abandon them. The result is that her text "subverts, reverses, burlesques, and just generally scatters asunder the fairy tale's sacrosanct notions about the agenda for happily-ever-after living" (M. Arnold 33). By rejecting the clarity and simplicity of the fairy tale in favor of complexity and ambiguity, Welty blurs not only the genre's unambiguous moral distinctions between good and evil, truth and lies, and right and wrong but also introduces inappropriate elements, particularly in the treatment of the romance between Jamie and Rosamond. Arnold points out that "the two of them have all the physical characteristics and even many of the adventures of fairy tale lovers, but their courtship and marriage would be an absolute scandal in any proper fairy tale" (36). Among those scandals, foremost are Jamie's rape of Rosamond, their life together without the sanction of marriage, and her pregnancy. "Whoever heard of a fairy tale heroine delivering twins just moments after her wedding?" (36). And worse, perhaps: fornication, cohabitation, lying, banditry, faithlessness, and lack of trust are not something that merits punishment or condemnation by the author (36). Indeed, Welty is not interested in moralizing but rather in mocking the rules of plot and morality of this particular discourse. By producing an ironic gap between the discursive rules of the fairy tale and their abandonment in the narrative, Welty's text opens a space for a linguistic "trace" to appear that leads into absurdity and parody.

In this way, the "fairy tale" not only seduces us into laughing but, more importantly, creates a realm of a clearly marked "imaginary" in order to make us believe that the rest of the text, its "history," is real and serious. However, the text's "history" participates in the same linguistic structures that make up its "fictional" world. So it only passes itself off as an authoritative discourse, but like the fairy tale into which it is bound, it is not. There is no residue of "serious History" left in the story when Welty gets done with it, or after critics have subtracted the "fairy tale" part from it. History—specifically in the form of the southern plantation economy, slavery, and westward expansion—is an inextricable part of Welty's postcolonial parody from the first sentence of the narrative on: "It was the close of day when a boat touched Rodney's Landing on the Mississippi River and Clement Musgrove, an innocent planter, with a bag of gold and many presents, disembarked" (1). From the start, history and fiction enter into easy textual hybridity. Rodney's Landing, a historical and geographical marker pointing to an "extinct" town (according to the 1938 *Guide to the Magnolia State*), provides a trace into the colonial history and the commercial geography of Mississippi Territory. The narrative sets into motion a historical discourse of a distinctly southern plantation economy and the American capitalist marketplace at the same time that it signals its fairy-tale mode. The opening phrase—not "once upon a time" but the similar "it was the close of day"—and another fairy tale standard, the "bag of gold," indicate the literary genre. What emerges from this semantic knotting of historical and fictional markers is a hybridization of discourses that results in aesthetic and political polyphony. From this act of grafting different discursive elements onto each other, the text gets its disruptive and transfigurative power. It at once reveals the interdependence of historical and fictional discourses and yet is transformed into something new. The mutual constitution of these discourses results in a hybrid mode of narration marked by numerous ironic paradoxes such as that of the "innocent planter" which radically destabilize the narrative.

Welty's interest in precisely such a disruption of discursive distinctions between history and fiction becomes clear in her 1975 discussion of *The Robber Bridegroom* at a meeting of the Mississippi Historical Society. In this talk, Welty slips in and out of history and fiction with an easy playfulness that amounts to a skillful performance similar to the one in her novella. Commenting on the opening of the novella, she explains that "the story is laid in an actual place, traces of which still exist": "Rodney just before 1798" (*Eye* 302).[16] These historical traces into a specific time and place make us believe that the text presents a "serious" historical perspective. But this is not so. In the context of late-eighteenth-century Spanish colonialism, slavery, and plantation economy, no planter is ever "innocent." As Welty says, "'innocent' has nothing to do with the historical point of view; and it shines like a cautionary blinker to what lies on the road ahead" (*Eye* 301). The irony of the "innocent planter" signals indeed a warning against proceeding to read him as offering any "serious" commentary on history. Limited by his naïveté, Clement is trapped in his own historical moment, from which he offers a shortsighted endorsement of popular theories of Manifest Destiny and a condemnation of the "violent Indians" who stand in the way of settlement and progress.

Welty rehearses these discourses at the beginning of the narrative and uses them to sketch a national framework to the fairy-tale and romance plot. When Clement tells the story of his Indian captivity, he and Jamie speculate about the persistence of the Indian foe. Jamie offers that "the savages are so clever, they are liable to last out, no matter how we stamp upon them," and Clement responds: "The Indians know their time has come. . . . They are sure of the future growing smaller always, and that let's them be infinitely gay and cruel" (21). And when Clement tells of his humiliation by the Indians, Jamie remarks: "This must have been long ago . . . for they are not so fine now and cannot do so much to prisoners as that" (23). The rhetoric of Manifest Destiny, the idea that Indians once strong will give way to the superior forces of American civilization as a result of a natural selection process that marks their "doom," of course enforced and supported self-serving designs of imperialist expansion. Such rhetoric of progress, extinction, and change—the theme of the vanishing Indian—is rehearsed not only in Welty's description of the frontier but in the critical discourse as well. Kreyling writes, "every step that the white pioneers confidently take is shadowed by the unseen, doomed Indians, whose harmonious relationship with the forest is coming to an end. The Indians enjoy an organic union with the place, appearing and dissolving in the surrounding forest, to the eyes of the pioneers, as if Indian nature were not restricted merely to the human but partook of the animal and the vegetable as well" ("*The Robber*" 138). This image of the Indians' intimate union with nature as it appears "to the eyes of the pioneers" is a common stylistic strategy of nineteenth-century writers who depicted Native Americans as part of the natural environment and accordingly explained their perishing as part of a natural process like the change of the seasons, the coming of nightfall, or the melting of snow.[17] Alluding to the pervasive discourse of Manifest Destiny and the "problems of Indian civilization," Thomas Jefferson in 1824 ventured to say that "Barbarism has . . . been receding before the steady step of amelioration; and will in time, I trust, disappear from the earth" (qtd. in Dippie 12). But the Indians had refused to "vanish," and fifty years later, Seldon Clark, who was charged with establishing Indian population estimates, summarizes the assumptions of many policy makers of the 1870s:

> If, as generally believed, the Indians are a vanishing race, doomed to disappear at a not remote period, because of their contact with civilization . . . then the efforts in behalf of their civilization will assume in most minds, a sentimental aspect. . . . But, on the contrary, if it is shown that the Indians, instead of being doomed by circumstances to extinction within a limited period, are, as a rule, not deceasing in numbers . . . the necessity of their civilization will be at once recognized, and all efforts in that direction will be treated as their importance demands. (qtd. in Dippie 125)

Unfortunately, the discourse of Manifest Destiny keeps lurking even in contemporary discussions of Welty's thematic concern with change. Kreyling revives not only the idea of the vanishing Indian but also the passive rhetorical stance: "Time and events make ghosts of the Indians and the town, and these forces neither the Indians nor the conquering white pioneers can control or foresee. . . . The Indians are in the throes of change and extinction; Rodney is a static omen of the same imminent change. The Indians' way of life and its passing dramatize the meaning of change; the presence of Rodney bodes it" ("Clement" 32). In presenting history as the agent of change, such a reading masks and distorts the political realities of conquest by accounting for white dominance and Indian extinction as a phenomenon of chronological progression. In addition, I suggest that the formal characteristics of Welty's text operate against such a reading of national history as "progression" by presenting it in the timeless setting of the fairy tale, a genre that works to arrest the time-bound explanation of the nation and dismantles its mythical and fictional grounding.

When Welty evokes the familiar assumptions about national progress and vanishing Indians, she plays with these conventions of historical representation in order to parody them. In the 1940s, Native Americans had not vanished, nor were most of them an integral part of mainstream "civilization." Popular images in movies and literature, while highlighting Native American visibility, returned Indians to their frontier settings and their "proper" place as doomed opponents to the advance of Anglo-American civilization, thereby reinforcing romantic, primitivist, and Darwinian beliefs. Astutely aware of these discursive and visual traditions, Welty reproduces them with subtle ironic overtones. Her representations of Indians owe as much to the romantic tradition of the "noble savage" as they do to contemporary movies and cartoons. From both media, Welty borrows a visual style that relies on synecdoche and fragmentation as techniques for representing the Indian body as it emerges ever so briefly from the wilderness. Notice the mocking, humorous intent in these passages: As Clement is contemplating the "lateness of the age" in the wilderness just a few steps off the Natchez Trace, "the Indians came closer and found him. A red hand dragged him to his feet. He looked into large, worldly eyes" (144). Similarly, as Salome is out in the woods looking for Jamie, she does not see that "dark was close around her now, and while she scanned the sky the bush at her side came alive, and folded her to the ground" (145). And just as the Little Harp, a bandit modeled on the dreaded Harp brothers, is at the brink of his most profound insight—that the way to get ahead is to cut a head off—the face that looks at him through the trees "was redskinned and surrounded by feathers, and it wore a terrible frown" and "red arms twined around him like a soft net" (145). Welty's use of synecdoche—the Indian as a "red hand," "red arms," "worldly eyes," or a bush come alive—results in a style of representation that has less to do with a serious historical discourse about Native Americans and more with popular Hollywood images. Hollywood movies of the period helped to reinforce a view of Indians as anachronism by portraying them through the use of grunts and alien-sounding language—Hollywood Indian English—and an emphasis on body language that was a carryover from the silent films.[18] Kreyling is right when he suggests that *The Robber Bridegroom* is "frankly more akin to an animated Disney feature . . . than to the actual history of the Natchez Trace" ("Welty as Novelist" 4–5). Using these cinematic techniques for her treatment of the Indians, Welty puns on the "cunning art of their disguise" as she draws images of "savages" in bearskins and masks "of a spotty leopard" (147).

Welty's satirical play with the conventions of Indian representation contains every conceivable stereotype from the "red hand" that grabs the unsuspecting white settler in the forest to the random violence committed by proud and fierce savages. Her postcolonial parody delights in toying with familiar representations of "otherness" such as the standard binary opposition between good and bad Indians. Welty's bad Indians wear blazing feathers, dance in circles, wield glittery weapons, and enjoy torturing and scalping prisoners. They are as unreal as every other character in her fairy tale, and they set into motion a concern with alterity, specifically the split and doubled identities that emerge in the encounter with the other. Indian "savagery" first occurs at the beginning of the novella in Clement's captivity narrative. This episode evokes the discourse of cannibalism, when Clement's son is dropped into a pot of burning oil by the Indians; of sentimentalism, when his beloved wife, Amalie, dies of grief as a result; and of comic sadism, when the Indians put a punishing "mark" on Clement in their "infinite cruelty" by tying him to Salome and setting them loose in the wilderness. The beginning of Clement's story is also the beginning of the American national narrative: the story of how the nation produced itself in violent contact experiences with Indians. But Indian violence remains abstract; the evil Indians themselves remain flat stereotypes who are used as a deus ex machina device in order to begin and end the plot. At the end, the narrative circles back on itself when all the main characters—Clement, Jamie, Rosamond, and Salome—find themselves in Indian captivity, all except for Goat, who "escaped, for the Indians searched in devious and secret ways only" (148).

Welty's text activates not only discourses of depraved and hostile Indians but also those of their noble counterparts. The Little Harp's brutal killing of the Indian maiden, a young, innocent, beautiful native girl, alludes to this tradition. In an act of textual revision, Welty changes the details of the original Grimms version of *The Robber Bridegroom* not only by giving it a specific locality (the Mississippi frontier) and changing the maiden into an *Indian* maiden, but also by displacing the monstrous act of killing the girl from the robber (Jamie) to his real-life historical counterpart, the Little Harp, who, she speculates "might have done it" (*Eye* 308). To substitute a historical character for something too terrible for a fictional one constitutes a particular kind of irony: history is worse than any grim fairy tale, as Welty believes. "History tells us worse things than fairy tales do. People were scalped. Babies had their brains dashed out against tree trunks or were thrown into boiling oil when the Indians made their captures. Slavery was the order on the plantations. The Natchez Trace outlaws eviscerated their victims and rolled their bodies downhill, filled with stones, into the Mississippi River. War, bloodshed, massacre were all part of the times" (*Eye* 309). Welty's act of substituting an "Indian maiden"—"And for a joke, it was an Indian girl" (131)—taps a whole host of familiar frontier narratives about rape, mutilation, and violent "conquest." But Welty touches lightly on the violation and murder of the "Indian maiden," a serious subject presented in a mocking tone whose jarring inconsistency is often understood as revealing the bitter edges of her parody. Barbara Carson sums up the critical consensus when she writes that "in the death of the Indian girl we are about as far as we can be from lighthearted innocence and from gay soaring dreams without nightmares" (71). A comparison with the original source reveals, however, that such violence is precisely part of the cruel fantasy of the fairy tale, and that Welty's substitution reveals less about a specific case of American frontier cruelty and more about the traditions of historical representation. Welty dishes up the image of the noble savage—here a beautiful *Indian* "maiden," an innocent and random victim of duplicitous, treacherous, and lecherous "robbers" of the New World. She "transposes" these real-life horrors of the American frontier—captivity, slavery, torture, and murder—into the fairy-tale format in order to question the traditions of representation that activate our understanding of Indians in terms of simple dualisms: the noble savage and her barbarian counterpart, the settler and the robber of the land.[19] Welty's narrative negotiates and collapses these binaries with satirical precision as they double up on themselves, matching Rosamond's rape with the Indian maiden's. By trapping her Indian characters in the contact zone between fiction and history, Welty explores the schism in the American psyche in which Indians register precisely *between* fiction and history, dream and nightmare, guilt and innocence.

Welty's "innocent planter," then, is a bad guide through the national narrative. His perception of reality is so flawed that he does not recognize the famous rogues surrounding him, and with his naively trusting attitude he is vulnerable, gullible, and easily duped. Through Clement's lack of perception, of motivation, and of financial ambition behind his cotton empire, Welty parodies the pioneering enterprise. Clement appears as a caricatured opposite of Faulkner's Thomas Sutpen, who, driven by desire and design, stamps his plantation out of the wilderness. By contrast, Clement chooses to remain forever innocent; or as he says, "cunning is of a world I will have no part in" (142). His resistance to the "time of cunning"—the epoch of deception, craftiness, and guile that marks the loss of Edenic innocence in the New World—is also a refusal to "know and see," as the Old English root of the word "to cunn(an)" indicates. His most profound insights into the nature of the world with its "massacre" and "murder" is rudely and comically interrupted when the Indians snatch him out of his reverie. His story begins with the familiar script of "discovery" and migration that represses the motives of national expansion such as profit, exploitation, and slavery. Clement admits: "The reason I ever came is forgotten now. . . . [I]t seemed as if I was caught up by what came over the others, and they were the same. There was a great tug at the whole world, to go down over the edge, and one and all we were changed into pioneers, and our hearts and our own lonely will may have had nothing to do with it" (20–21).

Welty pokes fun at the economic trajectory of the pioneers by linking her critique of the plantation economy both to the "innocent planter" and to the character of the bad stepmother, Salome, who scans "the lands from east to west" with her eagle eyes. Salome embodies the ruthless principle of westward expansion and greed as she counsels Clement: "we must cut down more of the forest, and stretch away the fields until we grow twice as much of everything. Twice as much indigo, twice as much cotton, twice as much tobacco. For the land is there for the taking, and I say, if it can be taken, take it" (99). The idea that the "land is for the taking" echoes early-nineteenth-century beliefs that Indians had too much land that they were not properly using. As we have seen, this is also a belief that Caroline Gordon addresses in *Green Centuries* when her settler character Rion admits: "I never had it in mind to pay anybody for the land after I got here. The Indians ain't using it. They ain't got a right to keep people from settling on it" (183). Colonists felt that they were right to take "unused" land from the Indians in order to cultivate it because agricultural labor was understood as part of the gospel of progress and blessed by God. As Thomas Jefferson professed: "Those who labor in the earth are the chosen people of God, if ever he had a chosen people" (qtd. in Andrews 53). Even though the lifestyle of southeastern Indians in the eighteenth and nineteenth centuries was based in agriculture, American settlers, blinded by expansionist goals and politics, ignored the common agricultural basis of early southern culture. In 1802, John Quincy Adams asked: "What is the right of a huntsman to the forest of a thousand miles over which he has accidentally ranged in quest of prey? . . . Shall the fields and vallies, which a beneficent God has formed to teem with the life of innumerable multitudes, be condemned to everlasting barrenness?" (qtd. in Berkhofer 138). The assumption here is that only land that is put to agricultural use is fruitful and properly used. As Robert Berkhofer explains, at the end of the eighteenth century "geography took on a moral as well as an economic dimension under the ideology of Americanism that had direct implications for Native American occupancy. First, to preserve the American political and social system, certain ways of using the land were preferred to others, and the idea of the Indian and his way opposed these modes. . . . Second, American ways of life were fated to expand within the boundaries of the United States and even beyond in accord with the ideas of progress and history" (138). Welty rehearses these discourses of economic expansion and superiority, but unlike Gordon, she presents them jokingly and thinly disguised as greed. "If we have this much, we can have more," says Salome (99). As the embodiment of the capitalist principle of surplus value, Salome ensures that Clement is planting the right crops, expanding the property, and building a better house every year. Clement remembers, "well, before long a little gallery with four posts appeared across the front of my house, and we were sitting there in the evening; and new slaves sent out with axes were felling more trees, and indigo and tobacco were growing nearer and nearer to the river there under the black shadow of the forest. Then in one of the years she made me try cotton, and my fortune was made" (28). Salome, however, will not be satisfied until she can live in a mansion "at least five stories high, with an observatory of the river on top of that, with twenty-two Corinthian columns to hold up the roof" (100).[20] She represents the obsession with possession—the desire for land, slaves, and ever-bigger plantations—as part of a southern *and* a national narrative of progress that is satirized and ironically endorsed at the end of the narrative when Rosamond happily shows off her own mansion "on the shores of Lake Pontchartrain with a hundred slaves" (184).

The myth of national innocence—evoked in the same stroke in which it is undercut by the casual references to slavery and colonialism—and the reality of capitalist greed are represented through Clement and Salome, who espouse two diametrically opposed worldviews that make up the dialectic of modern times. Wedded into Welty's double discourse, this doubling and splitting of the national narrative exposes the everlasting ambiguity of its own project. Welty articulates this ambivalence by presenting Indian violence, slavery, land acquisition, and the cotton economy casually in a pseudo-evolutionary narrative that shrinks chronological time and mocks the master narrative of History. By hybridizing history and fantasy, Welty presents what Bhabha terms "the disjunctive time of the nation's modernity" (142). In order to emphasize this disjunction, Welty plays with double structures, echoes, mirror images, reflections, and repetitions on all narrative levels, including plot, character, theme, and language. These double structures are intended to disrupt homogeneous and progressive constructions of (national) identity. When they occur in the novella, binary structures seem to make sense by their diametrical opposition, but far from providing certainty or truth, they are self-conscious strategies that resolve themselves into new mysteries. Meaning slips away. Welty comments on her narrative technique of splitting and doubling in *The Robber Bridegroom:* "There is a doubleness in respect to identity that runs in a strong thread through all the wild happenings—indeed, this thread is their connection, and everything that happens hangs upon it. . . . In the doubleness there was narrative truth that I felt the times themselves had justified (*Eye* 310–11). Barbara Carson argues that Welty's dual vision reveals "reality" not as "an either/or matter" but as a "dynamic tension of co-existing opposites." Carson, however, understands Welty's vision as essentially ontological when she writes, "The challenge of life is thus not choosing between opposites—joy or sorrow, true or false, beginnings or endings, life or death—but coming to see a whole with both poles as inseparably united, as interdependent as two poles of a magnet" (65–66). I agree that the double narrative movement of Welty's text does produce a tension, but it does not resolve itself into neatly formed, matching opposites. On the contrary, Welty's text in its very self-conscious play with binaries raises questions not about ontology but rather about language and epistemology; it reflects on acts of misrecognition grounded in discursive doublings that resist unified concepts of identity and nationality. Most characters in the story have a double identity—including the Indians, who are both savage and "noble," as we have seen[21]—but these identities are misrecognitions of opposites that, when put together, do not produce a "fit" but something extra, a kind of supplement. As in "First Love," the philosophical underpinnings of Welty's text broach the question of the production of knowledge and point to the slippage of the signifier that results in the misrecognition of the other.

The robber bridegroom himself, Jamie Lockhart, is a case in point. Of all the characters who are double, Jamie's doubleness as robber and bridegroom is most fully dramatized. The two sides of Jamie's identity—his two faces—are kept apart with help of the berry juice with which he stains his face when he operates as a robber. When Rosamond first meets Jamie, his face is all stained. When she meets him later without his disguise when her father brings him home as her bridegroom, she does not recognize him, nor does he recognize her, because her own face is "stained" from the smudges of ashes from a fire she was tending. This theme of misrecognition explicitly begs an epistemological question: Can we ever know the other? Jamie and Rosamond are happy with each other as long as they do not desire to discover their "true" identities. Rosamond grows increasingly curious, however, and begs Jamie to wipe the stains from his face so that she can see him. When he refuses, she spends sleepless nights peering into the face of her lover: "Sometimes she would wake up out of her first sleep and study his sleeping face, but she did not know the language it was written in" (84). Her attempt to read the language of Jamie's face is an inquiry into the identity of the other beyond the stained surface. In her desire to "read" and know the other, she seeks to penetrate this sur/face. Derrida writes on the meaning of the face in discourses of otherness: "the other is not signaled by his face, he is this face: 'Absolutely present, in his face, the Other—without any metaphor—faces me'" ("Violence" 100). In Rosamond's nightly "face to face," she tries to discover the identity of her lover, whose face "does not signify, does not present itself as a sign, but expresses itself, offering itself in person" (101). When Rosamond wipes the berry juice off Jamie's sleeping face "to learn the identity of her true love," she not only destroys the trust between them but, in peering behind the surface of otherness, seeks to erase Jamie's otherness, and in doing so she destroys it. Her discovery constitutes an act of epistemic violence driven by a desire to constitute the other and simultaneously to obliterate the trace of this other in its subjectivity. Derrida writes that "in the face, the other is given over in person as other, that is as that which does not reveal itself, as that which cannot be made thematic" (103). The face, and the body more generally, is a language that speaks otherness, and its discovery and reconstitution constitutes an act of both knowledge and violence.

Welty's narrative dramatizes such acts of reading and misreading. Clement cannot "read" Jamie, who in turn cannot "read" Rosamond, who cannot "read" Salome, who cannot "read" the Indians—the chain is infinite. These misreadings are grounded in Welty's play with doubles and binaries, not all of which form neat pairs made of symmetrical opposites. The robber/bridegroom opposition, for example, is not a match of semantic opposites such as day/night, sun/moon, or body/soul seem to be. What is the antonym of a robber or a bridegroom? According to the laws of Cartesian dualism, the work of doubling is limited; not everything can be neatly understood or even recognized in terms of its opposite or its negative mirror image. Clement's insight into difference and doubleness, which has been read as the text's central epiphany, rehearses these Cartesian epistemologies. Clement concludes about Jamie: "he must not be one man, but two, and I should be afraid of killing the second. For all things are double, and this should keep us from taking liberties with the outside world, and acting too quickly to finish things off. All things are divided in half—night and day, the soul and the body, and sorrow and joy and youth and age" (126). The discovery that the opposition robber/bridegroom is not an opposition at all produces a crisis within the process of signification that leaves an uncanny textual residue. By privileging doubling over splitting, Welty's text turns on this "residue" as it showcases discourses of identity based on difference only in order to deconstruct them. The split of self and other results not in meaningful identification or matching opposites but rather in the fantastic chaos of ambiguity and misrecognition in which Welty's text luxuriates.

Welty's concern with the linguistic construction of the Indian other and corresponding attempts at "reading" such otherness raises problems of signification and representation. Indians, robbers, planters, and bridegrooms are not what they appear to be. For example, in Welty's short story "Keela, the Outcast Indian Maiden" (1941), Keela turns out to be a crippled black man named Little Lee Roy, who was forced to act the part of a savage, bloodthirsty Indian woman. Significantly, the transformation of the black man into the freakish Indian maiden is accomplished through language, and this is why Steve, the circus drummer who is showing off Keela, feels guilty about his participation in the construction of a monstrous other: "It was me what I said out front through the megaphone" (*Collected Stories* 40). Steve's words produce the shameful misrecognition that results in Keela's isolation and monstrousness. He remembers: "I was yellin', 'Ladies and gents! Do not try to touch Keela, the Outcast Indian Maiden—she will only beat your brains out with her iron rod, and eat them alive! . . . Do not go near her, ladies and gents! I'm warning you!' So nobody ever did" (41). As the ultimate freak, Keela is silenced (she is only allowed to growl) and "othered" through the language of the white man. Quite appropriately, it is not language but touch that leads to her recovery and to the revelation of her "true" identity. It is only when a circus visitor approaches her and offers his hand in friendship that Keela breaks down, the "fake" is revealed, and the identity of Keela is transformed. Traumatized by his experience with Keela, Steve concludes: "I can't look at nothin' and be sure what it is" (43). When his friend Max responds, "Bet I could tell a man from a woman and an Indian from a nigger though" (44), Steve hits Max so hard for his confident assertion of epistemological certainty that Max falls off the porch. The conflict between Steve and Max is over the knowledge and the production of the other who remains mute. All that Little Lee Roy contributes to the conversation about him is a "soft almost incredulous laugh" (reminding us perhaps of the laughter of the Indians in "First Love") that is neither an assertion nor a denial of the "truth," the past, his identity, or even Steve's guilt. The trace that leads Steve to Little Lee Roy's house is shaped out of the desire to recover the past and atone for his cruel act of signification. But the meaning of the encounter remains obscure, leaving only the trace itself, in search of which Steve must forever wander.

In this bizarre story, as in "First Love" and *The Robber Bridegroom,* meaning is never simply present but is available only as a "trace." By following this trace, Welty becomes an archaeologist of knowledge who seeks to uncover and present those mute monuments for contemplation, and often she relies on history for making sense of them. Patricia Yaeger suggests that the historical traces underlying the story of the grotesque freak show in "Keela, the Outcast Indian Maiden" point toward "archaic national themes" (96), one of which is the violent crippling of racial others. She proposes that in Welty's omission of the act of crippling itself we can read the historical background of "man catchers" in the South who pressed African Americans into forced labor as well as more generally "the 'history' imposed on Native and African Americans in the circus of U.S. civic life" (158). Welty's treatment of the Native American signifier—whether as freakish representation of otherness or as "historical" discourse of "doom"—always returns to the national narrative. Welty says about the "historical spirit" that governs *The Robber Bridegroom:* "if I carried out well enough my strongest intentions, fantasy does not take precedence over that spirit, but serves the better to show it forth" (*Eye* 314). Welty's "fantasmatic representation" of history (borrowing Yaeger's term) does not seek to repress or displace the violence of the racial encounter into the dreamlike land of fantasy. Welty denies that her novella works like a "dream," as some reviewers have suggested. She writes, "I think it is more accurate to call it an awakening to a dear native land and its own story of early life, made and offered by a novelists's imagination in exuberance and joy" (314). It is in this spirit of joy and celebration, of exhilarating and irreverent pastiche, that Welty offers the Native American signifier as part of the national narrative. In *The Robber Bridegroom,* she ultimately rejects the modernist narratives of lament and despair about the vanishing world of the Indians. She renounces the mournful elegies that Andrew Lytle and William Faulkner wrote for the "vanishing Indians." Instead, she presents the wild gaudiness of the violence, the chance and randomness that make up history in the spirit of postmodern jouissance. When bizarrely colorful images of Indians show up on the surface of Welty's Natchez Trace fiction, they point toward a narrative of "dear" national history whose plot Welty questions and whose fairy-tale logic she exposes.

And yet, there remains an uneasy tension between the tall-tale boast of American origins and Welty's own historical moment. Merrill Skaggs speculates, "one easily guesses what historical facts might have provoked a desire to escape into fantasy in 1942 when Welty published her novella." Citing the work of Bruno Bettelheim, who argues that fairy tales function as "cultural escape valves," Skaggs suggests that Welty's return to the violence of the frontier might displace the violence elsewhere (57). Certainly Welty's turn to national history at a time of international political crisis might constitute a response to the threat of totalitarianism and fascism in Europe. Welty's frontier fantasy responds in many ways to what Alfred Kazin termed "the spirit of new nationalism," but it is by far not an expression of "reflex patriotism and hungry traditionalism of a culture fighting for its life as it moved into war" (487). Welty's text, though dipping into the "national inventory," remains self-consciously skeptical, if playful, about the meaning of the national narrative. In a review of Welty's novella long before the Derridean idea of linguistic "play" was in circulation, Lionel Trilling wrote: "Miss Welty is being playful and that is perfectly all right, but she is also aware of how playful she is and that is wearisome" (56). I beg to disagree. Welty's self-conscious "play" with the national narrative constitutes her political response to (as opposed to flight from) the contemporary conventions of genre, language, and history. By yielding to neither a historical nor an ahistorical framework in *The Robber Bridegroom,* Welty presents a postcolonial parody of (Native) American history suspended between fantasy and anxiety.

5
Mimesis and Mimicry

William Faulkner's Postcolonial Yoknapatawpha

> There was no time; the next act and scene itself clearing its own stage without waiting for property-men; or rather not even bothering to clear the stage but commencing the new act and scene right in the midst of the phantoms, the fading wraiths of that old time which had been exhausted, used up, to be no more and never return.
>
> —William Faulkner, *Requiem for a Nun*

From his earliest Indian story, "Red Leaves" (1930), to *Requiem for a Nun* (1950), William Faulkner returned repeatedly to the Indian origins of his imaginary landscape, Yoknapatawpha County, Mississippi. A complex and ideologically charged place, Yoknapatawpha provides a site for Faulkner's imaginary excavations of a cultural past that contributes to a knowledge of the region and the people who inhabit it. Itself a Native American signifier, Yoknapatawpha, which supposedly translates from Chickasaw as "split land"—*yaakni* (land) and *patafa* (split)—inscribes the Indian origins of Faulkner's imaginary community into the landscape itself.[1] This fictional terrain reaches deep down to a "prehistoric" strata in the soil and to a time in the remote past to which not only the names but the numerous Indian mounds of Mississippi bear testimony. Faulkner's cultural geography yields the roots and origin stories of his imaginary community which begins in the remote Native American past of the Mound Building periods, a past whose memories and ghosts are stored in the remaining mound monuments.[2] "The State of Mississippi," writes archaeologist Calvin S. Brown in 1926, "abounds in those ancient remains known as Indian mounds or tumuli," and he goes on to catalog each of them and describe their purposes and contents (1). Commenting on what can be found in these mounds, Brown asserts that "most of them contain nothing, except perhaps potsherds and frag-

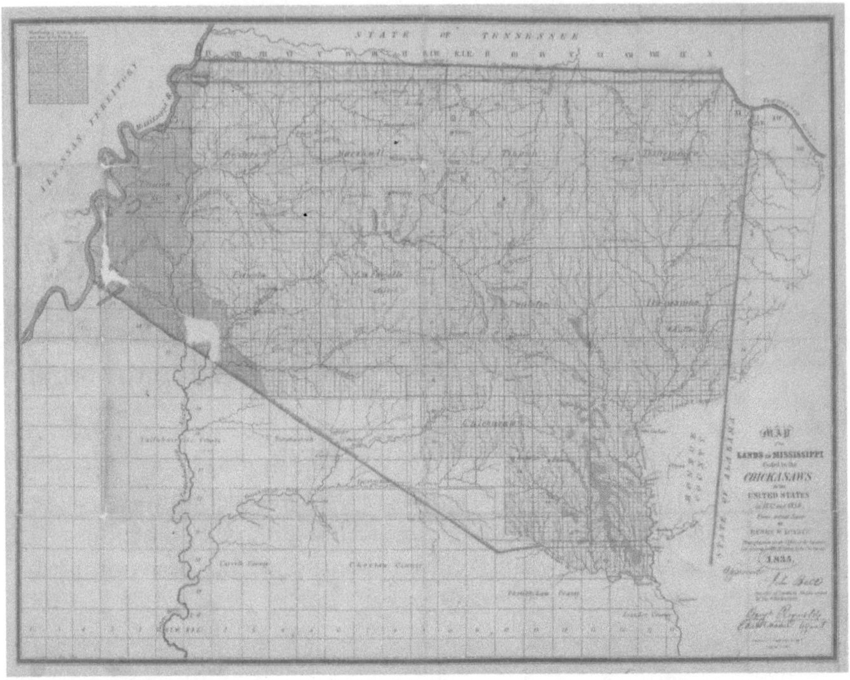

Map 5. "Lands in Mississippi Ceded by the Chickasaws to the United States in 1832 and 1834." Henry M. Lusher, draughtsman in the office of the Surveyor General. 1835. Courtesy of the Mississippi Department of Archives and History

ments of flint and such other refuse as was lying about on the surface when the mound was being constructed. Some contain beds of ashes, charcoal, and burnt clay. Posts and pieces of wood are sometimes found. The burial mounds contain skeletons or parts of skeletons and sometimes beads, pottery, stone implements, and other objects of ancient workmanship" (3). Brown goes on to dispel a popular and persistent myth that set many an amateur archaeologist digging during the depression years: "The mounds do not contain treasure; gold and silver were virtually unknown to the Amerind in this part of the country upon the coming of the white man" (3). This comment reminds us that Faulkner, who owned a copy of Brown's book, sets Lucas Beauchamp on a futile and comic search for precisely such treasures in *Go Down, Moses.*

The treasures that the mounds yield for Faulkner himself are histories of cultural identity and narratives of ancestry that provide the basis for a "deep mapping" of his southern site of excavation. When Faulkner digs deep into the structure of this landscape and unburies the Indian signifier, the Indian ghosts and phantoms of dispossession begin to haunt his landscape. The Indian mounds of his fiction are monuments of a bygone era and symbols of dispossession testifying to a "vanished" population. In the layered strata of the southern soil, these are the ineradicable remains of pre-colonial cultures long gone.[3] Their visible traces, inscribed in the landscape itself, are "overwritten" by cultures that have come after them. Their "vacated" space is now the dwelling place of Faulkner's Chickasaws and Choctaws who gather around the ancient mounds but who, in time, will also be displaced from the South to make room for a culture of white frontier settlers. Faulkner's multiple cultural and textual accretions convey not only a layering of history but also a kind of linear chronology and narrative of succession whose logic is clear: like the ancient Indians who have left only their traces in the landscape, the modern Indians of the South are on the brink of "vanishing." By connecting the ancient past of the Mound Builders with the recent past of Indian removal, Faulkner centers the Native American signifier in acts of dispossession and in the white colonial culture's imaginary repossession of their "vanished" identities and "vacated" spaces.

These acts of seizing possession of Indian territory apply not only to the characters in Faulkner's fictional universe but also to the writer himself. Like Eudora Welty, Faulkner predicates his own role and authority as a writer partially on his knowledge of local Indian cultures. In a letter to *Scribner's* accompanying the submission of "Red Leaves," Faulkner quips: "So here is another story. Few people know that Miss. Indians owned slaves; that's why I suggest you all buy it. Not because it is a good story; you can find lots of good stories. It's because I need the money" (Blotner, *Selected Letters* 46–47). Revealing his own role in acts of white imaginary reinscriptions of the vacated Indian space, Faulkner, like Welty, claims special access to knowledge about Indians on which he fashions his own authority as a writer. In order to do so, "Faulkner at once exoticizes the South and claims it as its own territory," writes Robert Dale Parker. "Both strategies mimic the contradictory way that his Indian stories at once seek closeness and distance between races (red, black and white) and seek both to identify with the scars of Southern history (slavery and Indian removal) and to distance those scars from the white masculine culture of the stories' authorship" (82). In 1930, white masculine identity formation for Faulkner was predicated both on the successful possession of Indian territory in acts of authorship (of Indian stories) as well as on landownership (of Chickasaw land). In April 1930 Faulkner bought Rowan Oak, his house in Oxford, Mississippi, and shortly after moving in he wrote "Red Leaves," probably during the late-summer months of the same year.[4] Assuming real and imaginary possession of lands that belonged to the Chickasaws just one hundred years earlier, Faulkner creates himself as the "sole owner and proprietor" of his Yoknapatawpha County.

The internal chronology of the Yoknapatawpha saga begins with colonial conquests before the time of the Louisiana Purchase of 1803, when this territory became American. Faulkner creates a narrative of origins by embedding references to colonial struggles of British, French, Spanish, and American colonial powers over trading rights and lands in many of his texts and by centering the Native American signifier in the geography of colonialism and removal. In fact, the invention of Yoknapatawpha is based on the dispossession and "disappearance" of Indians from the land, which is taken over by some of his most famous southern families, with names such as Sartoris and Stevens, Compson and McCaslin, and Sutpen and Coldfield. In both history and fiction, the Indian removal laid the groundwork not only for the rise of southern regional dynasties of power based in a blooming cotton empire but also for the prospering of the nation. The expansion of the American nation-state and the firming of national identities was equally grounded in the Indian removal and in those treaties with the Choctaws and Chickasaws that freed up large parts of Mississippi for settlement by whites. This dual function of the Indian removal for local *and* national economies is signified in the name of the town at the center of Faulkner's fictional universe: Jefferson. The small hamlet that is to become the town of Jefferson is named after Thomas Jefferson Pettigrew, the postal rider from "old Ferginny" who brings into the "pathless wilderness, the whole vast incalculable weight of federality" and the laws of the United States government (*Requiem* 23). Centered in the historical and symbolic significance of nation-building, westward expansion, and removal, Faulkner's Jefferson is inscribed over a Native American geography buried beneath. Faulkner's Native American signifiers, inscribed as place-names, monuments, and characters, are part of an important cultural strata in these political and historical landscapes. By emphasizing the historical role of the Indian "ancestors" to the southern community he invents, Faulkner engages in both a regionalist and a nationalist archaeology whose excavations give rise to corresponding discourses not only of "vanishing Indians" but of cultural transformation and transmission.

Tracing these cultural transformations, Faulkner mapped this imaginary county onto a "real" place—Oxford and Lafayette County, Mississippi—and onto the historical events that led to its existence.[5] In the process he not only fashioned fiction out of history but also fashioned "history" out of fiction so that "the two worlds of fiction and history become at times difficult to keep separate" (Doyle 9). By exhuming the historical and archaeological records of Lafayette County through stories, legends, documents, and accounts of oral and written history, Faulkner created a foundational narrative out of the confluence of history and fiction for his particular locale. This history begins with the Chickasaw removal, an idea first suggested during Thomas Jefferson's administration but not put into legislation until the early part of the nineteenth century, when white settlers increasingly clamored for Indian lands on the southwestern frontier. Pressure to remove Native Americans increased dramatically in the 1820s, and in 1830 Congress passed Andrew Jackson's Indian Removal Act. With the passage of this law, the Choctaws and Chickasaws who occupied the northern and central part of Mississippi were forced from their homes and lands. Like most other Native Americans, the Chickasaws who lived in what is today Lafayette County were at first resistant to the government's offer to "exchange" lands with them. "We never had a thought of exchanging our land for any other, as we think that we would not find a country that would suit us as well as this we now occupy, it being the land of our forefathers," said Chickasaw chief Levi Colbert, who likened the proposal of removal to the act of "transplanting an old tree" (Nabokov 151). However, Chickasaw resistance to vacating their lands was broken by legislation on national and local levels. The Indian Removal Act in conjunction with state legislation—"the extension of Mississippi (and Alabama) state law over the Chickasaw nation," which abolished "tribal government and law and all authority of the chiefs"—left the Chickasaws unprotected (Doyle 43–44). They signed the Treaty of Pontotoc in 1832, but it would be another five years until a majority of the Chickasaws left for Indian Territory.

In the 1930s, when Faulkner was writing his first Indian stories, he must have been particularly conscious of the Indian removal one hundred years earlier as an event that led to the historical founding of Oxford and Lafayette County in 1836. As Lafayette County was preparing to celebrate is foundational centennial in 1936, Faulkner's imagination centered on the Native American signifier in many of his stories, including "Red Leaves" (1930), "A Justice" (1931), "Lo!" (1934), "Mountain Victory" (1930), and "A Bear Hunt" (1933). Three of these stories—"Red Leaves," "A Justice" and "Lo!"—are set during the period leading up to and following the passing of the Indian Removal Act.[6] Given the history of Chickasaw land cession and removal that preceded the founding of Lafayette County and the building of Oxford, it is not surprising that the Indians who appear around the perimeters of Faulkner's fictional Yoknapatawpha gesture in many ways to this act of "disappearance."

Twenty years later, when Faulkner reconstructed the beginnings of Jefferson in the prologues to *Requiem for a Nun* (1950), he was well aware that the Native American signifiers he had inscribed into the cartography of his Yoknapatawpha County were like actors on a stage poised to leave the scene in time for the next acts of history to occur. His construction of his imaginary community is predicated on the correlating disappearance of the Indians who, "not so wild anymore, familiar now, harmless now, just obsolete" are pushed out west to Oklahoma. In *Requiem for a Nun,* the scene of the Indian exodus in which the fictional Chickasaw matriarch Mohataha signs the removal papers and "vanishes" from Mississippi is repeated several times throughout the text as if to underline by repetition the incredibility and the fantastic unreality of this act:

> Then she said, "Where is this Indian territory?" And they told her: West. "Turn the mules west," she said, and someone did so, and she took the pen from the agent and made her X on the paper and handed the pen back and the wagon moved, the young men rising too, and she vanished so across that summer afternoon to that terrific and infinitesimal creak and creep of ungreased wheels, herself immobile beneath the rigid parasol, grotesque and regal, bizarre and moribund, like obsolescence's self riding off the stage enthroned on its obsolete catafalque, looking not once back, not once back toward home. (217)

Like so many other Indian scenes in Faulkner's fiction, this passage straddles the borderlines among pathos, parody, and pastiche. All these elements mix as Faulkner firmly moves his Indians offstage. But it is the accumulation of these images and the repetition of the exodus—its constant reinvention and re-imagination—that signifies its historical and psychological trauma at the same time that it also renders the scene suspect as "serious" history. Four pages later the scene is self-consciously replayed with a vocabulary that highlights its exaggerated theatricality, this time inviting the reader to imagine that all that was required to lose the land was

> the single light touch of the pen in that brown illiterate hand, and the wagon did not vanish slowly and terrifically from the scene to the terrific sound of its ungreased wheels, but was swept, hurled, flung not only out of Yoknapatawpha County and Mississippi but the United States too, immobile and intact—the wagon, the mules, the rigid shapeless old Indian woman and the nine heads which surrounded her—like a float or a piece of stage property dragged rapidly into the wings across the very backdrop and amid the very bustle of the property-men setting up for the next scene and act before the curtain had even had time to fall. (222)

The excessiveness of Faulkner's descriptions is characteristic of a postmodern troping that moves into the foreground the very unreality and absurdity of the removal itself. Faulkner "plays" with these scenes and replays them with the breathless rhythm of his long sentences, a style that underscores with systematic mimicry its own eccentricity at the same time that it characterizes the Indians as grotesquely eccentric. Verging close to the satiric edge but devoid of laughter, the prose that captures the Indian exodus does not settle for a stable sense of irony; instead, Faulkner provides a collection of variations of the same scene—Mohataha in her soiled purple silk gown with the parasol held by a slave leaving for the West—in a replay that cannot be described as "pure" modernist nostalgia but rather as a fascination with an image whose compulsive repetition of past referents reveals the metonymic logic of displacement. Moving back and forth between elegy and grotesque comedy, Faulkner's linguistic performance turns the Indian removal into a theatrical play and the Indians into "stage property dragged rapidly into the wings." Even if Faulkner is forcefully suggesting the absurdity of the Indian removal here, we might ask, What ideological or political currency does absurdity or parody have? As we will see, Faulkner's modernism is an intellectual gesture that makes Indian removal a theatrical play, but it is a drama in which the Indians are finally still doomed—though the linguistic conventions of "doom" hailing from the nineteenth century and Faulkner's literary ancestors are themselves problematized and mimicked in a highly self-conscious fashion.

The above scene shows that the Native American signifier is part of a linguistic play with the conventions of a discourse of "Indianness" and the rhetoric of extinction that Faulkner stages for the reader. Using the metaphor of the stage, Patricia Galloway has recently corroborated the opinions of most Faulkner critics, who argue that from an ethnographic and historic point of view Faulkner's Indians are "constructions, stage properties, not modified portraits of real individuals" ("Construction" 13). Although Faulkner's fiction gives us an illusion of the embeddedness of his Indians in real historical, cultural, and political landscapes, the ethnographic contexts for his Indian characters are mostly products of Faulkner's pseudo-ethnographic imagination. In studying Faulkner's representations of Indians it is tempting to get caught up in questions of historical accuracy, ethnographic authenticity, and political correctness. These are appropriate questions, because the history and culture of Native Americans have been miscommunicated in American literature since the captivity narratives, and such distortions continue to be misrepresented as truth. Faulkner is no exception to the long list of American authors, some of them examined here, who employ and perpetuate in their work stereotypes about Native American culture. Almost all scholars mention Faulkner's inconsistencies in tribal names, dates, and ethnographic details, and as Howard Horsford points out, "Indians were indeed not central to Faulkner's own experience; nor for that matter does he seem to have had a developed historical sense for anything much preceding the Civil War" (312). Listing the misuses to which Native American culture has been put in Faulkner, studies like Horsford's tend to have an irritated if not genuinely angry tone. Setting out to examine the authenticity of Faulkner's knowledge of the native inhabitants of his own "little postage stamp of native soil," Horsford lists many of the ethnographic and historical mistakes in Faulkner's Indian fiction, including issues of black and red miscegenation, intergenerational relationships, the power of chieftains, burial rituals, and the lurid allusions to cannibalism. Spreading the historical evidence before us, he concludes that "with all due respect for the fictions as fictions, the blunt truth is that he shows very little familiarity with early Mississippi history or with the Choctaws and Chickasaws who were its victims" (310). Robert Dale Parker is even more blunt when he asserts that "as a larger picture of early nineteenth-century Chickasaw or Choctaw culture, Faulkner's stories are nonsense" (81). Of course, this is not a new conclusion.

Elmo Howell, writing about "Red Leaves" in 1970, argued that Faulkner's Indian stories are "almost wholly the product of the author's fancy" (293). He explains that Faulkner's Indians are different from his other characters, white or black, for whom he had living models and with whom he had personal contact. But, argues Howell, Faulkner was left without the benefit of living witnesses when he reached one hundred years back into history for his Indian stories, which are set before removal in the 1830s.[7] At the time Faulkner composed these stories in the 1930s, apparently "little of the past remained except the legends taken indiscriminately from the Chickasaws and Choctaws and other tribes perhaps of the lower South" (Howell 293). Except for Malcolm Cowley's assertion that "Faulkner was always a great reader . . . [of] Southern history and books about the Indians," the critical consensus seems to be that Faulkner "did not value history itself so much as the meaning he could impose upon it. Consequently, he felt no qualms about reconstructing the Indian past in lavish detail, although he had little knowledge of what it was like" (Howell 293). Add to that Faulkner's own comment—"I don't care much for facts, am not much interested in them"—and you get a perfect platform for ethnic stereotypes and sociological implausibility (qtd. in Horsford 311). When it comes to Native Americans, Faulkner seems to typify the attitude most non-Indians have about Indians: they prefer the mythical Indians of their own imagination.[8]

A close examination of the Native American signifier in Faulkner's fiction shows us that Faulkner's Indian texts do not participate in a mimetic understanding of literature as simply reflecting a (historical) reality outside the text, but instead in the distortion and displacement of these "historical realities." In this chapter I argue that Faulkner's Indian signifier is part of a self-reflexive production that highlights the discursive construction of Indians. The sign "Indian" is always wrought by fiction. The Native American signifier, while bound by existing discursive practices and reified by a familiar set of polarities (of savagery and civilization, e.g.), is open to reinvention and resignification. Always captured at the stage of "vanishing" from Yoknapatawpha, the Indian represents an unrepresentable absence and a denial that grounds the signifying economy through exclusion. As a lingering cultural residue inscribed in the land itself, Indianness is always discursively constructed or theatrically produced in attempts at covering up the inherent instability of the meaning of the sign. On the one hand, then, Faulkner plays self-consciously with the instability of the Native American signifier by opening up ironic gaps in the modernist text that highlight the parody, theatricality, and mimicry of the signifier's production. This discursive strategy serves to interrogate if not criticize the continuing power of ethnographic fictions and points to the valuable insight that "Indianness" is only performatively available. On the other hand, however, Faulkner's own language exerts a pressure that threatens to close this gap by reinscribing the Native American signifier within a hegemonic discourse that privileges the masculinist national narrative of expansion. We must ask critically, then, What does Faulkner's play with discourse, language, and history mean if this language game ends up affirming colonial and patriarchal power? What do threats, ruptures, and slippages of the Native American signifier mean if Faulkner re-stabilizes the identities and histories of his white male protagonists and narratively "dooms" the Indians? The tension between deconstruction and hegemonic reconstruction of the Native American signifier in Faulkner's texts indicates, first, that as a southern writer, Faulkner attempted to distance himself from the predominant construction of Indians as part of the national narrative of expansion, but like many of his American and southern contemporaries, he ultimately surrendered to this very narrative in the elegies he wrote for his "doomed" Indians. From the particular locus of the South, Faulkner participates in national narratives about Native Americans and shares those anxieties, endemic to these discourses, triggered by genocide, removal, and dispossession. Second, as a modernist writer, Faulkner privileges linguistic ambiguity, not political activism; that is, with his preference for irony, parody, and mimicry he reveals a problem in the construction of the Native American signifier and in the language of identity that underlies U.S. policy, but he does not attempt to solve it.

I begin with a brief discussion of Faulkner's short story "A Bear Hunt" (1933), which explicitly addresses the theatrical production of the Native American signifier. In this story, Indians are not only rhetorically created in the language of the white community, but they enter the stage to play a parodic copy of themselves. The role of parody and mimicry is crucial to most of Faulkner's Indian stories of the 1930s, particularly those that address colonial contact in the pre-removal setting of "Red Leaves" (1930) and the removal setting of "Lo!" (1934).[9] In these two stories, Faulkner comments on the cultural transformations of Indians, who are presented as grotesque and orientalized effigies. However, by the time he published *Go Down, Moses* in 1942, there is a shift in mood away from mimicry and orientalist depictions of Indians that render them as national others toward an embrace of Indians—now "noble savages"—as part of the national family. Moving from the grotesque cultural transformation of Indians to their importance as agents of cultural transmission, Faulkner reintroduces in the figure of Sam Fathers not only nineteenth-century discourses of vanishing Indians but a contemporary modernist desire for a national heritage based in Native American cultural roots. This shift from "othering" to embracing the Native American figure corresponds with the disillusionment of the war years and the rise of a new national(ist) climate.

Playing Indian: Are There Any Real Indians Here?

As in *Requiem for a Nun,* in the earlier short story "A Bear Hunt" Faulkner presents the Indian signifier as part of a "play," a linguistic trick and a "practical joke" that produces its presence. This trick is embedded in a signifying economy that activates fictions of "Indianness" and opens an ironic gap between those fictions and the apparent sociological "realities" of Native Americans. The story begins by evoking the locus of the Native American past, symbolized by an Indian mound and characterized by its distance from white civilization. Far away even from the remote hunting camp of Major de Spain, the mound is located "in an even wilder part of the river's jungle. . . . Aboriginal, it rises profoundly and darkly enigmatic, the only elevation of any kind in the wild, flat jungle of river bottom" (*Collected Stories* [*CS*] 65). In the white imagination, Indian signifiers in the cultural strata of the southern landscape connote the aboriginal, the wild, and the mysterious. Located beyond the comprehensible and the present, Indians are part of a "dark" remote past and a guilty historical conscience that is forever haunted.[10] As part of such a dialectic between past and present, Faulkner's Indian signifier is situated in the borderland between the imaginary and the real. For the fifteen-year-old boy narrator, the mound functions as part of the imaginary:

> it possessed inferences of secret and violent blood, of savage and sudden destruction, as though the yells and hatchets which we associated with Indians through the hidden and secret dime novels which we passed among ourselves were but trivial and momentary manifestations of what dark power still dwelled or lurked there, sinister, a little

> sardonic, like a dark and nameless beast lightly and lazily slumbering with bloody jaws—this perhaps due to the fact that a remnant of a once powerful clan of the Chickasaw tribe still lived beside it under Government protection. They now had American names and they lived as the sparse white people who surrounded them in turn lived. (*CS* 65)

By simultaneously evoking both a mythical and a sociological discourse, Faulkner produces an ironic gap, a slippage in the sign "Indian." The pervasive fictional discourse of Indian savagery and violence perpetrated with the stereotypical hatchets of the "dime novels" clashes with the counterdiscourse of assimilation and reservation life for the remaining Chickasaws, who live under government "protection" and have assumed American names. By exposing the fictional foundations of Indians whose lives are associated with a mysterious, dark power emanating from the mound of the ancestors whose spirits they are apparently guarding, Faulkner's text simultaneously evokes and dispels these fictions. The Native American specter, raised by past acts of colonialism and continuing dispossession, haunts the imagination and the conscience of boys and adults alike.

For the boys who camp overnight on the Indian mound, the Indian encounter is a complex and somewhat ambiguous experience. What the boys felt or understood about the mound is actually eclipsed by the text. They may have been in the grip of fear and superstition, but their silence might also be expressive of their sadness and sudden adult understanding of the situation of Native Americans so incongruent with the fantasy Indians of their childhood imagination. As the narrator grows up and awakens to the reality of Native American poverty and dispossession, he comes to understand that Indians "were no wilder or more illiterate than white people, and that probably their greatest deviation from the norm—and this, in our country, no especial deviation—was the fact that they were a little better than suspect to manufacture moonshine whisky back in the swamps" (*CS* 65).

For the adults of the hunting camp, Indians also remain suspended between myth and demystification. The trick that is played on Luke Provine, who is cured of his hiccups by a frightening encounter with Indians, shows that the mythical discourse about Indians is still very powerful. The first myth is that Indians are natural healers. Ratliff suggests to Luke that "them Indians knows all sorts of dodges that white doctors ain't hyeard about yet" (71) and that they might be able to cure his hiccups. But Ratliff is also plainly sarcastic when he implies that old John Basket would love to help a white man out and cure him of his hiccups: "He'd be glad to do that much for a white man, too, them pore aboriginees would, because the white folks have been so good to them—not only letting them keep that ere hump of dirt that don't nobody want noways, but letting them use names like ourn and selling them flour and sugar and farm tools at not no more than fair profit above what they would cost a white man. I hyear tell how pretty soon they are even going to start letting them come to town once a week. Old Basket would be glad to cure them hiccups for you" (71–72). Ratliffe's real intention is to send Luke several miles out of camp so that the hunting party kept awake by Luke's hiccups will be able to sleep. Again, the text opens up an ironic gap between fantasies of Indians' supernatural healing powers and the reality of their discrimination and dispossession, a gap that mobilizes white guilt, anxieties, and fears of revenge.

The second myth is that Indians are violent, hatchet-swinging savages who are out to kill the white man. Both myths combine in the story. When Ratliff suggests that Luke go to see "old John Basket," Ash, the black cook, overhears the conversation and sneaks to the Indian camp to set up a scare for Luke that will get him back for his racism some years ago when Luke molested and humiliated him and a group of his friends at a picnic by burning cigar holes into their new shirt collars. Ash tells the Indians that a new revenue agent is on his way to their still and that all they have to do to get rid of him is give him a good scare. When the Indians hear Luke approach in the dark, they seize him, tie him, and act as if they were going to harm him. Luke escapes, and in his shock and terror he loses his hiccups. Faulkner implies in this episode that blacks and Indians share a connection—Ash knows some of the Indians—and a common past of discrimination and racist abuse. It is through these cultural alliances that the trick works. The second, more interesting implication in this story of successful revenge is that whites, blacks, and the Indians themselves constantly play with the storehouse of Indian myths. As Jay Winston points out, the Indians end up feigning savagery, "consciously playing the role of the wild savages of the captivity narratives to their own advantage" (134). In an ironic twist, the Indians are "playing Indian" in order to scare off a white man. But the character who really gets his revenge is the black man, Ash, who is repaid for the cruelty he suffered in the past. He, too, knows the enduring power of the myths of savage Indians, and he uses them to his advantage.

In this story, Faulkner plays with discourses of Indian identity, both real and mythical, past and present. The narrative results in a demystification of imaginary Indians not only by clearly revealing their ethnographic realities—poverty and whiskey manufacture—but by exposing the continuing power of ethnographic fictions and their own parodic inversion. Taking possession of the Indian signifier, all the characters in the story—blacks, whites, and Indians themselves—are filling the perceived vacuum, the absence that the sign "Indian" signifies, with an invented and distorted discourse that mimics Indian identity.

Indianness is not available as an ontology; it is only discursively and performatively available in a production that awakens the ghosts slumbering in the popular imagination and in the guilty colonial conscience.

Postcolonial Displacements in "Red Leaves" and "Lo!"

Of the four stories that comprise "The Wilderness" section of Faulkner's 1950 *Collected Stories,* "Red Leaves" and "Lo!" are most interesting for the purposes of my investigation because they explicitly address Euro-American colonial aspirations. Loosely based in Mississippi Indian history and set during the early decades of the nineteenth century, these stories hold up a skewed mirror to national history that, in its imaginary reflection, transforms "reality" and "history." In re-imagining the colonial encounter, Faulkner's Indian stories participate in a tradition of postcolonial literature that is, as Homi Bhabha claims, rich in "trompe-l'oeil, irony, mimicry and repetition" (85). Mimicry is different from repetition because what is repeated is always represented with a difference. Mimicry is different from trompe l'oeil because, unlike trompe l'oeil, where something seems to be what it is not, mimicry can hold several meanings at once. Mimicry is different from irony because whereas the ironic mode derives its power from a perceptible and intentional difference between context and representation or articulation, that difference often goes undetected in mimicry. Hence mimicry, unlike irony, both critiques *and* reinscribes. It works, not by highlighting the difference between what is said and what *is,* but by camouflaging that difference. In Lacan's words, mimicry "is not a question of harmonizing with the background, but against a mottled background, of becoming mottled" (qtd. in Bhabha 85). In literary texts that address colonial situations, including Faulkner's, "what emerges between mimesis and mimicry is a *writing,* a mode of representation, that marginalizes the monumentality of history, quite simply mocks its power to be a model, that power which supposedly makes it imitable" (Bhabha 87–88). Bhabha contends that by mocking history, mimicry "problematizes the signs of racial and cultural priority, so that the 'national' is no longer naturalizable" (87). I suggest that the power of Faulkner's "writing" in "Red Leaves" and "Lo!" resides in such mimicry and in the ironic transformation of the concerns and rhetoric of early-nineteenth-century national politics.

I would like to begin this discussion by showing how Faulkner ironically inverts the positions of "savage" and "civilized." In "Red Leaves," Faulkner's Indians are not living in a pristine wilderness but rather in a grotesque environment transformed by the introduction of European surplus economy and American slavery. Such colonial contact, Faulkner seems to suggest, has taken its toll on the integrity of Native American cultures and has caused their dynasties to decay. In the second section of my argument I will show that the binary opposition between "savagery" and "civilization" is not simply inverted, as it first seems, but that the positions of "colonized" and "colonizer" are constantly changing places. In other words, Faulkner's texts do not simply produce a dualism that is inverted, two positions that change places; rather, by engaging in mimicry, they produce an uncomfortable doubleness that blurs any clear hierarchical distinctions. The colonial mirror Faulkner turns onto the South as a cultural frontier merges the images of colonizer and colonized and splits each image in half, ultimately mocking the process of self-reflection and national mastery in "Lo!" Because Faulkner's texts operate through a complex strategy of displacement, in which what is displaced is repeated but with a difference, they produce a kind of mimicry that ultimately results in a reading experience characterized by discomfort or discontent, or as Freud would say, a kind of *Unbehagen.*[11] This term suggests the malaise or unease of civilization also characterizing Faulkner's own representations of the nature of (national) guilt that haunts his Indian stories. By shifting the analysis from the field of vision to the space of writing in the last section of my argument, we will discover a third dimension to Faulkner's Indian stories. Despite Faulkner's efforts at deconstructing ethnic and political binaries, his own language cancels his critique of colonialism by reinscribing it with a hegemonic discourse. Faulkner's language, which characterizes the Indians as oriental and feminized, activates the discourse of orientalism that ultimately serves to stabilize traditional hierarchies and the masculinist power of the "West."

Civilized or Savage? Faulkner's Game of Inversion

Let's begin with Faulkner's game of ironic inversion in "Red Leaves." The story opens with Louis Berry and Herman Three Basket, two Indians who have returned to the Chickasaw plantation for Chief Issetibbeha's funeral. As tribal elders they want to see that the traditional funeral rites are carried out. These rites involve burying the chief with his dog, his horse, and his black body servant. The unnamed body servant, Issetibbeha's lifelong slave, has not surprisingly disappeared. The story focuses on the manhunt for the slave and the shift in power from Issetibbeha to his son Mokketubbe, who must accept the responsibilities of being a leader to his people, or as they say, being "the Man." The narrative is written in six sections, and the third-person point of view of the omniscient narrator shifts from the Indians in sections one through three to the runaway slave in section four and back to the Indians in sections five and six. Although the surface action centers on the preparations for the funeral and the slave hunt, which lasts for more than a week, the real narrative interest is the story of

Issetibbeha's dynasty, which spans three generations and begins with his father, Ikkemotubbe, also named Doom.

In the first two sections, Faulkner intersperses the story of Doom's rise to power with Berry's and Three Basket's comments about the escaped slave and slavery among their nation more generally. Many critics have commented on Faulkner's use of slavery in "Red Leaves." Slavery, according to Edmund Volpe, is "the major symbol of corruption" that provides an opportunity to portray Euro-Americans as a damaging influence on the attitudes and values of Indians (122). Gilbert Muller, for example, has explained that in "Red Leaves" Faulkner invents the "earliest history of Yoknapatawpha, that transitional period in which the last vestiges of Chickasaw culture were being corrupted by the plantation South" (244). But rather than attacking the ethics of the American culture directly, Faulkner, Muller argues, "creates a parable on slavery by casting the Indians in the role of plantation masters, while the blacks, rather than being an economic asset, become useless chattel" (245). Scholars agree that by using this technique of displacement, where "red men stand in for white men," as Arthur Kinney ("Faulkner's" 199) argues, Faulkner rearticulates his well-worn theme of the burden of slavery in an ironically reversed way through the Indian elders. But why go through such an elaborate charade?

I believe that Faulkner's displacement of the narrative voice from Anglo-American culture to Native American culture achieves two main goals: one is to estrange the familiar American logic of economic production and consumption; the second is to signify on nineteenth-century discourses about "savagery" and "civilization" from the more unfamiliar perspective of the "savage." Faulkner seems to suggest that the native population's entry into an economy based on the capitalist marketplace of production, consumption, and slave labor results in significant changes to native cultures and lifestyles—changes that do not represent "progress" but, on the contrary, problems.[12] Echoing Faulkner's white characters, the Indians of "Red Leaves" complain about the burden of slavery. Their complaints are not motivated by pious humanitarian interests or superior moral convictions, however, but by economic ones. Now that they own slaves, the Indians have to keep them busy. Three Basket explains: "A[n Indian] man's time was his own then. He had time. Now he must spend most of it finding work for them [blacks] who prefer sweating to do" (314). This crucial change in the native economy causes fundamental cultural problems, and in order to solve them Three Basket and Berry absurdly contemplate eating the slaves, that is, replacing the capitalist economy of consumption with a more literal (and primitive?) version of consumption. However, Faulkner's Indians realize that eating the slaves offends the laws of the marketplace, and they decide that profit-producing labor must be conserved. Faulkner's vision of excess is rendered in comic form. When Three Basket and Berry speak about the burdens of slavery, the following exchange takes place:

> "Man was not made to sweat."[13]
> "That's so. See what it has done to their flesh."
> "Yes. Black. It has a bitter taste, too."
> "You have eaten of it?"
> "Once. I was young then, and more hardy in the appetite than now. Now it is different with me."
> "Yes. They are too valuable to eat now." (*CS* 314)

Besides the fact that none of the civilized tribes was known to practice cannibalism, Faulkner revives the stereotypical image of "savages" as cannibals, a popular practice of representing utter alterity and inhumanity. Faulkner, however, seems to suggest that the Indians are savage not because they have tasted the flesh of a fellow human but because their appetite for the flesh is restrained only by economic considerations that the "white man" has taught them. Ergo the "white man" is the greater savage: he has dehumanized other human beings by reducing them to the status of commodities and passed on this cursed system of cultural and economic incorporation to those he failed to successfully enslave. In this ironic reversal of the positions of "savage" and "civilized," Faulkner suggests that what the Indians have learned from "civilization" is everything that is "uncivilized" in Western society.

This message with its cannibal metaphor is reminiscent of nineteenth-century arguments, popularized in the American context, for example, by Herman Melville in novels such as *Typee* (1846), in which the narrator deplores the European corruption of unspoiled cannibalistic savages in the Marquesas: "Alas for the poor savages when exposed to the influence of these [Western European] polluting examples! Unsophisticated and confiding, they are easily led into every vice, and humanity weeps over the ruin thus remorselessly inflicted upon them by their European civilizers" (16). Sarah Winnemucca Hopkins's *Life among the Piutes,* a late-nineteenth-century Native American text, also inverts the positions of savage and civilized. Hopkins casts the white American intruder into Paiute country into the role of cannibal as well: "Our mothers told us that the whites were killing everybody and eating them" (11). When whites indeed approach their camp, frightened women and children run to hide, but progress with small children is slow and the women decide to bury their children instead: "So they went to work and buried us, and told us if we heard any noise not to cry out, for if we did they would surely kill us and eat us" (11). Caused by rumors about the fate of the Donner party, the image of white cannibalism renders the

American colonizers as inhuman savages whose approach literally and symbolically buries the Native American lives and cultures. Although Faulkner's text seems to reactivate these nineteenth-century arguments and perhaps even shares their message of blame, his narrative mode is radically different. Unlike Hopkins's traumatic personal narrative and Melville's open didacticism, Faulkner's twentieth-century modernist revision of arguments about primitivism and cannibalism privileges strategies of displacement and mimicry that result in literary and political irony. Peter Mallios argues that "neither Faulkner nor the overwhelming majority of his readers would likely have taken seriously—which is to say, taken *as historical representations*—any claims that they [Faulkner's Indians] *were* cannibals" (150). Therefore the absurd discussion about cannibalism in "Red Leaves" can only be taken seriously as self-referentially fictional. Cannibalism, Mallios concludes, "may be understood in the Indian stories as an overarching and omnipresent sign of that which is historically, politically, and rhetorically 'cooked up'" (151). What Faulkner dishes up here is cannibalism as a modernist sign that belongs to a discourse of economic consumption, but one that has a very different flavor from Andrew Lytle's treatment of cannibalism as rooted historically in seventeenth-century discourses about Indians. By choosing the perspective of "primitive outsiders" to inspect the economics of consumption and the production of surplus through slavery, Faulkner mocks the ways of modern American society. Through the lens of Indians, the practice of slavery is rendered alien, and this estrangement effect helps Faulkner criticize this most unsavorable by-product of civilization.

Faulkner's critique of slavery continues in section four of "Red Leaves" when the narrative focus shifts to the escaped slave and his vivid recollection of the Middle Passage. Faulkner again is careful to evoke a hint of cannibalism in the description of the slave, a "Guinea man" who "had been taken at fourteen by a trader off Kamerun, before his teeth had been filed" (328). In the slave's recollection of the Middle Passage, Faulkner links his critique of civilization even more clearly with images of consumption: "they had lived ninety days in a three-foot-high tween-deck in tropic latitudes, hearing from topside the drunken New England captain intoning aloud from a book which he did not recognize for ten years afterward to be the Bible. Squatting in the stable so, he had watched the rat, civilized, by association with man reft of its inherent cunning of limb and eye; he had caught it without difficulty, with scarce a movement of his hand, and he ate it slowly, wondering how any of the rats had escaped so long" (*CS* 330). Linking literal and political levels of incorporation, the text produces a clear message: by comparison with the man who enslaves others and reads from the Bible—a major civilizing and colonizing instrument—the rat is civilized. In the narrative present of the manhunt, the black man who survived the Middle Passage is meeting his fate like the ants he eats, who walk into "oblivious doom with a steady and terrific undeviation" (334). Faulkner leaves no doubt that the slave is "doomed" by the larger economic system and haunted by the tribal chief of the same name whose legacy overshadows the events. The black man whose body is "gaunt, lean, hard, tireless and desperate" (334) fights hard until he is struck by a cottonmouth moccasin and his arm begins to swell and smell of death and decaying flesh, like Issetibbeha's body. When the black man becomes delirious from the snake poison, the Indians capture him and ready him for the sacrifice. Faulkner returns the black man to a primeval condition: naked, mud-caked, singing and speaking in his native tongue. He is a man whom the Indians respect for his endurance. "'Come,' the Indian said. 'You ran well. Do not be ashamed'" (338).[14] In the end, the human sacrifice, which remains outside the textual boundaries, seems like a relief, a humane ending to the man's fight.

These narrative events have given rise to critical arguments that seek to universalize Faulkner's narrative. Floyd Watkins argues that human sacrifice "is part of the long history of the life of every race that ever existed" (73), and Edmund Volpe agrees that "Man is part of nature, and in the immutable pattern of natural existence, all things living live by feeding upon one another, and all living things must die" (122). Faulkner has always attracted criticism of the universal and symbolic school, and in this perspective "Red Leaves" has been seen as symbolic of man's fall from grace in a wilderness that is "a dim reflection of that original Garden that man lost when evil came into the world" (Muller 248). Superimposed on a history of slavery, removal, and extermination, such a typological reading successfully replaces specific historical and political referents in the text with a Western Christian theological blanket statement. This kind of rhetoric perpetuates and reinscribes an ahistorical understanding of native peoples that makes them part of a vanished world, a "primeval past," a rhetoric that ensures their continued invisibility even today. Part of this myth is also perpetuated by Faulkner himself, who, when asked about his representations of African Americans versus Native Americans, answered that the black man "has a force, a power of his own that will enable him to survive. He won't vanish as the Indian did, because he is stronger and tougher than the Indian" (Meriwether and Millgate 182–83).[15] Arguments that aim to justify the "vanishing of the Indian" on the basis of racial fitness also get perpetuated in Faulkner criticism. Based on Faulkner's comment, Gene Moore, for example, argues that Faulkner contrasts the slaves' "progenitive vitality" and "cultural integrity" with the Indians' loss of these qualities and that Faulkner's depiction of the slaves in "Red Leaves" suggests that "the slaves have preserved a far more natural and unified culture than the borrowed and degraded cultural trappings of their masters" who suffer from "cultural alienation and loss of integrity" (" 'European Finery' " 265). By inverting the positions of "civilized" and "savage" in such a way that the most "uncultured" group of black slaves seems superior to Indians and whites, Faulkner critiques the dominant culture's colonizing practices, but he also reinscribes cultural and racial hierarchies. Nostalgic for a myth of pure cultural origins, Faulkner's text (or Moore's reading of it) replicates the hierarchical ranking of people on the basis of race by assuming some sort of "natural" state of nature (the African's) that is better than a (semi)civilized state of culture (the Indian's).

The Danger of Looking into French Mirrors: Doubling Identities

On a closer look, however, Faulkner's text supports a different kind of reading, one in which differences between Indians, whites, and blacks on the colonial frontier are not stable and interchangeable but merging and blurring and indeed becoming "mottled." Both "Red Leaves" and "Lo!" also yield a reading against the grain in which ethnic identities do not simply change places; rather, each identity changes as it occupies the place of the other. As a result, hierarchies are not clearly inverted, as it first seems, but transformed. Even the black slave who appears as an uncorrupted example of "progenitive vitality," according to Moore, wears a charm that "consisted of one half of a mother-of-pearl lorgnon which Issetibbeha had brought back from Paris, and the skull of a cottonmouth moccasin" (*CS* 330). By designating this hybrid amulet half-French, half-American, Faulkner seems to suggest that in the colonial context of the southern frontier, there are no "pure" cultural identities. The lorgnon, an instrument of French specularity slung around the hips of an African man, suggests the hybridity of colonial identities and environments. Homi Bhabha argues that the production of colonial identity is never simply based on a binary opposition between colonizer and colonized, even if that binary is presented as inverted, but on a doubling of identities. Such doubling is not a form of "dialectical contradiction" but rather something that exceeds the frame of simple binaries and, in the production of cultural hybridity, gives rise to something new (Bhabha 49). Faulkner, I propose, explores such cultural hybridity by means of a number of mirror images.

We encounter the first mirror in Issetibbeha's steamboat residence. The decaying steamboat, which has been turned into a residence for the new chief, has traditionally been read as a central symbol both of the Indian's greed for European things and of those things' ultimate corruptive power. Once a splendid symbol of civilization, "the saloon of the steamboat was now a shell rotting slowly; the polished mahagony, the carving glinting momentarily and fading through the mold in figures cabalistic and profound; the gutted windows were like cataracted eyes" (324). Blinded and estranged from their original purposes, European things take on a new life as signifiers of cultural subversion. By absorbing and transforming the steamboat, the Indians have inscribed it with a new significance. Like the coveted red slippers from France which have become a sign of native power, the hybrid items we find in Faulkner's "wilderness" transform the native culture as well as the colonizing culture. Inside the steamboat are the gilt bed and the girandoles that Issetibbeha brings back from Paris. "From the ceiling [of the steamboat], suspended by four deer thongs, hung the gilt bed which Issetibbeha had fetched from Paris. It had neither mattress nor springs, the frame crisscrossed now by a neat hammocking of thongs" (324). Like the gilt bed with the deer thongs, Faulkner's text itself is a hybrid object crisscrossed with historical and political determinations that mark the Indians as the inheritors of eighteenth-century French history. The pair of girandoles, ornate brackets for a candelabra with a reflecting mirror at the back of the shelf, insert French history into Faulkner's hybrid environment. Louis XV and Madame Pompadour enter the text (and the lives of the Indians) with the girandoles, "by whose light it was said that Pompadour arranged her hair while Louis smirked at his mirrored face across her powdered shoulder" (320). Why did Faulkner insert these historical figures into his Indian "wilderness"? What is he reflecting on? Is the indirect evocation of Louis XV a reference to French and British colonialism, of which North American Indian tribes felt the vicious and lasting effects?[16] Is it a reference to the decadence of style and decorative self-aggrandizement mirrored in the stylistic confusions of Issetibbeha's "house"? Or is it an indirect comment on the failure of political leadership? Louis XV is the French king who is supposed to have said "After me, the deluge," a policy that Faulkner's lethargic Indian chiefs also seem to follow. It seems that Faulkner's text crisscrosses back on itself with this reference to the age of Enlightenment, the starting point for European colonialism and race theories that helped justify the enterprise of exploration and subjugation. The mirrors behind the candles of the girandoles are part of a system of colonial specularity that does not produce clear-cut reflections of colonizer and colonized. Instead, the figures of Louis XV and Issetibbeha are refracted and reflected back doubly inscribed.

Faulkner also uses the colonial mirror for breaking down the symmetry and duality between self and other in the opening passages of "Lo!" when the president (we assume it is Andrew Jackson) looks at himself in a "hand mirror of elegant French design" (381) and beholds his own image blended and blurred with that of his Indian opponent:

> he raised and advanced the mirror. For an instant he caught his own reflection in it and he paused for a time and with a kind of cold unbelief he examined his own face—the face of the shrewd and courageous fighter, of that wellnigh infallible expert in the anticipation of and controlling of man and his doings, overlaid new with the baffled helplessness of a child. Then he slanted the glass a little further. . . . Squatting and facing one another across the carpet as across a stream of water were two men. He did not know the faces, though he knew the Face, since he had looked upon it by day and dreamed upon it by night for three weeks now. It was a squat face, dark, a little flat, a little Mongol; secret, decorous, impenetrable, and grave . . . it seemed to him that in some idiotic moment out of attenuated sleeplessness and strain he looked upon a single man facing himself in a mirror. (381–82)

Presented in the mirror is not the subject of authority but precisely the want of authority: Jackson is helpless like a child overwhelmed by the task of controlling the children of the Nation, the Indians. The colonial roles of father and child, Nation and nations, powerful and powerless, are not only inverted here but doubled. The Indian presence (which should be an absence) in the mirror of the nation confounds the boundaries of colonial authority and besieges the president with his own nightmarish phantoms of otherness and the persistence of a so-called problem that will not be solved. What is visible in the mirror is not only the gaze of the colonizer looking at the Indian other but also the Indian who holds and returns the look. In the mirror, the return of the repressed has literally manifested itself and negated the visibility of difference: the president's own face merges with the "squat face" of the Indian other so that "he looked upon a single man facing himself in a mirror." Bhabha comments on the effect of the kind of hybridity Faulkner produces here: "The display of hybridity—its peculiar 'replication'—terrorizes authority with the *ruse* of recognition, its mimicry, its mockery" (115). The hybridity of colonial authority reflected in the mirror literally unsettles the figure at the center of the American credo of democratic ideals. The personal trauma of the president *is* the political trauma of the entire nation, whose Indian policies alienate its own language of liberty. The president knows that "he faced not an enemy in the open field, but was besieged *within* his very high and lonely office by them to whom he was, by legal if not divine appointment, father" (383, emphasis added). The enemy within—as U.S. internal colonization more generally—produces a schizophrenic split mocking the patronizing Enlightenment rhetoric of legal and divine fatherhood by its contrast with political reality. The interior warfare on Native Americans, the numerous land treaties, and the impending radical removal of Native Americans east of the Mississippi all mar the language of democracy, threaten the rationalist hegemony, and open a wide schism for national anxieties. This is even more interesting and ironic in 1934 considering that the United States was once again gearing up to defend democracy, this time against the irrationality of the rise of fascism in Europe.

Faulkner locates the Indian "problem" at the heart of the nation, centered "in the very rotunda [of the White House] itself of this concrete and visible apotheosis of the youthful Nation's pride" (384). The Indian crisis in America does not go unnoticed abroad: the Indians camped out at the White House are "serene beneath the astonished faces and golden braid, the swords and ribbons and stars, of European diplomats" (384). The European diplomats might be astonished indeed because the American nation was originally built on the rejection of its status as a British colony, yet the "young Nation" went on to colonize other nations in its interior. Renee Bergland addresses the shame and resulting repression associated with American colonialism: "American nationalist subjectivity internalizes the colonial relation, but, since the nation was established by denying the validity of colonialism, American subjects repress this interiorized colonialism far more deeply than do Europeans" (13). Seizing on this American anxiety, Faulkner hones in on the national irony even more when he describes the avenue leading to the White House as "the stage upon which each four years would parade the proud panoply of the young Nation's lusty man's estate for the admiration and envy and astonishment of the weary world" (385). The term "estate" is not accidental, since land acquisition is the crucial issue and root cause for national anxieties. From Thomas Jefferson to Andrew Jackson and beyond, land was exchanged for "civilization," as each president hoped that with increasing acculturation the Indians would need less land.[17]

Faulkner signifies upon this acculturation process and the national civilizing missions through the metaphor of dress. When the Indians travel to Washington in "Lo!" their invisibility, suddenly become visible, marks an unruly threat to civilized order and political procedure. The president complains that his house is blocked by "half-naked Chickasaw Indians asleep on the floor or gnawing at half-raw ribs of meat" (388). The state of Indian civilization, half-naked and half-raw, signifies an ethnographic and political ambivalence: Faulkner's Indians, neither civilized nor savage, continuously elude clear classification and identification. The desire of the colonizing power for clear-cut identities and a reformed, recognizable other leads the president to order Western clothes for them, a gesture that makes them worthy of the negotiating table but is also intended to mask the threat that their presence in the U.S. capital presents. But the threat of the other cannot be properly masked by superficial civilizing missions. The Indians accept the clothes but invert the strategy intended to reform and discipline them. They wear all the clothing items, but with an essential difference. In Faulkner's words, the Indians "wore beaver hats and new frock coats; save for the minor detail of collars and waistcoats they were impeccably dressed . . . down to the waist. But from there down credulity, all sense of fitness and decorum, was outraged" (382). The outrage stems from the imitation of Western dress codes that produces similarity with a difference, a difference that slides the meaning of Western decorum into the absurd and marks a threat rather than the civilized safety the president had hoped for. That this threat is also sexual is implied in the fact that they wear everything but their pants and that the president's wife no longer dares to leave the sanctity of her bedroom, "let alone receive lady guests" (388). The excess or slippage produced by this instance of colonial imitation—this "almost the same"—ruptures the social order and transforms stability into uncertainty and mimicry. Such mimicry functions both as "a sign of the inappropriate and as threat to disciplinary powers" (Bhabha 86). This threat is so real that the president pays for the new clothing "out of his own pocket" in the same fashion "as he would have commanded gunsmiths and bulletmakers in war emergency" (389). But the president's war strategy backfires, and the ensuing mimicry, instead of securing the signs of racial and cultural priority, problematizes and destabilizes the situation.

Reciprocating the "gift" of clothing from the president, the Indians present the president with a ludicrous and colorful costume: "a mass, a network, of gold braid—frogs, epaulets, sash and sword—held loosely together by bright green cloth" (390). As a carnival costume that undermines rather than confirms national authority, the outfit has the same destabilizing power and traumatic effect as the president's look in the mirror: the performance of personal and national identity becomes difficult if not impossible because the other *is* the self. When the phantom Indians crowd into the president's most intimate hiding spot, his bedroom, the colonial fantasy quickly turns into a nightmare as the president is losing his grip on personal and political space. This scene seems to confirm Bhabha's insight that "the place of difference and otherness, or the space of the adversarial . . . is never entirely on the outside or implacably oppositional. It is a pressure and a presence, that acts constantly, if unevenly, along the entire boundary of authorization" (109). Questioning national authority, Faulkner's colonial mirror produces an uncomfortable ambiguity that collapses inside and outside spaces not in order to reverse authority or history, but in order to destabilize the very terms that make such opposition possible. Put simply, Faulkner does not merely reverse the roles of "victim" and "victors" in "Lo!"; rather, in splitting and doubling these roles he produces multiple ironies and a textual excess that slips away from clear classification toward the complexity and cloudiness of mimicry.[18] Faulkner dramatizes the Indians' quest for "justice" in a doubly ironic gesture when the secretary of state echoes the request in an "almost exact imitation" of the Indians' plea. But instead of ensuring justice, the president and his secretary deceive the Indians and appease them by playing around with "dummy papers" and reading Petrarch sonnets to them instead of the law. From long years of experience, the Indians know of the white man's ignorance and arrogance toward them, and they, in turn, masterfully mimic the mainstream beliefs on which the nation operates: "Weddel or Vidal. What does it matter by what name the White Chief calls us? We are but Indians: remembered yesterday and forgotten tomorrow" (396). This ironic echo of the "white man's" belief that the Indians are vanishing finds expression in the Indian Removal Act, section 3, which states that "the President solemnly . . . assure[s] the tribe or nation with which the exchange is made, that the United States will forever secure and guaranty to them, and their heirs or successors, the country so exchanged with them. . . . Provided always, That such lands shall revert to the United States, *if the Indians become extinct*, or abandon the same" (emphasis added). Faulkner's parodic language in which Indians echo the laws and beliefs of "white men" and they, on their part, echo Indians ("you found good hunting," the president says to a group of Indians) turns political negotiations into a game of mimicry. In this game, the Indians trick the president into affirming their status as equals: "To me, my Indian and my white people are the same" (397), an obvious falsity because, while presidents tried to protect Native American interests, they have always protected the interests of the settlers. In the end, the presidential ruse will not bring peace; it brings a false peace. Just when the president thinks he has taken care of the "Indian problem," the nightmarish scenario threatens to begin again. Another white man has come among the Chickasaws and has died. By the end of the story, the Indians have changed from "charges" and "children" into the enemies of the nation. Lothar Hönnighausen writes that "what Faulkner invites us to witness in 'Lo!' . . . is Andrew Jackson's experience of the 'return of the vanishing American' (Fiedler) as an embodiment of the uncanny and the parodic rewriting of the historical event, whose tragic aspect Tocqueville witnessed in 1831, as an act of 'poetic justice'" (343). But if Faulkner is indeed interested in justice, the "poetic justice" he exercises on the surface level of the story—his critique of American expansion politics—is strangely undercut by his own rhetoric. On a closer look, the images of Indians he activates in his stories serve to reinforce instead of upset the hegemony.

Ethnological Images from the Far East: Faulkner's Orientalism

Faulkner's language, his mode of writing and representation, participates in America's desire to homogenize native people and, in this case, to orientalize them. This tendency can be seen clearly in Faulkner's exotic description of "the Indians" that opens "Red Leaves": "The first Indian's name was Three Basket. He was perhaps sixty. They were both squat men, a little solid, burgher-like; paunchy, with big heads, big, broad, dust-colored faces of certain blurred serenity like carved heads on a ruined wall in Siam or Sumatra, looming out of the mist" (*CS* 313). This description draws on ethnological images from the Far East—or to be more precise, Indonesia—and immediately superimposes a worldwide colonial geography upon the events at home in Mississippi. Exotic and "oriental," Faulkner's Indians resemble the "carved heads on a ruined wall in Siam or Sumatra," countries securely under English and Dutch colonial control in the 1930s. The description of the Indian chief in "Lo!" similarly orientalizes Native American identities. The chief is a "soft paunchy man facing them with his soft, bland, inscrutable face—the long monk-like nose, the slumbrous lids, the flabby, café-au-lait-colored jowls above a froth of soiled lace of an elegance fifty years outmoded and vanished; the mouth was full, small and very red. Yet somewhere behind the face's expression of flaccid and weary disillusion, as behind the bland voice and the almost feminine mannerisms, there lurked something else: something willful, shrewd, unpredictable and despotic" (*CS* 395). This description combines the racist stereotype of the feminine Asiatic and the 1930s Hollywood stereotype of the "inscrutable Indian." In contradictory articulations of desire and revulsion, the Indian is projected as ultimately other: not white but "coffee-colored," not firm but flabby, not masculine but feminine, not logical but unpredictable, not democratic but despotic. Fleshy to the point of disease, Faulkner's Indian bodies are not the trim and athletic Indians of Cooper's nineteenth-century imagination but rather obese, diseased, and lethargic. In the description of Mokketubbe, Faulkner represents the disease of the entire lineage of Indian rulers. "At three years of age Mokketubbe has a broad, flat, Mongolian face that appeared to exist in a complete and unfathomable lethargy" (320). At twenty-five, Mokketubbe "was already diseased with flesh, with a pale, broad, inert face and dropsical hands and feet" (321). Because Mokketubbe's feet cannot carry him much less fit into the coveted red slippers, he is being carried around by his people in "a litter made of buckskin and persimmon poles" like a king.

By coding Indian bodies as fat, inert, and feminized, Faulkner delivers a twofold message: the fat, docile body of the Indian signifies an absence of self-discipline and a central vulnerability to his own person that translates into a vulnerability of his tribe. Mokketubbe's fleshy body represents by extension the diseased and dying social body, a society out of control, operating out of unrestrained hunger and uncontrolled impulses, "doomed" to expire. Because in Western society the body is often imagined as belonging to the "nature" side of a nature/culture duality, excessive body fat generally represents the uncultured and uncivilized (Bordo 295). But not only does the Indian body implicitly reject Western cultural ideals; it also explicitly evokes Eastern ones. Mokketubbe seems at once grotesque and Buddha-like with his "round, smooth copper balloon of belly swelling above the bottom piece of a suit of linen underwear" (*CS* 325). With his "broad, yellow face with its closed eyes and flat nostrils," the motionless Mokketubbe "looked like an effigy, like a Malay god" (325). Coded as an Eastern idol with the swelling belly of a Buddha or a pregnant woman, the Indian body signifies ultimate otherness, a sort of ontological difference that points to a difference in Eastern and Western economic and cultural mentalities. The cultural identity Faulkner assigns to Native Americans clearly makes them part of a discourse of orientalism in which the East is discursively produced as the West's inferior other. Edward Said argues that orientalism operates in the service of the West's hegemony over the East in order to construct the West's own image as a superior civilization. In this context, it is interesting to note that Native Americans have been traditionally misrepresented in the West, beginning with the name "Indian" that makes them part of a discursive system inscribing them as Asian or "Eastern." Representations—including misrepresentations—usually serve a purpose in a specific historical, intellectual, and economic setting (Said, *Orientalism* 272).

Considering this setting, we must ask what Faulkner's purpose is in (mis)-representing Native Americans as orientalized figures in his stories of the 1930s. One answer is that the orientalist traces in Faulkner's Indian stories are part of the general interest American modernists had in the Orient. During the period of high modernism, poets such as Ezra Pound and William Carlos Williams were inspired by the cultures and languages of China, Japan, and the legendary "Cathay," which they sought to "translate" in their poetry. While modernists were rediscovering the Orient, they were also sifting through the history of the Occident, particularly the "discovery" of the New World. In search of a national heritage expressed in a distinctly American language, William Carlos Williams—in his book *In the American Grain* (1925), for example—reconstructed some of the main chapters in the history of the nation, including Columbus's discovery of the Indies as well as the adventures of Ponce de León and Hernando de Soto. This quest for a subject matter able to serve the goals of American nation-building in a language that attempted to express a sacred essence of nationality led some of the modernists to Native American poetry. It is perhaps no coincidence that George Cronyn's *The Path on the Rainbow: An Anthology of Songs and Chants from the Indians of North America* (1918) was republished in 1934 when Faulkner was writing and marketing his Indian stories.[19] Public interest in Native American poetry during the 1920s and 1930s was part of the modernist movement of primitivism, which often availed itself of an orientalist discourse even as it was discussing the work and expressions of "Indians." In Alice Corbin Henderson's review of the special issue of *Poetry* (1918), this discursive conflation between orientalism, nationalism, and modernism is clearly displayed. After asserting that "these Indian poems are very similar in spirit and method to the poetry of our most modern American poets," Henderson claims that "the whole art character of the Indian is of course more Oriental than European," and she speculates that "perhaps that is why we have failed to appreciate it" (qtd. in Carr 226). By both nativizing and orientalizing the Native American signifier, Faulkner's modernist contemporaries model a discourse that simultaneously others and integrates the Indian into the foundations of national history and narrative. Faulkner's orientalized Native American figures share this political and aesthetic agenda as they bear the imprint of his own colonizing language.[20]

Faulkner's paunchy, orientalized Indians are the sorry products of cultural assimilation and transformation. Orientalism in Faulkner's text signals a kind of cultural degeneracy that is the result of cultural and racial assimilation, a position that by implication romanticizes the apparent health and vitality of pre-contact Indians. For all the grotesque troping with orientalist signifiers and the playful and irreverent mood with which Faulkner introduces his Indians, there is a deep-seated romanticism that forms the basis for his critique of modern materialism: when Indian cultures get caught up in the forces of Western civilization, their political, moral, and economic power is doomed to wane.[21] The discourse that warns of the disastrous effects of assimilation is compatible with the contemporary perception that the Native Americans who were least integrated and assimilated into American mainstream civilization—Native Americans out "West" such as the Hopis, Zunis, and Navajos—retained the most valuable cultural power and strength. Those Native Americans who remained the most culturally independent were celebrated and even fetishized by American writers and intellectuals during the 1920s and 1930s. Those same Native Americans also inspired John Collier's Indian Reorganization Act (1934), which worked against the past dictum of forced assimilation and attempted to reverse the political legacy of dispossession. I suggest that Faulkner's preoccupation with Native American cultural assimilation and transformation in his stories of the 1930s becomes particularly relevant when read against the concurrent shift in federal Indian policy. Robert Dale Parker also sees this connection: "By the summer of 1933, when Faulkner sent out 'Lo!' Collier was Commissioner of Indian Affairs in the new Roosevelt administration and was controversially turning federal policy towards Indians upside down, trying to support Native sovereignty and communal land ownership" (96). Despite the intended benefits of this policy shift, which bore the imprint of Collier's own conception of "Indianness," the policy that emphasized Native American self-determination nevertheless showed signs of Collier's own deep-seated paternalism. Helen Carr argues that Collier "failed to see that his paternalism was a continuation of the oppression of the past," a blind spot that "may perhaps have been intimately bound up with the feminization of the Indian" (229). Faulkner shares this paternalism in his fictional representation of Indians on which he superimposes images of a feminized, despotic, irrational, and backward East, a technique of representation that leaves intact the masculinist colonial power of the "West" and his own masculinity as a white southern male.[22]

Fathering Sam Fathers: From Orientalism to Modernist Nostalgia

Faulkner's orientalization and feminization of Indians in his stories of the 1930s may be puzzling considering that his most famous Indian figure, Sam Fathers of *Go Down, Moses,* is not flabby but hard, not feminine but masculine, not an absurdly comic but an essentially tragic figure. This shift in mood away from the mimicry of orientalist inscriptions of Indians in Faulkner's earlier stories toward an embrace of Indians as members of the national family marks both a change in the author's mood and a rising national trend. Like Caroline Gordon in *Green Centuries,* published the same year as *Go Down, Moses,* Faulkner engages a discourse of national ancestry and heritage. Sam Fathers, in his early incarnation in "A Justice" (1934) and in his reappearance in the stories of *Go Down, Moses* eight years later, is explicitly linked to a discourse of blood and ancestry. A hybrid figure of African-American and Indian descent, Sam Fathers *performs* the role of the "Indian" ancestor, a guiding paternal figure to Ike McCaslin, the white inheritor of the land to whom he teaches his knowledge of the rapidly receding wilderness. Very much the noble savage who is part of Doom's lineage, and therefore clearly "doomed" to extinction, Sam Fathers does not have any children of his own, and in the course of the novel he vanishes like the wilderness itself.

Sam Fathers is most commonly understood within the tradition of the romantic and sentimentalized stereotype of the noble savage of the nineteenth-century imagination. In an early portrait of Sam Fathers in "A Justice," he smokes the stereotypical Indian pipe of "creek clay with a reed stem" and moves about straight-backed and stoic like a Hollywood Indian. A decade later, in *Go Down, Moses,* Faulkner excavates the stereotype of the vanishing Indian on which he models Sam Fathers, a characterization that most critics find limited and disappointing.[23] It seems that recently Faulkner scholars prefer the politics of his seemingly more radical and subversive Indian stories of the 1930s to the agenda of his more canonical text, and most critics concur that Faulkner's modernist nostalgia in *Go Down, Moses* is different altogether from the mimicry of his earlier stories.[24]

However, despite this apparent shift in representation, the ideological function of Faulkner's Native American signifier in *Go Down, Moses* is similar to that of his stories. Sam Fathers remains a foundational figure in the saga of Yoknapatawpha; he is a cultural and racial hybrid who vanishes to make room for white southern communities. What has changed is Faulkner's emphasis: whereas the exotic and doomed inhabitants of his Indian stories illustrate the process of cultural transformation and assimilation, Sam Fathers performs the important lesson of cultural transmission. He belongs to two discursive realms: as part of the cultural archive of the nineteenth century, he is the Indian in the act of vanishing before civilized progress who elicits our sympathy, regret, and shame; as an anthropological object, an archaic exotic anachronism who must give way to a new world, he represents the American past linked to a rhetoric of racial extinction. But as part of Faulkner's time and the twentieth-century discourses surrounding Indians, Sam Fathers articulates a new desire for cultural and national union. What Faulkner depicts in the hunting rituals of "The Old People" and "The Bear" is a momentary bond between whites, blacks, and Indians, rich men like Major de Spain and poor swamp hunters who come together drawn by the spectacle of nature. But what makes this ritual so special is the fact that it will disappear—that even as Ike McCaslin is still a boy, the group of men bonding over the traditional ritual of the hunt find themselves at the end point of the advancing edge of history. This is not only part of Faulkner's romantic understanding of a primitive life that was good and unspoiled; it is also a powerful fantasy of masculinity and brotherhood, a bonding between men of different races and classes.[25]

What makes this fantasy of a bond between the white boy and the Indian hunter particularly urgent for Faulkner is the perceived "lack" of Native Americans from the South. In the 1940s what seemed to have remained of the Indians were the inscriptions in the land: the names, mounds, and archaeological remains engraved in the Mississippi landscape. When Faulkner's characters in "Delta Autumn" look around their ever-receding hunting grounds, they see "no gradient anywhere and no elevation save those raised by forgotten aboriginal hands as refugees from the yearly water and used by their Indian successors to sepulchre their fathers' bones, and all that remained of that old time were the Indian names on the little towns and usually pertaining to water—Aluschaskuna, Tillatoba, Homochitto, Yazoo" (325). Set during Faulkner's contemporary moment, this story famously laments the disappearance of the wilderness and the transformation of the land "across which there came now no scream of panther but instead the long hooting locomotives" (325). Like Welty, Faulkner memorializes the Native American inscriptions in the land as evidence of a bygone presence, although he knows very well that the Chickasaws and Choctaws had not vanished but continued to live in Oklahoma and on reservations, including the Choctaw Reservation in Philadelphia, Mississippi.[26] Faulkner, however, is not interested in representing the realities of contemporary Native American life; instead, he presents the discursive conventions that contribute to the construction of the Native American signifier as "lack." This representation of native space as "empty" is part of the appropriation of Native Americans in the white imagination and their subsequent erasure from the American South. By colonizing the narrative space of Indians through representations that focus on their receding space (the wilderness), the text opens a gap that can be filled with the fantasies, needs, and desires of the white hegemony. This blank spot and the empty sign "Indian" become the host for hegemonic discourses of Indianness important to the shaping of white masculinity and to concepts of nationhood and political power centered in this sign.

Faulkner's textual production of the Native American signifier taps into those needs by articulating anxieties around concepts of race, culture, and nationhood relevant to his time and place. Faulkner's frequent self-conscious references to Sam Fathers's "blood" engage racialist discourses based in biology that still carried much weight in the segregated South.[27] By creating Sam Fathers, a figure in whom black, white, and Indian "blood" flow together, Faulkner opens up the text for an investigation of the complicated relationship between biological and cultural heritage in the construction of the racial signifier. He introduces racially based definitions of identity in blood quantum theories—one drop of black blood, or the designation full-blood, half-blood, mixed-blood, and so on—as markers of identity and cultural memory that are clearly unstable and insufficient. The son of a Chickasaw chief and a black female slave, Sam Fathers is a man "not tall, squat rather, almost sedentary, flabby-looking though he actually was not, with hair like a horse's mane which even at seventy showed no trace of white and a face which showed no age until he smiled, whose only visible trace of negro blood was a slight dullness of the hair and the fingernails" (160–61). This overtly racialist characterization, which recalls the squat, sedentary Indians of Faulkner's earlier stories, is grounded in the biological signs of hair and fingernails. A "negro" by the legal definition of the "one drop rule," Sam Fathers is imagined simultaneously as caged by the bondage of his "black blood" and free by the privilege of his "Indian blood." Such racialist discourse, dating from the nineteenth century, links biological characteristics with other inherited intellectual and moral qualities. The claim that there is a racial essence that is connected to knowledge and behavior is of course a racist stereotype that is best articulated by Ike's cousin McCaslin, who believes that the wilderness resides in Sam Fathers's blood: "He was a wild man. When he was born, all his blood on both sides, except the little white part, knew things that had been tamed out of our blood so long ago that we have not only forgotten them, we have to live together in herds to protect ourselves from our own sources" (161). These racialist (and racist) ideas perform important functions in Faulkner's text. By linking knowledge to race, these discourses seek to naturalize racial hierarchies on the basis of biological heredity, thereby conflating epistemology with ontology. Because Sam Fathers's knowledge of the wilderness is in his "blood," his death means a terrible loss not only of "native" knowledge but of the American wilderness itself. This threat, in turn, necessitates a shift from the concept of *racial* knowledge to the new idea of *cultural* knowledge and the importance of Native American cultural transmission.

Faulkner undercuts the discourse of "blood" with the new anthropological discourse of culture. We learn that although Sam Fathers lives in the slave quarters and dresses and talks like a black man, he does "white man's work" (carpentry) and takes liberties that others cannot afford because "he was still the son of that Chickasaw chief and the negroes knew it" (163). Sam Fathers bears himself like a noble savage with gravity, dignity, and lack of servility toward white men. At stake in the text is his cultural *performance* as an Indian—not as an African American—that makes him valuable to the cultural heritage of white southern men. Sam Fathers plays the role of a hunting guide who passes on the codes of the wilderness and the history of the "old days." In this transmission of knowledge, the "native" past becomes part of Ike's living present. Sam Fathers's oral tradition functions as "the mouthpiece of the host" to a world primeval of which the boy becomes "a guest." As a figure who is key to the transmission of an essential aspect of American culture, the Indian articulates codes of behavior and essences of "Indianness" that are imagined to impart to Americans a sense of indigenousness that will distinguish them from other (Euro-American) nationals. Whether or not this transmission of cultural knowledge from Sam Fathers to Ike McCaslin is successful is a point of debate among critics. Some read Ike's famous renunciation of the land as a result of Sam Fathers's teachings, while others argue that the transmission and preservation of Native American knowledge is ultimately unsuccessful and that "Ike's mimicry of Sam's Native American traditions more accurately highlights the white culture's appropriation of the Indians' doomed heritage" (Johnson 119).[28]

I want to propose that mimicry of Native American culture is all there is for Faulkner. If the Indian Citizenship Act of 1924 meant the absorption of Indians into national life as Americans,[29] then the impending crisis of World War

II meant the reinvention of Americans as "Indians." It is for this reason that Sam Fathers must be "barren." His name expresses Faulkner's sharply calculated pun and a deep-seated irony: Sam Fathers does not "father" anything but an imagined cultural heritage that Ike seeks to imitate. Sam Fathers is "an old man past seventy whose grandfathers had owned the land long before the white men ever saw it, and who had vanished from it now with all their kind, what of blood they left behind them running now in another race and for a while even in bondage and now drawing towards the end of its alien and irrevocable course, barren, since Sam Fathers had no children" (159). Alluding to the discourse of citizenship, Faulkner makes it clear: Sam Fathers's blood is alien, a word that transforms the native insider into the foreign outsider to make room for the new white "natives." When Sam Fathers is first introduced in "A Justice" his name is Had-Two-Fathers, and the story is about the cruel joke that his biological father, Doom, played on a slave woman with whom he conceived a child but whom he then married off to a slave. This name symbolizes Sam Fathers's dual ancestry, referring both to his Indian and his black father, and the patriarchal betrayal that silences and erases the slave woman in an act of paternal rivalry and dominance. Originally, then, Sam Fathers is conceived of "two fathers." The name change from Had-Two-Fathers in "A Justice" to Sam Fathers in *Go Down, Moses* is indicative of the new role he plays here: his identity moves from having two fathers to being a father. Fathers is the grammatical plural of the noun that connotes his dual ancestry, but it also functions as the verb "to father." Of course, Sam Fathers does not have any offspring. Like the feminized and orientalized Indians of Faulkner's stories, he is not a rival to the imagined political and sexual potency of the white man. Conveniently, he leaves no biological trace but a rich cultural heritage ready to be embraced by the white southerner. What Sam fathers are the customs, rituals, and stories that are transmitted to Ike. More so, he passes on the property and the spirit of the land that is important not only for the shaping of white southern masculinity but for the idea of the nation more generally. In other words, he passes on "native" cultural memory crucial to the nationalist imaginary of America at the brink of entering a major international crisis. Like Caroline Gordon, Faulkner imagines a white-Indian connection crucial to articulations of American national identity, but unlike Gordon, who proposes a brotherhood of white and red men, Faulkner constructs a flawed fatherhood as the paradigm that characterizes the relation between Indians and whites. In either case, Native Americans as "native" *Americans* are crucial for the articulation of national self-definition and the need to locate indigenous roots in the South and elsewhere as the United States is heading into World War II.

Published on May 11, 1942, *Go Down, Moses* is in some ways Faulkner's response to the traumatic events of World War II. This is apparent even on the textual surface of a story like "Delta Autumn," which explicitly refers to a changed political landscape. Adolf Hitler appears on Faulkner's map as hunting camp members discuss the threat of European fascism, and Ike, now "Uncle Ike," patriotically argues that America is "a little mite stronger than any one man or group of men, outside of it or even inside of it either. . . . It will cope with one Austrian paper-hanger, no matter what he will be calling himself" (322–23). The entry of fascism into the novel points toward an anxiety in the linkages among nation, race, and culture. When European nations identified themselves as biological and not just cultural units beginning in the nineteenth century, the door was opened for an understanding of a hierarchy of races and the kind of nationalism that resulted in Hitler's holocaust. In *Go Down, Moses* the textual tension in the triangular relationships among nation, race, and culture is centered in the theme of Sam Fathers's "heritage." Here, not only does the Indian transmit a "native" tradition that unites the rivaling narratives of racial and cultural inheritance (red, white, and black), but, more importantly, Indian-white relations are imagined as shoring up a native nationalism against the foreign fascist threat. Sam Fathers is imagined as an ancestor to white southerners, and his relationship with Ike McCaslin is expressive of a desire for a bonding that results in a collective national identity and the affirmation of a national culture.

Faulkner's embrace of Sam Fathers expresses a changed Indian-white relationship that pop culture and Hollywood movies were also portraying. In the prewar years, as they fostered national unity in the face of foreign fascism, Hollywood studios participated in the antifascist mood best exemplified by the Hollywood Anti-Nazi League. "National unity was a powerful weapon against fascism, and Blacks, Indians and Mexicans soon joined their white counterparts in the movies' effort to 'racially integrate' the home front" (Aleiss 25). In this political climate, Indians were quickly changed from the stereotypical "hostile warrior" to the white man's brothers, and this "concept of racial brotherhood began to influence its Indian/white portrayals at least two years before America's entry into the war" (29). Indian characters were designed to strengthen national unity and to articulate concepts of American freedom and cultural heritage. The frontier's new villain became the advance of technology symbolized by the ever-encroaching railroad. In "Delta Autumn" the wilderness makes room for "trains of incredible length" whose steam whistles tear through the once-primeval landscape (*CS* 325).[30] The new interracial alliance between Indians and whites and the changing depiction of Indians as supporters and friends of white Americans in Hollywood films helped boost the construction of a national union. Faulkner and his contemporaries were aware of these changing representations of Indians not only in the movie industry but also in the rhetoric of a war effort that rallied Native Americans to defend the country both on and off the movie set. In a 1942 article titled "The Indian in a Wartime Nation," John Collier writes that despite continued discrimination against Indians, "the Indians have responded earnestly and even enthusiastically to the challenge of the war" (29). And he cites enrollment figures showing that after Pearl Harbor Indian enrollment in the armed forces quickly climbed from 4,481 to more than 7,500 (29).

Read against the background of America's fight for freedom overseas that included Native Americans and African Americans, Faulkner's choice of the title for his novel is doubly ironic. *Go Down, Moses* alludes to one of the best-known African-American spirituals, a "song of struggle" that takes its political message of freedom from the biblical story of the Exodus.[31] The title of the song is applicable not only to American slavery and human bondage but also to the black/Indian character at the center of Faulkner's novel who is confined by the bondage of his black blood and freed by the imagined liberty of his Indian blood. Uniting bondage and freedom, Sam Fathers demands his release not by imploring "Let my People go" but by informing Major de Spain: "I'm going now" (167). Although he is by blood associated with blacks and their history of enslavement, Sam Fathers does not ask for his release from bondage but firmly demands it. His departure, however, results not in a better lifestyle for him and changed power relationships to whites and blacks, but, in contrast to the children of Israel, in a self-chosen exile. For the Indian, freedom means, ironically, permission to vanish into oblivion, to participate in his own "vanquishment and the mausoleum of his defeat" (162). It means his total dispossession (he does not have any possessions) and disappearance. Thus vanished, he is only visited by Ike and the other white men in the wilderness where and when his guiding "spirit" is needed. It is this lingering spirit, and not the physical presence of Indians, that is essential to the concept of American nationhood. Faulkner's novel presents the American doctrine of freedom to which the title alludes as hollow rhetoric in the face of the exploitation of slaves and the dispossession and displacement of Native Americans. The novel shows that such dispossession gives rise to certain perverse performances, such as Sam Fathers's self-effacement. "In these performances," writes Gyan Prakash, "as the myths of the civilizing mission and historical progress find perverse expressions in caricatures of indigenous traditions and racist stereotyping and exploitation of blacks [and Native Americans], the colonial reality appears in its estranged representation" (4).

Go Down, Moses presents some of these colonizing contortions of discourse in familiar myths about Native Americans as noble savages on the brink of extinction at the same time that the political potential of the "native figure" is rallied for a politically important imagined union with the white man. The enduring circulation of such myths in white southern culture and American culture more generally is intended to justify the white man's right to political power and property "vacated" by the Indians. Whether Faulkner embraces the Indians in the tragically ironic "father figure role" of Sam Fathers or rejects them as comically orientalized characters of the likes of Mokketubbe and Doom, he creates them to probe concepts of regional and national inheritance. In either case, his Indians serve to negotiate the boundaries of American culture and the processes of inclusion and exclusion needed to maintain those boundaries and police their limits.

Conclusion

Written during the period between the two world wars, Faulkner's Indian narratives seem to justify American national history even as they question it. Taken together, these narratives form a showcase for the way in which American systems of cultural description are deeply informed by national strategies of power. What Said says about scholars is also true about writers: "there is in each scholar some awareness, partly conscious and partly non-conscious, of national tradition, if not national ideology" (*Orientalism* 263).[1] If that is so, we could ascribe the political currents that run through Faulkner's texts to the cultural traditions and the national ambience of the 1930s and 1940s, more specifically perhaps to Faulkner's modernism. The oriental hues in Faulkner's Indian stories and the resuscitation of a rhetoric of extinction in his 1942 novel are both part of a modernist aesthetic and a southern paternalism that grants control of the land and mastery of the cultural heritage to the white southern male. Faulkner's thematic concern with cultural assimilation and transmission as well as his language of orientalism and pastoralism produce national discourses of power that give rise to the narratives' cultural overdetermination and heterogeneity. The closure of the plot in any of Faulkner's Indian narratives does not reduce the contradictory energies the reader experiences; it does not ease the ideological tension or the sense of *Unbehagen*. Hidden behind the lighthearted tone and the comic mode of narration, Faulkner's Indian stories are plagued by questions of national guilt and haunted by American colonization even as they endorse the mythology of the West and American nationalism.

In style and spirit, Faulkner's approach to Native American history resembles Eudora Welty's playful celebration of historical pastiche in *The Robber Bridegroom*. Like Welty, Faulkner presents the Native American signifier in an utterly self-conscious production that has more to do with a postmodernist performance than with historical "reality." Preferring mimicry to mimesis, Faulkner rejects traditional realism and approaches the Indian foundations of Yoknapatawpha with a solid dose of self-conscious irreverence. But as we have seen, under the pressure of political and personal events, this irreverent mood changes to a more traditional modernist nostalgia in *Go Down, Moses*. By emphasizing the moral implications of the history of Native American dispossession and the enslavement of blacks, Faulkner shares with other writers of the period, including Lytle and Gordon, a sense of shame and guilt over past and present acts of racial injustice. Thadious Davis argues that Faulkner's change in mood may have stemmed from his personal grief over the death of Caroline Barr, to whom his novel is dedicated; she suggests that as a white southern man, Faulkner felt guilty over the treatment of the black servant woman in the southern household (5). But Faulkner's anxiety over racial injustices may also have had an international cause in the politics of racial genocide and fascism threatening from abroad. These national and international offenses to racial justice may have altered not only Faulkner's awareness of the contemporary situation of southern segregation and national apartheid as America was on the brink of entering World War II to fight for freedom abroad, but also his awareness of a national heritage of dispossession on which America was founded. These sentiments of guilt infuse his text to create the elegiac tone that Faulkner shares with Andrew Lytle. Both authors deplore the abuses Native Americans suffered as a result of cultural conquest and exploitation, and in the process they romanticize the Indian figure as a venue for regionalist and nationalist identification. Like Caroline Gordon, Faulkner seeks to capture this nationalist identification in the controversial discourses of "blood" and genealogy, and in imaginary kinship relations with Indians.

Together, Faulkner's Indian narratives mirror the continuing political ambivalence toward Native Americans. In a gesture of mimicry and mournfulness, they ironically echo the problems caused by Euro-American intrusion into Indian territories, the "civilizing missions" of the U.S. government with its policy of forced cultural assimilation, and the land treaties and negotiations between the U.S. government and the Indian nations. In reflecting on these geographical and political transgressions, Faulkner substitutes fantasy for anthropology in narratives that are themselves deeply entrenched in the climate and language of Western colonialism. The mythology he invents in his Indian stories participates in a historical discourse that reflects national interests, a discourse that keeps haunting American writers, scholars, and politicians. Lewis Dabney argues that because Faulkner realized that Native Americans were the "first dispossessed and ravaged people of the South," he was haunted by their ghosts (21). Faulkner said in 1957: "I think the ghost of that ravishment lingers in the land, that the land is inimical to the white man because of the unjust way in which it was taken from Ikkemotubbe and his people" (Gwynn and Blotner 43). Faulkner's admission of guilt typifies the shameful and traumatic origins of the nation. "For is it not well said that the graves of a man's fathers are never quiet in his absence?" asks the secretary of state in "Lo!" (398). Built on the graves of

Native Americans, the United States is a nation haunted by these ghosts, a nation whose conscience is never quiet in the absence of its fathers.

On June 22, 2000, President Bill Clinton again raised this ghost by citing America's failed treaty obligations at an Indian town hall meeting in Phoenix, Arizona. He admitted that "the relationship between our national government and the Native American tribes, in my judgment, has never really been as it should have been, and certainly has never been consistent with the promises we made in return for all the land and minerals and other things that we took so long ago" (Norrell A1, A3). Guilt, according to Freud, is the most important problem in the development of civilization, and the white southern writers' reconstruction of the Indian past with all its displacements, ironies, and mimicries functions as a mirror of a national unconscious plagued to this day by its "Indian policies." The excavation of the Native American past in the South between the two world wars brings to the surface not only such a sense of guilt but also an anxiety about regional and national identity. In the South, the Indian civilizations that apparently "vanished" warn of the possibility of southern culture's own disappearance into the hegemonic national culture or a homogenized global culture. By offering a strategy for nativist and regionalist identification, the Native American signifier tells a story of cultural and political colonization that struck a chord with southern writers of the 1930s. At the height of their regionalist self-articulation, these writers not only struggled with narratives of cultural conquest but also embraced the regional essence and the historical depth that they felt this signifier could offer to narratives about the South. But as they were digging deep into the past to trace the Native American history of their region, they discovered a history deeply entwined with national policy and international politics. Writing about Indians meant always also writing about national ideology; it meant coming to terms with anxieties about the fragility not only of an imagined white southern identity but of an American national identity.

Notes

Introduction

1. See Dippie, Maddox, and Bergland for discussions of the impact of the Indian Removal Act on public debates and literary representations of Native Americans as "vanishing" or "extinct."

2. For TVA archaeology see Lyon 37–50.

3. The issue of language and terminology is particularly important for Native American critics and can be found in the writings of Vine Deloria, Philip Deloria, Craig Womack, Jace Weaver, Louis Owens, and many others who argue that the appellation "Indian" is a problematic Euro-American imposition that silences native voices and invents their existence in accordance with the power structure of the hegemonic settler culture.

4. The most important ones are by Lewis Dabney, whose 1974 study *The Indians of Yoknapatawpha* laid the groundwork for a serious consideration of this topic, and more recently by Don Doyle's *Faulkner's County* and Gene Moore's special issue "Faulkner's Indians" in the *Faulkner Journal* (Fall 2002/Spring 2003).

Chapter 1

1. Helen Carr sums up the cultural climate when she writes that "by the early twentieth century, the modern world had become the place of fragmentation, root-

lessness and dissolution: Indian culture is the place of wholeness, both of the psyche and of Nature. This view is still very much with us" (203).

2. Walter Benn Michaels characterizes the 1920s as a decade marked by a "rhetoric of racial extinction" (30) and by a cultural redefinition that is grounded in two legislative acts: the Johnson Act (1924), which was designed to restrict European immigration according to national origin, and the Indian Citizenship Act (1924), which sought to include into the concept of American national identity formerly excluded "native" populations.

3. Renee Bergland argues that American literature is haunted by spectralized Indians who express doubts about American national ideology. Her study concentrates on the New England area prior to the twentieth century.

4. William Alexander concurs: "A sense of nationalism underlay both attacks on and defenses of individualistic capitalism. Nationalism found expression in both national and regional planning movements, and in both the glorification of national tradition and the rejection of tradition" (23).

5. The term "usable past" was coined by Van Wyck Brooks in 1938 in search of cultural and historical roots for American writers. In his slender volume *On Literature Today* (1941), Brooks laments that the absence of deep roots such as those of "men of older countries" causes Americans to live on the surface (23).

6. Beidler and Egge's *Native Americans in the Saturday Evening Post* is a great bibliographic resource for popular perceptions of Indians in artwork, illustration, fiction, and nonfiction.

7. Before the relief programs of the New Deal, southeastern archaeology was developing very slowly because many southern universities were unable to support archaeological and anthropological research, which was then mostly supported by northern museums such as the Smithsonian Institution, the Peabody Museum, and the American Museum of Natural History, in addition to some support from amateurs. See Lyon 6.

8. Gordon may have also been familiar with William D. Funkhouser and William S. Webb's *Ancient Life in Kentucky* (1928). Webb was a professor at the University of Kentucky who, in partnership with Funkhouser, revolutionized the study of Kentucky prehistory. Webb and Funkhouser worked at a time during the pre-New Deal era when archaeology was still in an "undeveloped state" (Lyon 23). Written for a general audience, their book may have been particularly important to the work of Caroline Gordon.

9. See Scott Romine's discussion of the role of place in southern literature in "Where Is Southern Literature?" (36). Romine predicts that "almost certainly, place as a marker of southern literary identity cannot continue under the aegis of verisimilitude and mimesis, although this is not certainly to pronounce a postmortem" (41). See also Barbara Ladd's suggestion for reading place as a "site of cultural dynamism" that helps access cultural memory outside its traditional boundaries of region and nation. "Places, like memories, are always in transition, always redefined, resituated, by experience over time" ("Dismantling the Monolith" 56).

10. See Suzanne Jones and Sharon Monteith's introduction to *South to a New Place.* Suggesting that "Southern place-ness" has obsessed those both inside and outside the South (6), they present critical approaches that seek to break open the boundaries drawn around the traditional South and instead propose new ways of remapping its geography. See also Robert Brinkmeyer's *Remapping Southern Literature* (2000) and Deborah Cohn's study of Faulkner and Latin American writers. For a discussion of the continuing dichotomy between South and North see Richard Gray's foreword to *South to a New Place.*

11. This "relocation" of the field of southern studies and the desire for theoretical and cultural remappings was also expressed in the December 2003 meeting of the Society for the Study of Southern Literature, held in Puerto Vallarta, Mexico, at which scholars discussed the U.S. South and its relation to postcolonialism and New World studies.

12. Edward Said's work, which marks the beginning of the postcolonial enterprise, is continued in the U.S. context by scholars such as Mary Louise Pratt, Anne McClintock, Peter Hulme, Francis Barker, Margaret Iversen, Renato Rosaldo, Benita Parry, and Gayatri Spivak, among others.

13. Broadly speaking, the term "colonial discourse" implies two distinct ideas: "firstly, it directs attention towards the interrelatedness of a whole variety of texts and practices that were conventionally seen as belonging to their 'own' disciplinary realms, and then, secondly, it politicises that network by implicating it with the power relations of colonial hegemony" (Barker, Hulme, and Iverson, *Colonial Discourse* 2).

14. According to *Key Concepts in Post-Colonial Studies,* by Ashcroft, Griffiths, and Tiffin, a *palimpsest* is "a process in language: the naming by which imperial discourse brings the colonized space 'into being,' the subsequent rewritings and overwritings, the imaging of the place in the consciousness of its occupants, all of which constitute the contemporary place observed by the subject" (175).

15. Craig Womack argues that "even postcolonial approaches, with so much emphasis on how the settler culture views the other, largely miss an incredibly important point: how do Indians view Indians?" (13). He proceeds to mount an argument for a Native American literary separatism. Although I question his proposal of a more authentic insider's perspective, I share his conviction that "outsiders" to native culture, in this case white southerners, have often been the ones to shape historical reality and misinterpret "things Indian" (7).

Chapter 2

1. With the exception of Swanton from the Smithsonian, the members of the commission came from southern states (Alabama, Arkansas, Florida, Louisiana, Mississippi, and Tennessee). For a discussion of the commemorative activities of the de Soto expedition, see Patricia Galloway's "Commemorative History and Hernando de Soto."

2. For detailed discussions of de Soto's historic route through Florida, see Galloway, *The Hernando de Soto Expedition;* Charles Hudson, "The Historical Significance of the de Soto Route"; and Jay K. Johnson, "From Chiefdom to Tribe in Northeast Mississippi."

3. In "The Historical Significance of the de Soto Route," Hudson writes that the work of the de Soto commission in postulating the location of Native American towns remained authoritative into the late 1970s.

4. In January 1938, Lytle wrote to Laurance Chambers, his editor at Bobbs-Merrill, that although he was still puzzling over "unresolved problems," he had a clear idea of the concepts and themes governing the novel: "First it is gold and Spain's lust for it. Later it will be another sort of exploitation. But for the first book it must be gold" (Polk 453). He also understood at this time that *Alchemy,* the "first book," would be a separate work, "a sort of introductory novel" that "will stand by itself" (453).

5. Helen Carr explains that it was out of a general sense of the malaise of modernity that "modernists in America, as elsewhere, drew on 'primitive' art as a critique of bourgeois philistine modernity. Native Americans were now seen not as an 'immature race' but as inheritors of ancient wisdom. Primitivism was reborn" (200).

6. Lytle was not alone in reading native rhetoric as polluted by years of forced assimilation. Helen Carr points out that Mary Austin also felt that the best of native expression was lost through assimilation (3).

7. See Carr for an extensive discussion of the role of Boasian anthropology in changing the scientific understanding of Native Americans and other "primitive" peoples (229–37).

8. In his introduction to *The Indian in Latin American History,* John Kicza estimates that "some tens of millions of peoples organized into distinct polities and ethnic groups had already lived in this vast region for thousands of years before Europeans reached the hemisphere" (xiii).

9. Published only two years after the Inca conquest, Francisco de Jerez's report is the first historical document about the conquest. Subsequent versions were published by native authors such as Titu Cusi Yupanqui (1570), Guaman Poma de Ayala (1615), and Garcilaso de la Vega (1617). Each document takes a different rhetorical stance toward the encounter. See Hemming and Seed.

10. Keen (168) highlights the neo-romantic studies of Robert Redfield, *Tepozlan* (1930); George Valliant, *Aztecs of Mexico* (1944); and Philip A. Means, *Ancient Civilizations of the Andes* (1931). All of these accounts romanticize the harmony of pre-capitalist native communities.

11. Lytle might have read Frank Shay's 1932 biography of Pizarro, *Incredible Pizarro: Conqueror of Peru,* Hyatt Verrill's 1929 *Great Conquerors of South and Central America,* and F. A. Kirkpatrick's 1934 *The Spanish Conquistadores.*

12. Keen writes that "only recently has the legend of Inca 'socialism' been dis-

pelled, and it may still linger in some minds" (156). In my own research I found the Incan empire described as "socialist" as recently as Jean Descola's 1957 history *The Conquistadores,* perhaps reflecting the cold war climate.

13. Alchemy operates like the concept of invention, which according to Derrida signifies two essential linguistic values: "the constative—discovering or unveiling, pointing out or saying what is—and the performative—producing, instituting, transforming" (qtd. in Kamuf 206).

14. Abdul JanMohamed usefully distinguishes between the covert and overt aspects of colonialism, arguing that "while the covert purpose is to exploit the colony's natural resources thoroughly and ruthlessly through the various imperialist material practices, the overt aim, as articulated by colonialist discourse, is to 'civilize' the savage, to introduce him to all the benefits of Western cultures" (81). In *Alchemy,* Lytle reverses the covert and overt aims of such colonialist discourse by laying bare the profit motive and by questioning the role of Christianity in colonial conquests.

15. Some years after the conquest of the Incan empire, Pedro de Cieza de Leon wrote in 1550: "I am of the opinion . . . that there is no kingdom in the world more rich in precious ore, for every day great lodes are discovered both of gold and of silver" (qtd. in Starn 1).

16. Unlike Europeans, the Incas did not use gold as an exchange commodity.

17. John Murra documents European comments on the Incan art of weaving. He points out that comparisons between Incan and European cloth manufacture in the early days of the invasion were all unfavorable to European weaving skills. Pedro Pizarro, for example, notes that the Incas weave so smoothly that "no thread could be seen" (qtd. in Murra 57).

18. Patricia Seed explores this encounter in the historical narratives and shows that how the meeting is depicted depends on the ideological slant of the historian. Native historians and early Spanish eyewitnesses quite predictably differ in their readings of the encounter.

19. According to Seed, Francisco de Jerez seems disturbed that Atahuallpa refused to be awed by European accomplishments, a refusal Jerez attributes to the Indian's overweening pride and disrespect. By contrast, Titu Cusi, who writes from a native perspective, thinks that Atahuallpa's gesture of dropping the book is a sign of disrespect for the Europeans provoked by earlier acts of Spanish disrespect for Indian culture and customs.

20. Instead of a writing system, the Incas had developed a sophisticated tallying system with knots by which they kept track of accounts and debts. Tzvetan Todorov explains that "the three great Amerindian civilizations encountered by the Spaniards are not located on precisely the same level of evolution of writing. The Incas are the most unfamiliar with writing (they possess a mnemotechnical use of braided cords, moreover one that is highly elaborated); the Aztecs have pictograms; among Mayas we find certain rudiments of phonetic writing" (80).

21. Peter Mason comments on early European constructions of the native body.

He shows how sexual and economic arguments in colonial narratives, including Columbus's, become complicit with justifications for colonial rule.

22. Commenting on the allegorical meanings of East and West, Lytle writes that "as a term for our society the West is too geographical; it is to the secular society of our day a submerged half-truth, for the symbolic meaning of the West is death, the grave, the night sea journey; and in spite of the blatant political public assertion that the West is power, underneath we feel the threat of its eternal mythological meaning. And this makes for fearful speculation in so far as it is separated from its completing symbol, the East, which promises renewal of life and light" (*Hero* 22).

23. De Soto died of a fever in 1542 and was buried in the famous river—the Mississippi—that he "discovered."

24. Stephen Slemons argues that cannibalism functions textually in two ways: as metaphor in order to set into motion a dialectic between self and other, and as metonymy in order to subsume the colonized into a "tropics of the body" (169).

25. Slemons suggests that the trope of cannibalism in postcolonial writing is often operated by strategies of reversal, overdetermination, and fragmentation so that the textual meaning of cannibalism appears multiple, deferred, and refracted into different determinations.

26. According to Jerald Milanich, the plundering of native food resources began not very far from the coastal base camp in present-day Tampa, where, as in most of the American Southeast, native peoples were largely corn agriculturalists. De Soto's plan to winter the army in Ocale—a larger town some miles inland—during the first year failed because there was not enough food there for the entire regiment even for just a few days, forcing some foot soldiers to forage for edible roots to sustain themselves (Milanich 131).

27. Such an individual, Kilgour writes, is "free from dependence upon others or relations other than those he chooses to enter into in his own self-interest. A society made up of such individuals must therefore be based on market relations, regulated by laws that attempt to determine and preserve the right to private property" (144).

28. This is Richard Gray's characterization of Lytle's fiction. Gray reads *At the Moon's Inn* and *Alchemy* as "arguments for agrarian simplicity" dramatizing the conflict between "the capitalist and the agrarian" (*Aberrations* 135).

Chapter 3

1. Under the influences of archaeological discovery work in the South, Andrew Lytle was writing his conquest narratives while Caroline Gordon, his close friend, was at work on narratives about the Indian frontier in Kentucky. During the late 1930s, Gordon and Lytle often visited each other and spent extended time at Lytle's mountain cabin in Monteagle, Tennessee, where the Tates and Lytles were enjoying their remote writers' retreat. Gordon and Lytle shared a vocation as novel-

ists, and they often discussed their craft. In 1941, when Gordon had just finished her novel *Green Centuries* and Lytle was in the last stages of *At the Moon's Inn,* they discussed the impact and meaning of Euro-American imperialism on Native American life.

2. Funkhouser and Webb who provided an accessible survey of prehistoric Kentucky in their 1928 study *Ancient Life in Kentucky.* Complete with photographs and detailed descriptions of various archaeological sites, this book serves as a solid foundation and as a guide through the Native American past—both historic and prehistoric.

3. Anne Goodwyn Jones, Carol S. Manning, and Patricia Yaeger are among those pioneering critics who have effectively challenged this paradigm.

4. I agree with Nancylee Jonza that "this is unfortunate. Gordon's marriage may have been a large portion of and controlling influence on her life, but Gordon lived more years of her life without Tate than she did with him" (x).

5. Gordon claimed, for example, that Tate "practically wrote the last chapter" of *Green Centuries* (qtd. in Jonza 208).

6. In her biography, Veronica Makowsky includes several episodes that show Gordon's irritation and hurt pride as a result of being referred to as the poet genius's wife. For example, in September 1928, when Tate and Gordon sailed to England—Tate surrounded by props signaling his intellectual status such as "his grandfather's gold-headed cane and two volumes of *The Rise and Fall of the Confederacy* and Gordon with Nancy on one hand and a toy on the other—a member of a traveling group of Rhodes Scholars "had the effrontery to refer to me as the wife," Gordon complained (77). In 1939, when Gordon and Tate lived at Princeton, where he had accepted a prestigious teaching position, Gordon was "soon to be demoted to the rank of faculty wife; similarly her reputation would decline while Allen's skyrocketed during the 1940s" (152).

7. Sensing Gordon's preference for "male forms of heroism," early critics like William J. Stuckey characterized the protagonists of her narratives as the sportsman, the soldier, the agrarian, and the pioneer.

8. I caution readers of a sort of ideological backlash: what is often considered Gordon's political conservatism keeps circulating within and haunting even the most recent criticism. When Gordon's style gets cited as a "masculine style" and her subject matter as "violent stories about such 'manly' subjects as war and life on the American frontier" (Boyle 46), we need to question our own constructions of gender. What should women write about? Is there a proper female subject? Was is a "masculine style"? Gordon's frontier subjects can hardly be taken as evidence for her desire to be a masculinist writer; on the contrary, Gordon meticulously deconstructs the workings of gender and the definitions of masculinity and femininity. At stake in understanding her politics is not the choice of her subject but rather how she uses it.

9. Gordon's fascination with America's colonial frontier, I suggest, was not in-

spired by Allen Tate, as Makowsky claims, but by the history of her own family, particularly the connection with Meriwether Lewis, with whom she identified.

10. William Elsey Connelley, who has written the most complete account of the Wiley captivity, says that most historians agree on two possible dates: 1789 and 1787. The first date is supported by Walter Crockett, County Lieutenant of Montgomery County, who is said to have reported the captivity. The second is given by Jennie Wiley's son, Adam P. Wiley, on whose account Connelley bases his history. Among fifteen different authorities who were consulted concerning the exact date of the Wiley captivity, seven point to 1787, six to 1789, one to 1788, and one to 1790.

11. In the historical sources the spelling of Wiley's first name appears as either "Jennie" or Jenny." Her given name was Jean. Hazelett points out that more historical evidence supports "Jennie," and this is also how the name appears in the Connelley document. The state park established in her honor in 1958 is called the Jenny Wiley State Park, however. Gordon cleverly avoids the controversy about her name by turning it into "Jinny," a spelling that echoes the dialect of the region and clearly indicates the fictionalization of the historical person.

12. Gordon planned a sequence of stories about early Tennessee but was discouraged from doing so by her editor, Maxwell Perkins, who thought it would be difficult to sell a short-story collection. Perkins also rejected the first version of "The Captive," feeling that it was too much like a historical chronicle and that the main character lacked "psychological depth." After his rejection, *Hound and Horn* published the story in their final issue of 1932. See Makowsky (107) for a brief discussion of the publication history of "The Captive."

13. Connelley, a historian, was particularly interested in Kentucky's pioneer life. He was the president of the Kansas Historical Society in 1912 and the president of the Mississippi Valley Historical Association in 1921 and 1922. See Edward Hazelett's introduction to Connelley's life and career preceding the Connelley reprint.

14. The size of the Cherokee population at the end of the eighteenth century, at the time of the story's setting, was already much diminished by numerous smallpox epidemics and wars, particularly the war of 1776. Russell Thornton estimates their numbers at this time as no more than 16,000 (*American Indian Holocaust* 43). A 1930 census counted 45,238 Cherokees and shows that "of the total Cherokee population, there were 40,904 Cherokees in Oklahoma and 1,963 in North Carolina; the rest were in 43 other states, particularly Alabama, Virginia, and California" (Thornton, *The Cherokees* 129).

15. Neither Connelley nor other sources on Tennessee or Cherokee history that I have consulted mention a Cherokee chief named Mad Dog. I believe Gordon invented the name.

16. In the late eighteenth century, mixed bands of Indians such as the Shawnee/Cherokee group mentioned in the narrative were common. Under the stress of Euro-American warfare, many smaller tribes such as the Shawnees were increasingly conscious of the need for Indian unity. Tecumseh, who died for the goal of a united

front against white settlers, is a famous example of a Shawnee leader who envisioned the establishment of an intertribal confederacy.

17. Examining the construction of racialized subjectivity from a psychoanalytic perspective in the colonial context, Seshadri-Crooks links theories of sexual identification with racial anxieties.

18. By inventing Jinny's "light eyes," Gordon differed from the historical record. Connelley writes: "Her son informed me that she had black hair through which ran a tinge of auburn in her youth. Others say her hair was coal black. . . . Her eyes were black" (67).

19. In his preface to Connelley's history, Edward Hazelett writes, "the Scotch-Irish have been called the true pioneers of the early frontier. At the beginning of the American Revolution they were more numerous and far more important than all other nationality groups in the back settlements" (29). Connelley also emphasizes the Scotch-Irish genealogy of Jennie Wiley's father, Hezekiah Sellards (60).

20. Foucault reminds us that blood is traditionally "*a reality with a symbolic function*" (*History* 147).

21. Although Foucault locates the transition between two different regimes of power structured around blood and sex mostly in the nineteenth century—that is, much later than the American colonial context of Gordon's story—he also says that the "symbolics of blood" and the "analytics of sex" did not come about "without overlappings, interactions, and echoes" (*History* 149).

22. Hale summarizes the Supreme Court's justification for the ruling against Homer Plessy, a light-skinned black man who challenged segregated seating on Louisiana streetcars in 1896, as follows: "The law, the Court decided, could only reflect the sense of racial difference that was a part of human nature itself. Plessy could not be both black and white. He could follow law and custom, the 'one drop rule,' and despite his predominantly white ancestry choose 'For Colored.' Or, in an option the Court in no way promoted, he could deny his African-American heritage and by 'passing' choose 'For White'" (23).

23. Christopher Castiglia writes that "dominant narratives of manifest destiny, from the colonial era through the present day, have relied for dramatic tension on the threatened sexualization of white women by men of color who possess uncontrollable, violent, and animalistic lusts. The persistent belief in the sexual 'tainting' of white women through captivity, which exposes the captive to men of color, is revealed in the etymology of 'rape,' the root of which is the Latin verb, rapere, to seize, to capture, or to carry away" (123).

24. The Mound Builder period refers to the time of the Woodland Indians, who used the mounds as religious and ceremonial sites. This period dates to about 1000 B.C..

25. Castiglia argues that the fictional captivity narrative in particular provides new possibilities for women to express their resistance to domesticity and to imagine positive and empowering ways of self-representation.

26. Carl S. Smith points out that American writers often explore human values in conflict with legal prescriptions, most famously perhaps in case of Natty Bumppo and Huck Finn: "it is the lawless Natty Bumppo in Cooper's *The Pioneers* who has to lecture Judge Temple on what travesties have been committed in the name of law" (C. S. Smith et al. 32).

27. See, for example, David Hume's essay "Of National Characters" in *Essays Moral and Political* (1742), Immanuel Kant's *Observations on the Feeling of the Beautiful and the Sublime* (1764), and Thomas Jefferson's *Notes on the State of Virginia* (1787).

28. Reminding us "that slavery is an instance of the fundamental violence of colonialism" because it is "the conscious effort to take from others their very means of survival" (*Literary Culture* 53), Rowe urges us to consider "the similarities between the Southern colonization of Africans and the more general U.S. efforts to colonize the frontier by subjugating its native peoples" (54).

29. In the Holston area, in which Gordon's novel is set, the settlers did not buy the land from the Cherokees directly but rather "leased" the land for eight years in order to avoid violating the 1763 Proclamation by the King, which prohibited private purchases in British colonies. But despite this prohibition, some settlers—like Judge Richard Henderson, a lawyer from North Carolina who makes his appearance in Gordon's novel—had their own schemes for western colonization. Henderson employed Daniel Boone and others to scout out Kentucky lands and organized his own land company (Wallace 43).

30. Gordon consulted John P. Brown's 1938 book *Old Frontiers* as a source of information on Cherokee history. See acknowledgments to *Green Centuries.*

31. Perdue confirms Gordon's historical facts: "Nancy Ward achieved the title of War Woman in the 1750s when she seized her slain husband's gun and joined the battle against the Creeks. . . . [F]ew Cherokee women, however, played so central a role in military actions or strategy" (*Cherokee Women* 87).

32. In *Going Native,* Shari Hundorf writes that "over the last century, going native has become a cherished American tradition, an important even necessary means of defining European-American identities and histories. In its various forms, going native articulates and attempts to resolve widespread ambivalence about modernity as well as anxieties about the terrible violence marking the nation's origins" (2).

33. Ricardo Quinones, who examines variants of the Cain and Able myth, writes: "the fraternal context of the Cain-Abel story means that division becomes more emotionally vibrant as the tragedy of differentiation. Such differentiation is painfully realized at the moment of the offering, when one brother has his essential nature endorsed over that of the other brother" (9).

34. Shari Huhndorf links the cultural preoccupation with "going native" in the literature of the twentieth century to a crisis of modernity: in addition to "defining and regenerating racial whiteness and a racially inflected vision of Americanness," going native exhibits a "profound ambivalence about America's past as well as about modernity" (5).

Chapter 4

1. See Welty's correspondence with her agent Diarmuid Russell in Michael Kreyling's *Author and Agent,* which also includes a publication history of each of the stories in *The Wide Net.*

2. Welty speaks about her work for the WPA in an interview with Bill Ferris in Prenshaw's *Conversations with Eudora Welty* (155).

3. Chester E. Eisinger discusses Welty's work as situated between the "traditional novel" and the modernist novel. But in characterizing Welty's affinity for modernism, he groups under the rubric "modernist" many characteristics that are even more pronounced in the work of postmodernists, such as nonlinear concepts of time and space, reality as illusion, uncertainties concerning identity, and the critique of ontology (4).

4. These historical characters include, for example, Lorenzo Dow, a Methodist minister; James Murrell, the infamous bandit; John James Audubon, the well-known ornithologist and painter from "A Still Moment" (1942); and Mike Fink from *The Robber Bridegroom* (1942).

5. See Philip Deloria's *Playing Indian.*

6. Robert Penn Warren, in a perceptive review of *The Wide Net,* remarks that the opening sentence begins "as though the author cannot be quite sure what did happen, cannot quite undertake to resolve the meaning of the recorded event, cannot, in fact, be too sure of recording all of the event" (43). This "coyness" is more than the warning Warren takes it to be; it is a calculated effect that is thematically related to the meaning of the story. Granted, it is difficult to distinguish conscious from unconscious effects in literature; but Welty's narrative framework, her choice of subject matter, and her creation of Joel as a filtering consciousness to mediate historical "truth" strongly point toward her intention to question history.

7. Derrida sees the trace as taking shape particularly in the works of Nietzsche and Freud. The deconstruction of presence that Derrida discovers in their work "accomplishes itself through the deconstruction of consciousness, and therefore through the irreducible notion of the trace (Spur)" (Kamuf 42).

8. Suzanne Marrs argues that the only way Joel can move forward is by confronting his past. In this sense, Welty's story is a comment on the power of memory, and her choice of Liberty Road as a final setting is "an emblem of Joel's development and an ironic comment on Burr's" (77).

9. Lewis and Clark were scouting out new territories, apparently trying to gain favors with Indian tribes who were enlisted in the war against Spain. The Spanish clearly recognized the ulterior purpose of the expedition, which was ostensibly about the discovery of new territories but really designed to estrange the Indians from alliances with the Spanish. See McCaleb 12.

10. Settlers did not always wait for official decisions about new territories from Washington. For example, two frontier men, Nathan and Samuel Kemper, and about thirty followers marched on Baton Rouge in June 1804 with the intention of over-

throwing the Spanish regime. The revolt was quickly crushed, and the insurgents were forced to seek refuge in Mississippi Territory (DeConde 220).

11. Parmet and Hecht provide a good historical account of the flotilla incident. The purpose of this flotilla was apparently as unclear as Burr's plans. It is reported to have comprised "sixteen oars, eight flatboats, and six keels" (269). Apparently, no women and children were on the boats, which, according to eyewitnesses, seemed to have been loaded with boxes of muskets.

12. Parmet and Hecht write that Burr was disguised "as a riverboat man in an old blanket coat with a leather strap across from it which dangled a tin cup and a scalping knife. A broken down white hat almost completely obscuring his face, completed his attire" (282). Victor Thompson, who cites J. F. H. Claibourne's book as a historical source for Welty's image, believes that Burr was disguised as an Indian. Claibourne writes: "I cannot describe his dress; but from the description I have heard of it, it appeared to me to be that of an Indian country man carricatured [*sic*]" (qtd. in Thompson, "Burr" 80).

13. Kreyling argues that Welty was searching for a new narrative form that abandons chronological plot when she was writing *Delta Wedding* (1946). In this novel, Welty "fragments the monolithic obligation to form and content, and distributes it spatially among several characters, embedding it in an essentially modernist symbolic narrative" ("Welty as Novelist" 16). But Welty was already experimenting with breaking the logic of a particular narrative form—fairy tale, history, novel—in *The Robber Bridegroom,* which prepares us for those experiments in fragmentation that would later become important in *Delta Wedding* and for the essentially parodic voice that dominates *Ponder Heart.*

14. See also Kreyling's more extensive discussion of the early reviews in "Clement and the Indians" (25–27).

15. Marylin Arnold was the first to suggest that Welty creates a parody of the fairy tale to mock the limitations of its narrative form and its system of morality.

16. Mississippi Territory, which comprises the present states of Mississippi and Alabama, was formed in 1789. A historian writing for the newly formed *Journal of Mississippi History* argued in 1939 that "Nowhere in the country was there a more interesting region than the old Natchez district. . . . Soon to become rich and powerful, on the crest of a great cotton boom and the rise of the river trade, it took a prominent place in human and economic growth of the lower Mississippi Valley" (Hamilton 29).

17. See also Brian Dippie's discussion of the "anatomy of the vanishing American" in chapter 2 of *The Vanishing American* (12–31).

18. See Kilpatrick's discussion of cinematic language of movies from the 1930s and 1940s (37).

19. Kreyling believes that Welty's violation scene is a "departure from the fantasy of the fairy tale" ("Clement" 36), but the original Grimms tale actually depicts the robbers as cannibals who, after cutting up the body of the young girl, "strewed

salt thereon," as Welty tells us (*Eye* 307). In other words, the violence and violation in this scene are precisely part of the fantasy of the fairy tale.

20. When Salome wants "the mansion with the columns," Clement comments, "My poor wife, you are ahead of yourself" (100). Welty explains the joke: "(The reason she is ahead of herself, as you will know, is that she's describing Windsor Castle, out from Port Gibson, which did not get built until 1861)" (*Eye* 305). What counts as history (dates, facts, material evidence) assumes parenthetical status in the narrative. Welty skews chronology as she presents Clement's tale of the pioneer track from Virginia to the Old Southwest, and from the plantation economy based on slavery to the rise of urban mercantilism.

21. I question Warren French's assessment of the Indians as lacking this doubleness: "The Indians in this tale are even more clearly doomed, for they do not, like the white characters, have two faces; and this lack of doubleness works to their disadvantage" (185). The discourses of doom and civilization are precisely narratives that Welty's narrative parodies.

Chapter 5

1. For a discussion of the word *Yoknapatawpha* see Doyle, who sums up local lore on its meaning as well as translations from Chickasaw and Choctaw dictionaries. Doyle believes that the implications of the meaning of *Yoknapatawpha* as splitting or ripping the soil open, a meaning to which modern translations point, indicate Faulkner's ominous foreshadowing of Native American dispossession by a cotton economy (25). See also Dabney, who traces Yoknapatawpha to Faulkner's manuscripts of "Red Leaves," where the name is associated with the old name for the Yocona River (24).

2. In *The Southeastern Indians* Charles Hudson notes that some of the mounds date back as far as the Archaic tradition, but more typically most of the mounds date from the Woodland and Mississippian periods (44).

3. Mounds built during the Woodland period (1000 B.C.) are often taken as evidence for the increasing importance of agriculture among Native Americans and for leisure necessary to their construction (Hudson, *Southeastern Indians* 63). Mounds of the Mississippian period (between 700 and 900 A.D.) can be distinguished by their flat-topped pyramidal shape, onto which temples and other important buildings were built.

4. Parker sees the act of buying Rowan Oak as closely connected with Faulkner's awareness of the dispossession of the Chickasaws, since the house was built in 1844 on land bought from a Chickasaw named E-Ah-Nah-Yea.

5. In *Faulkner's County,* Don Doyle traces in detail the history of Lafayette County and suggests the historical sources and events for Faulkner's fiction. Using history to illuminate Faulkner's fictional world, Doyle suggests many correspondences between history and fiction.

6. Gene Moore dates the events in "A Justice" to the 1820s and those in "Red Leaves" to between 1833 and 1859, but the internal chronology of the stories is not very consistent ("Chronological Problems" 53–54).

7. In the light of the United States' continuing struggle with "Indian affairs," the question of Faulkner's knowledge of Native Americans cannot be brushed away, because together Faulkner's Indian stories are the product of particular forms of knowledge (factual or mythical), and the stories in turn produce specific kinds of ideologies and power relations. The precise extent of Faulkner's knowledge about southern history before the Civil War and what Faulkner did read about Native American tribes of the Southeast remains largely a matter of conjecture. Was he familiar with Angie Debo's 1934 book *The Rise and Fall of the Choctaw Republic*? Was he influenced by the chapter "Archeology and Indians" in the *WPA Guide to the Magnolia State*? Was he inspired by Calvin Brown's 1926 book *Archeology of Mississippi*, a book Faulkner owned? These questions remain open and are, on the whole, much less interesting for me than the kind of "history" Faulkner in turn produced.

8. Native American activist Vine Deloria argues in *Custer Died for Your Sins* that "the American public feels most comfortable with the mythical Indians of stereotype-land who were always THERE. These Indians are fierce, they wear feathers and grunt." He goes on to explain that "most of us don't fit this idealized figure since we grunt only when overeating, which is seldom" (10).

9. Since I wrote this chapter, several other critics have also pointed out the role of mimicry in Faulkner's Indian stories. Bruce Johnson finds Bhabha's concept of mimicry particularly useful for a study of Faulkner's Indian narratives. Robert Dale Parker and Peter Mallios also use Bhabha's postcolonial vocabulary for their reinterpretations of Faulkner's Indian stories.

10. Charles Hudson writes that the large mounds and earthworks in the South are so impressive that the popular press in the nineteenth century believed they could not have been built by "lazy" Indians. Around the time of Indian removal, the most accepted belief was that the mounds had been built by a race of "Mound Builders" who may have emigrated from the civilized part of the world. "Why these Mound Builder theories became so popular is not entirely clear," Hudson writes, "but they obviously fulfilled some need in nineteenth-century American thought" (*Southeastern Indians* 35). He suggests that one reason for the popularity of this theory was that it could have been used as a "justification for the way Southeastern Indians were treated in the early decades of the nineteenth century. 'Removing' them and seizing their lands seemed less unjust when viewed against the story of their having done the same thing to the Mound Builders. The Mound Builder myth began to decline in the late nineteenth and early twentieth centuries, when scientific archaeology began" (35).

11. Freud's original title for his essay *Civilization and Its Discontents* (1930) was "Das Unglück in the Kultur." The word *Unglück* (unhappiness) was later altered to *Unbehagen*, for which it was difficult to find an English equivalent but which catches the feeling of malaise and unease much better.

12. Slavery among the Choctaws and Chickasaws starts with the introduction of cotton farming to native farming communities. James Taylor Carson writes that the first federal Choctaw agent disbursed cottonseed to his Choctaw neighbors in 1800 and that women took to the new crop quickly (79).

13. Regarding Faulkner's Indians who refuse to sweat, James Taylor Carson explains that Choctaw men did not consider field work, including cotton farming, as suitable or appropriate for them. Biracial men, however, were free from such rules (79). In order to avoid the stigma of male farming, prominent leaders bought slaves to do the work for them. "Not surprisingly, the growth of the cotton economy paralleled the spread of slavery in the nation" (80).

14. Faulkner's Indians change their opinion about their slaves during the story. In the early part of the narrative, Basket and Berry spew insults about their black slaves, whom they call "savages," compare to horses and dogs, and describe as "worse than white people" (*CS* 314). Toward the end, when they have captured the slave, they seem to develop respect for him and patiently wait until he is ready to die.

15. This quotation is from an interview conducted in Japan in 1955. Faulkner's attitude about the helplessness of "vanishing Indians" in the 1930s is not much different, however. In 1937, when Faulkner and his friend Ben Wasson returned from California, they passed a group of Indians in the Southwest and Faulkner supposedly said, "This [the land] was theirs. All of it. This whole country. We took it away from them and shoved them off onto reservations. . . . I reckon it's bad enough the way we treat the black folks. But they're like children and need looking after, expect to be looked after" (qtd. in Williamson 257).

16. Louis XV's (1715–74) failure to provide strong leadership contributed to the crisis that brought on the French Revolution. During his reign France was involved in three wars, and during the last of them, the Seven Years' War (1756–63), it lost most of its overseas possessions to the British.

17. On Jefferson's Indian politics see, for example, Reginald Horsman's *Expansion and American Indian Policy, 1783–1812* and Anthony F. C. Wallace's *Jefferson and the Indians.* Jefferson imagined carrying out American expansion with justice toward the Indians. He saw Native Americans as capable and deserving of civilization, and he viewed American expansion in terms of spreading a superior culture. In Jefferson's Enlightenment view, land acquisition and the spread of civilization were intertwined. When Jefferson realized that he could not hope "both to obtain the land he wanted and at the same time gain land only when the Indians were happy to offer it to the United States" (Horsman 107), he suggested that lands east of the Mississippi be exchanged for lands west of the Mississippi. As early as 1803, Jefferson wrote on several occasions of the idea that Indian removal would eliminate the friction between settlers and Indians, an idea that was turned into practice during Andrew Jackson's administration nearly thirty years later.

18. In his essay "Faulkner Rewriting the Indian Removal," Lothar Hönnighausen proposes that Faulkner, in inventing the "burlesque invasion of Washington by the Indians as a backlash to their Washington directed removal, rewrites a

tragic chapter of history as a burlesque comedy and transforms the victims into victors" (339).

19. The republished edition was titled *American Indian Poetry: The Standard Anthology of Songs and Chants.*

20. In the nineteenth century, the celebration of the "noble savage" of the New World and of the romanticized Arab world often went hand in hand in order to support colonial interests. The writing of Karl May is ample proof of both Indian fantasies and orientalism. See Weaver 21.

21. Robert Woods Sayre argues that Faulkner's Indians are "an integral part of his larger romantic pattern of meaning" (38). Faulkner identifies "original Indian culture with the wild" as indicated by the title of the section that includes his Indian stories in *Collected Stories*—"The Wilderness." Sayre reads Faulkner's Indians as an antithesis to modernity.

22. On this point see Parker, who argues that Faulkner's Indian stories reveal his concerns about white masculinity in the segregated South: "Faulkner's Indian stories flutter back and forth over figures of masculinity, ownership, and agency, conflating masculinity, white masculinity, and whiteness itself" (82).

23. Parker argues that in *Go Down Moses,* "Faulkner describes Indians mostly through the sentimentalizing filters of Sam Fathers and Isaac McCaslin, who squeeze the past into the romanticized patterns of boyhood dream objects, cultural nostalgia, and faux anthropological ritual" (85).

24. Peter Mallios, for example, prefers Faulkner's critical and subversive relationship with the stereotypes of the Indian figure in his stories, and he argues that these stories constitute "a kind of analytic safety valve" for his more canonical work (147).

25. Such a bonding between Indian and white men in friendly competition also operates in "A Courtship," published six years later, a story that closely matches the critical paradigm of Leslie Fiedler's *Love and Death in the American Novel.*

26. Parker points out that the Choctaw Reservation in Philadelphia was set up between 1918 and 1944, "overlapping the years when Faulkner thought up Yoknapatawpha, with its Indian name, and wrote his Indian stories" (87).

27. Faulkner establishes a clear ranking of Indians according to their Indian blood. Jobaker, the last full-blood Chickasaw to disappear from Faulkner's Yoknapatawpha landscape, vanishes back into the wilderness without leaving a trace. The other two Indians—Sam Fathers and Boon Hoggenbeck—are mixed-bloods. In contrast to Boon, who had a Chickasaw grandmother and a white father and whose "blood" had "run white since," allowing him to live as a "white man," Sam Fathers was "doomed" by his inheritance of black and Indian "blood."

28. Robert Sayre and Bruce Johnson argue that Sam's cultural transmission fails. Sayre argues that there is a two-step transmission process: in the first transmission Sam's Indian qualities "cease to be specifically Indian as they pass to Ike, and in the second they are betrayed, for in 'Delta Autumn' the receivers of the tradition are shown to be unworthy heirs" (46). Johnson argues that Sam's "internal

conflicts prevent him from adequately mentoring Ike" and that his initiation of Ike into adulthood ultimately fails (121).

29. In *Our America,* Walter Benn Michaels discusses the concurrent passing of the immigration act (the Johnson Act), which was designed to exclude southern and eastern Europeans from American citizenship, and the Indian Citizenship Act, which did just the opposite. The inclusion of Indians into national life sought to transform Native Americans into "Americans." See Michaels's chapter on "The Vanishing American."

30. In *They Died with Their Boots On,* which premiered on November 20, 1941, only seventeen days prior to America's entry into World War II, the railroad owners similarly are the villains (Aleiss 30).

31. See Thadius Davis's *Games of Property* for an extended discussion of the function of Faulkner's title in the African-American context (20–25).

Conclusion

1. Although Said speaks mostly of scholars in the field of orientalism here, he makes clear that all writers are embedded in their national and institutional circumstances. See *Orientalism* 263 and 271, for example.

Bibliography

Achebe, Chinua. *Things Fall Apart.* 1959. New York: Doubleday, 1994.

Adair, James. *The History of the American Indians.* Ed. Samuel Cole Williams. 1775. Johnson City, TN: Watauga Press, 1930.

Aleiss, Angela. "Prelude to World War II: Racial Unity and the Hollywood Indian." *Journal of American Culture* 18.2 (1995): 25–34.

Alexander, Charles C. *Nationalism in American Thought, 1930–1945.* Chicago: Rand McNally, 1969.

Allen, Paula Gunn. *The Sacred Hoop: Recovering the Feminine in American Indian Traditions.* Boston: Beacon P, 1992.

——, ed. *Studies in American Indian Literature.* New York: Modern Language Association of America, 1983.

Allen, Theodore W. *The Invention of the White Race.* London: Verso, 1994.

Anderson, Benedict. *Imagined Communities: Reflections on the Origin and Spread of Nationalism.* London: Verso, 1991.

Anderson, Eric Gary. "Native American Literature, Ecocriticism, and the South: The Inaccessible Worlds of Linda Hogan's Power." S. W. Jones and Monteith 165–83.

Andrews, William L. ed. *The Literature of the American South.* New York: Norton, 1998.

Appiah, Kwame Anthony. "The Postcolonial and the Postmodern." *The Postcolonial Studies Reader.* Ed. Bill Ashcroft et al. New York: Routledge, 1995. 119–24.

Arnold, Marylin. "Eudora Welty's Parody." W. C. Turner and Harding 32–38.
Arnold, St. George Tucker. "Eudora Welty's *First Love* and the Personalizing of Southern Regional History" *Journal of Regional Cultures* 1.2 (1982): 97–105.
Ashcroft, Bill, Gareth Griffiths, and Helen Tiffin. *Key Concepts in Post-Colonial Studies.* New York: Routledge, 1998.
Axtell, James. *The European and the Indian: Essays in the Ethnohistory of Colonial America.* New York: Oxford UP, 1981.
Baker, Houston A., Jr. *Turning South Again: Rethinking Modernism/Re-reading Booker T.* Durham, NC: Duke UP, 2001.
Baker, Houston A., Jr., and Dana D. Nelson. "Preface: Violence, the Body, and 'The South.'" *American Literature* 73.2 (2001): 231–44.
Balibar, Etienne, and Immanuel Wallerstein. *Race, Nation, Class: Ambiguous Identities.* New York: Verso, 1991.
Barker, Francis, Peter Hulme, and Margaret Iversen, eds. *Cannibalism and the Colonial World.* New York: Cambridge UP, 1998.
———, eds. *Colonial Discourse/Postcolonial Theory.* Manchester and New York: Manchester UP and St. Martin's P, 1994.
Bartram, William. *Travels Through North and South Carolina, Georgia, East and West Florida, The Cherokee Country, The Extensive Territories of the Muscogulges, or Creek Confederacy, and the Country of the Chactaws.* 1791. Harmondsworth, UK: Penguin, 1988.
Basso, Matthew, Laura McCall, and Dee Garceau, eds. *Across the Great Divide: Cultures of Manhood in the American West.* New York: Routledge, 2001.
Baum, Catherine B., and Floyd C. Watkins. "Caroline Gordon and 'The Captive': An Interview." *Southern Review* 7.2 (1971): 447–62.
Beidler, Peter, and Marion F. Egge. *Native Americans in the* Saturday Evening Post. London: Scarecrow P, 2000.
Bellin, Joshua David. *The Demon of the Continent: Indians and the Shaping of American Literature.* Philadelphia: U of Pennsylvania P, 2001.
Benson, Robert G. "Yankees of the Race: The Decline and Fall of Hernando de Soto." Bradford, *The Form Discovered* 84–96.
Bergland, Renee L. *The National Uncanny: Indian Ghosts and American Subjects.* Hanover, NH: UP of New England for Dartmouth College, 2000.
Berkhofer, Robert F., Jr. *The White Man's Indian: Images of the Indian from Columbus to the Present.* New York: Knopf, 1978.
Bhabha, Homi K. *The Location of Culture.* New York: Routledge, 1994.
Bishop, John Peale. "The Violent Country." *The Critical Response to Eudora Welty's Fiction.* Ed. Laurie Champion. Westport, CN: Greenwood P, 1994. 53–54.
Black, Nancy, and Bette S. Weidman, eds. *White on Red: Images of the American Indian.* London: National University Publications, Kennikat P, 1976.
Bloom, Harold, ed. *Eudora Welty: Modern Critical Views.* New York: Chelsea House, 1986.

Blotner, Joseph L. *Faulkner: A Biography.* 2 vols. New York: Random House, 1974.

———, ed. *Selected Letters of William Faulkner.* New York: Random House, 1977.

Bordo, Susan. "Reading the Slender Body." *Body and Flesh: A Philosophical Reader.* Ed. Donn Welton. Oxford: Blackwell, 1998. 291–304.

Boyle, Anne M. *Strange and Lurid Bloom: A Study of the Fiction of Caroline Gordon.* Madison, NJ: Fairleigh Dickinson UP, 2002.

Bradford, M. E., ed. *The Form Discovered: Essays on the Achievement of Andrew Lytle.* Jackson: UP of Mississippi, 1973.

———, ed. *From Eden to Babylon: The Social and Political Essays of Andrew Nelson Lytle.* Washington, DC: Regnery Gateway, 1990.

———. "Toward a Dark Shape: Lytle's 'Alchemy' and the Conquest of the New World." Bradford, *The Form Discovered* 57–63.

Brinkmeyer, Robert H., Jr. "Fascism, the Democratic Revival, and the Southern Writer." Hönnighausen and Lerda 244–50.

———. "A Fighting Faith: Faulkner, Democratic Ideology, and the World War II Home Front." *William Faulkner's Short Stories: An International Symposium.* Ed. Hans Skei. Oslo: Solum Forlag, 1997. 306–15.

———. *Remapping Southern Literature: Contemporary Southern Writers and the West.* Athens: U of Georgia P, 2000.

Brookhart, Mary Hughes, and Suzanne Marrs. "More Notes on River Country." Devlin 82–95.

Brooks, Van Wyck. *On Literature Today.* New York: Dutton, 1941.

Brown, Calvin S. *Archeology of Mississippi.* University, MS: Mississippi Geological Survey, 1926.

Brown, Jane Gibson. "Woman in Nature: A Study of Caroline Gordon's 'The Captive.'" Landess 75–84.

Brown, John P. *Old Frontiers: The Story of the Cherokee Indians from Earliest Times to the Date of Their Removal to the West, 1838.* Kingsport, TN: Southern Publishers, 1938.

Butler, Judith. *Bodies That Matter: On the Discursive Limits of "Sex."* New York: Routledge, 1993.

Calloway, Colin G. *The American Revolution in Indian Country: Crisis and Diversity in Native American Communities.* Cambridge: Cambridge UP, 1995.

Carr, Helen. *Inventing the American Primitive: Politics, Gender, and the Representation of Native American Literary Traditions, 1789–1936.* New York: New York UP, 1996.

Carson, Barbara Harrell. "Eudora Welty's Dance with Darkness: *The Robber Bridegroom.*" W. C. Turner and Harding 64–81.

Carson, James Taylor. *Searching for the Bright Path: The Mississippi Choctaws from Prehistory to Removal.* Lincoln: U of Nebraska P, 1999.

Cash, Wilbur J. *The Mind of the South.* 1941. New York: Random House/Vintage, 1969.

Castiglia, Christopher. *Bound and Determined: Captivity, Culture-Crossing, and White Womanhood from Mary Rowlandson to Patty Hearst.* Chicago: U of Chicago P, 1996.

Cheyfitz, Eric. *The Poetics of Imperialism: Translation and Colonization from The Tempest to Tarzan.* Philadelphia: U of Pennsylvania P, 1991.

Chrisman, Laura. "The Imperial Unconscious? Representations of Imperial Discourse." P. Williams and Chrisman, *Colonial Discourse* 498–516.

Clark, Charles C. "Andrew Lytle." *Literature of Tennessee.* Ed. Ray Wilbanks. Macon, GA: Mercer UP, 1984. 115–29.

Clayton, Lawrence A., Vernon James Knight Jr., and Edward C. Moore, eds. *The De Soto Chronicles: The Expedition of Hernando de Soto to North America in 1539–1543.* 2 vols. Tuscaloosa: U of Alabama P, 1993.

Clifford, James. *The Predicament of Culture: Twentieth-Century Ethnography, Literature, and Art.* Cambridge: Harvard UP, 1988.

———. "Traveling Cultures." Grossberg, Nelson, and Treichler 96–112.

Coates, Robert M. *The Outlaw Years: The History of the Land Pirates of the Natchez Trace.* 1930. Gretna, LA: Pelican, 2002.

Cohn, Deborah N. *History and Memory in the Two Souths: Recent Southern and Spanish American Fiction.* Nashville: Vanderbilt UP, 1999.

Collier, John. "The Indian in a Wartime Nation." *Annals of the American Academy of Political and Social Science* 223 (Sept. 1942): 29–35.

———. *The Indians of the Americas.* New York: Norton, 1947.

Connelley, William Elsey. *The Founding of Harman's Station and the Wiley Captivity.* Preface by Edward Hazelett. 1910. Paintsville, KY: Harman Station, 1966.

Conrad, Joseph. *Heart of Darkness.* New York: Norton, 1971.

Corkran, David H. *The Cherokee Frontier: Conflict and Survival, 1740–62.* Norman: U of Oklahoma P, 1962.

Cotterill, Robert Spencer. *The Southern Indians: The Story of the Civilized Tribes before Removal.* Norman: U of Oklahoma P, 1954.

Cowley, Malcolm, ed. *The Faulkner-Cowley File: Letters and Memories, 1944–1962.* New York: Viking, 1966.

———, ed. *The Portable Faulkner.* 1946. Rev. ed. New York: Viking, 1967.

Critchley, Simon, and Peter Dews, eds. *Deconstructive Subjectivities.* New York: SUNY P, 1996.

Cronyn, George, ed. *The Path on the Rainbow: An Anthology of Songs and Chants from the Indians of North America.* 1918. Republished as *American Indian Poetry: The Standard Anthology of Songs and Chants.* New York: Liveright, 1934.

Cushman, H. B. *History of the Choctaw, Chickasaw, and Natchez Indians.* Ed. Angie Debo. 1962. Norman: U of Oklahoma P, 1999.

Dabney, Lewis M. *The Indians of Yoknapatawpha: A Study in Literature and History.* Baton Rouge: Louisiana State UP, 1974.

Daniels, Jonathan. *The Devil's Backbone: The Story of the Natchez Trace.* Gretna, LA: Pelican, 1992.

Davis, Thadious M. *Games of Property: Law, Race, Gender, and Faulkner's* Go Down, Moses. Durham, NC: Duke UP, 2003.
Dean, Robert D. *Imperial Brotherhood: Gender and the Making of Cold War Policy.* Amherst: U of Massachusetts P, 2001.
Debo, Angie. *The Rise and Fall of the Choctaw Republic.* 1934. Norman: U of Oklahoma P, 1961.
De Certeau, Michel. *Heterologies: Discourse on the Other.* Trans. Brian Massumi. Minneapolis: U of Minnesota P, 1986.
DeConde, Alexander. *This Affair of Louisiana.* New York: Scribner, 1976.
Deloria, Philip J. *Playing Indian.* New Haven: Yale UP, 1998.
Deloria, Vine, Jr. *Custer Died for Your Sins: An Indian Manifesto.* New York: Macmillan, 1969.
Deloria, Vine, Jr., and Clifford M. Lytle. *The Nations Within: The Past and Future of American Indian Sovereignty.* Austin: U of Texas P, 1984.
Derounian-Stodola, Kathryn Zabelle, ed. *Women's Indian Captivity Narratives.* New York: Penguin, 1998.
Derrida, Jacques. "Freud and the Scene of Writing." *Writing and Difference.* Trans. Alan Bass. London: Routledge & Kegan Paul, 1978. 196–231.
——. *Of Grammatology.* Trans. Gayatri Chakravorty Spivak. Baltimore: Johns Hopkins UP, 1976.
——. "Psyche: Inventions of the Other." Kamuf 200–220.
——. *Specters of Marx: The State of the Debt, the Work of Mourning, and the New International.* Trans. Peggy Kamuf. New York: Routledge, 1994.
——. "Structure, Sign, and Play in the Discourse of the Human Sciences." *Writing and Difference.* Trans. Alan Bass. London: Routledge & Kegan Paul, 1978. 278–93.
——. "Violence and Metaphysics." *Writing and Difference.* Trans. Alan Bass. London: Routledge & Kegan Paul, 1978. 79–153.
Descola, Jean. *The Conquistadores.* Trans. Malcolm Barnes. New York: Viking, 1957.
Devlin, Albert J., ed. *Welty: A Life in Literature.* Jackson: UP of Mississippi, 1987.
Diamond, Jared. *Guns, Germs, and Steel: The Fates of Human Societies.* New York: Norton, 1999.
Dippie, Brian W. *The Vanishing American: White Attitudes and U.S. Indian Policy.* Middletown, CT: Wesleyan UP, 1982.
Donaldson, Susan V. "Gender, Race, and Allen Tate's Profession of Letters in the South." *Haunted Bodies: Gender and Southern Texts.* Ed. Anne Goodwyn Jones and Susan V. Donaldson. Charlottesville: UP of Virginia, 1997. 492–518.
Doyle, Don H. *Faulkner's County: The Historical Roots of Yoknapatawpha.* Chapel Hill: U of North Carolina P, 2001.
Drinnon, Richard. *Facing West: The Metaphysics of Indian Hating and Empire Building.* New York: Schocken, 1990.
Early, James. *The Making of* Go Down, Moses. Dallas: Southern Methodist UP, 1972.
Ebersole, Gary L. *Captured by Texts: Puritan to Postmodern Images of Indian Captivity.* Charlottesville: UP of Virginia, 1995.

Eisinger, Chester E. "Traditionalism and Modernism in Eudora Welty." Prenshaw 3–25.

Erdrich, Louise. "Where I Ought to Be: A Writer's Sense of Place." *Louise Erdrich's* Love Medicine: *A Casebook.* Ed. and intro. Hertha D. Sweet. New York: Oxford UP, 2000. 43–50.

Fabion, James D., ed. *Michel Foucault: Aesthetics, Method, and Epistemology.* New York: The New P, 1994.

Faery, Rebecca Blevins. *Cartographies of Desire: Captivity, Race, and Sex in the Shaping of the American Nation.* Norman: U of Oklahoma P, 1999.

Faulkner, William. *Collected Stories of William Faulkner.* New York: Random House, 1950.

——. *Essays, Speeches, and Public Letters by William Faulkner.* Ed. James B. Meriwether. New York: Random, 1965.

——. *Go Down, Moses.* 1942. New York: Random House/Vintage, 1990.

——. *Requiem for a Nun.* 1950. New York: Random House Vintage, 1975.

——. *Uncollected Stories of William Faulkner.* Ed. Joseph Blotner. New York: Vintage, 1981.

Fiedler, Leslie A. *Love and Death in the American Novel.* 1960. Harmondsworth, UK: Penguin, 1984.

——. *The Return of the Vanishing American.* London: Paladin, 1968.

Fliegelman, Jay. *Prodigals and Pilgrims: The American Revolution against Patriarchal Authority, 1750–1800.* Cambridge: Cambridge UP, 1982.

Foucault, Michel. *The Archaeology of Knowledge and the Discourse on Language.* Trans. A. M. Sheridan Smith. New York: Pantheon Books, 1972.

——. *The History of Sexuality: An Introduction.* Vol. 1. Trans. Robert Hurley. New York: Vintage Books, 1990.

——. *The Order of Things: An Archaeology of the Human Sciences.* New York: Random House, 1970.

Fowler, Doreen, and Ann J. Abadie, eds. *Faulkner and Race.* Jackson: UP of Mississippi, 1987.

Franco, Jean. "The Nation as Imagined Community." McClintock, Mufti, and Shohat 130–40.

French, Warren. "'All Things Are Double': Eudora Welty as a Civilized Writer." Prenshaw 179–88.

Freud, Sigmund. *Civilization and Its Discontents.* Trans. and ed. James Strachey. 1930. New York: Norton, 1962.

——. *Das Unbehagen in der Kultur.* Intro. Alfred Lorenzer and Bernad Goerlich. Frankfurt am Main: Fischer Taschenbuch Verlag, 2001.

——. "The Uncanny." *The Standard Edition of the Complete Psychological Works of Sigmund Freud.* Vol. 17, *1917–19.* Ed. James Strachey. London: Hogarth, 1973. 219–56.

Friar, Ralph E., and Natasha A. Friar. *The Only Good Indian . . . : The Hollywood Gospel.* New York: Drama Book Specialists/Publishers, 1972.

Funkhouser, W. D., and W. S. Webb. *Ancient Life in Kentucky.* Frankfort: Kentucky Geological Survey, 1928.

Galloway, Patricia. "Commemorative History and Hernando de Soto." Galloway, *The Hernando de Soto Expedition* 410–35.

———. "Conjoncture and Longue Durée: History, Anthropology, and the Hernando de Soto Expedition." Galloway, *The Hernando de Soto Expedition* 283–94.

———. "The Construction of Faulkner's Indians." *Faulkner Journal* 18.1–2 (2003): 9–32.

———, ed. *The Hernando de Soto Expedition: History, Historiography, and "Discovery" in the Southeast.* Lincoln: U of Nebraska P, 1997.

Garrison, Tim Alan. *The Legal Ideology of Removal: The Southern Judiciary and the Sovereignty of Native American Nations.* Athens: U of Georgia P, 2002.

Gates, Henry Louis, Jr. "Writing 'Race' and the Difference It Makes." *"Race," Writing, and Difference.* Ed. Henry Louis Gates Jr. Chicago: U of Chicago P, 1985. 1–20.

Geertz, Clifford. *The Interpretation of Cultures.* New York: Basic Books, 1973.

———. *Local Knowledge: Further Essays in Interpretive Anthropology.* New York: Basic Books, 1983.

Gessner, Robert. *Massacre: A Survey of Today's American Indians.* New York: Jonathan Cape and Harrison Smith, 1931.

Gibson, Arrell. *The Chickasaws.* Norman: U of Oklahoma P, 1971.

Glancy, Diane. *The Relief of America.* Chicago: Tia Chucha P, 2000.

Gordon, Caroline. "The Captive." 1932. *Old Red and Other Stories.* New York: Scribner, 1963. 213–56.

———. *The Collected Stories of Caroline Gordon.* Intro. Robert Penn Warren. New York: Farrar, Straus & Giroux, 1981.

———. *Green Centuries.* 1941. Nashville: Sanders, 1992.

———. *Penhally.* 1931. Nashville: Sanders, 1991.

Gosden, Chris. "Postcolonial Archaeology: Issues of Culture, Identity, and Knowledge." Hodder, *Archaeological Theory Today* 241–61.

Gray, Richard. Foreword. "Inventing Communities, Imagining Places: Some Thoughts on Southern Self-Fashioning." S. W. Jones and Monteith xiii–xxiii.

———. *Southern Aberrations: Writers of the American South and the Problems of Regionalism.* Baton Rouge: Louisiana State UP, 2000.

———. *Writing the South: Ideas of an American Region.* Cambridge: Cambridge UP, 1986.

Green, Rayna. "The Tribe Called Wannabee: Playing Indian in America and Europe." *Folklore* 99 (1988): 50–55.

Grossberg, Lawrence, Cary Nelson, and Paula A. Treichler, eds. *Cultural Studies.* New York: Routledge, 1992.

Grosz, Elizabeth. *Jacques Lacan: A Feminist Introduction.* New York: Routledge, 1990.

Gwynn, Frederick L., and Joseph L. Blotner, eds. *Faulkner in the University.* Charlottesville: U of Virginia P, 1959.

Hale, Grace Elizabeth. *Making Whiteness: The Culture of Segregation in the South, 1890–1940.* New York: Vintage, 1999.

Hamilton, William B. "The Sources of History of the Mississippi Territory." *Journal of Mississippi History* 1.2 (1939): 29–70.

Hemming, John. *The Conquest of the Incas.* New York: Harcourt Brace Jovanovich, 1970.

Hodder, Ian, ed. *Archaeological Theory Today.* Oxford: Polity P/Blackwell, 2001.

———. *Theory and Practice in Archaeology.* New York: Routledge, 1992.

Holder, Alan. *The Imagined Past: Portrayals of Our History in Modern American Literature.* Lewisburg, PA: Bucknell UP, 1980.

Hönnighausen, Lothar. "Faulkner Rewriting the Indian Removal." Hönnighausen and Lerda 335–43.

Hönnighausen, Lothar, and Valeria Gennaro Lerda, eds. *Rewriting the South: History and Fiction.* Tübingen: Francke Verlag, 1993.

Hopkins, Sarah Winnemucca. *Life among the Piutes.* Reno: U of Nevada P, 1994.

Horsford, Howard C. "Faulkner's (Mostly) Unreal Indians in Early Mississippi History." *American Literature* 64.2 (1992): 311–30.

Horsman, Reginald. *Expansion and American Indian Policy, 1783–1812.* East Lansing: Michigan State UP, 1967.

Howell, Elmo. "Inversion and the 'Female' Principle: William Faulkner's 'A Courtship.'" *Studies in Short Fiction* 4 (1967): 308–14.

———. "William Faulkner and the Mississippi Indians." *Georgia Review* 21 (1967): 386–96.

———. "William Faulkner's Chickasaw Legacy: A Note on 'Red Leaves.'" *Arizona Quarterly* 26 (1970): 293–303.

Hudson, Charles. "The Historical Significance of the de Soto Route." Galloway, *The Hernando de Soto Expedition* 313–28.

———. *The Southeastern Indians.* Knoxville: U of Tennessee P, 1976.

Huhndorf, Shari M. *Going Native: Indians in the American Cultural Imagination.* Ithaca, NY: Cornell UP, 2001.

Hulme, Peter. *Colonial Encounters: Europe and the Native Caribbean.* London: Methuen, 1986.

———. "Including America." *Ariel: A Review of International English Literature* 26.1 (1995): 117–24.

I'll Take My Stand: The South and the Agrarian Tradition. Intro. Louis D. Rubin Jr. 1930. Baton Rouge: Louisiana State UP, 1977.

Jaimes, M. Annette, and Theresa Halsey. "American Indian Women: At the Center of Indigenous Resistance in Contemporary North America." McClintock, Mufti, and Shohat 298–329.

JanMohamed, Abdul R. "The Economy of Manichean Allegory." *The Postcolonial Studies Reader.* Ed. Bill Ashcroft et al. New York: Routledge, 1995. 18–23.

Jehlen, Myra. *American Incarnation: The Individual, the Nation, and the Continent.* Cambridge: Harvard UP, 1986.

Johnson, Bruce G. "Indigenous Doom: Colonial Mimicry in Faulkner's Indian Tales." *Faulkner Journal* 18.1–2 (2003): 101–28.

Johnson, Jay K. "From Chiefdom to Tribe in Northeast Mississippi: The de Soto Expedition as a Window on a Culture in Transition." Galloway, *The Hernando de Soto Expedition* 295–312.

Jones, Anne Goodwyn. "The Work of Gender in the Southern Renaissance." Morris and Reinhardt 41–56.

Jones, Billy M., ed. *The Heroes of Tennessee.* Memphis: Memphis State UP, 1979.

Jones, Suzanne W., and Sharon Monteith, eds. *South to a New Place: Region, Literature, Culture.* Baton Rouge: Louisiana State UP, 2002.

Jonza, Nancylee Novell. *The Underground Stream: The Life and Art of Caroline Gordon.* Athens: U of Georgia P, 1995.

Jordan, David, ed. *Regionalism Reconsidered: New Approaches to the Field.* New York: Garland, 1994.

Jung, Carl Gustav. *Psychology and Alchemy.* Ed. Herbert Read et al. New York: Princeton UP, 1968.

Kammen, Michael. *Mystic Chords of Memory: The Transformation of Tradition in American Culture.* New York: Knopf, 1991.

Kamuf, Peggy, ed. *A Derrida Reader: Between the Blinds.* New York: Columbia UP, 1991.

Kartiganer, Donald M., and Ann J. Abadie, eds. *Faulkner and the Natural World.* Jackson: UP of Mississippi, 1999.

Kazin, Alfred. *On Native Grounds: An Interpretation of Modern American Prose Literature.* New York: Harcourt Brace, 1942.

Keen, Benjamin. *Essays in the Intellectual History of Colonial Latin America.* Boulder: Westview P, 1998.

Keiser, Albert. *The Indian in American Literature.* New York: Oxford UP, 1933.

Kelly, Lawrence C. *The Assault on Assimilation: John Collier and the Origins of Indian Policy Reform.* Albuquerque: U of New Mexico P, 1983.

Kesselman, Steven. "The Frontier Thesis and the Great Depression." *Journal of the History of Ideas* 29.2 (1968): 253–68.

Kicza, John E., ed. *The Indian in Latin American History: Resistance, Resilience, and Acculturation.* Wilmington, DE: Scholarly Resources, 2000.

Kidwell, Clara Sue. *Choctaws and Missionaries in Mississippi, 1818–1918.* Norman: U of Oklahoma P, 1995.

Kilgour, Maggie. *From Communion to Cannibalism: An Anatomy of Metaphors of Incorporation.* Princeton: Princeton UP, 1990.

Kilpatrick, Jacqueline. *Celluloid Indians.* Lincoln: U of Nebraska P, 1999.

Kimmel, Michael. *Manhood in America: A Cultural History.* New York: The Free Press, 1996.

King, Duane H., ed. *The Cherokee Indian Nation: A Troubled History.* Knoxville: U of Tennessee P, 1979.

King, Richard H. "Cash and the Crisis of Political Modernity." *W. J. Cash and the Minds of the South.* Ed. Paul D. Escott. Baton Rouge: Louisiana State UP, 1992. 67–87.

Kinney, Arthur F., ed. *Critical Essays on William Faulkner: The McCaslin Family.* Boston: Hall, 1990.

———. "Faulkner's Other Others." *Faulkner at 100: Retrospect and Prospect.* Ed. Donald M. Kartiganer and Ann J. Abadie. Jackson: UP of Mississippi, 2000. 195–203.

———. Go Down, Moses: *The Miscegenation of Time.* New York: Twayne, 1996.

Kirkpatrick, F. A. *The Spanish Conquistadores.* Cleveland: Meridian Books, 1934.

Kohl, Philip L., and Clare Fawcett, eds. *Nationalism, Politics, and the Practice of Archaeology.* Cambridge: Cambridge UP, 1995.

Kolodny, Annette. *The Lay of the Land: Metaphor as Experience and History in American Life and Letters.* Chapel Hill: U of North Carolina P, 1975.

Kreyling, Michael. *Author and Agent: Eudora Welty and Diarmuid Russell.* New York: Farrar, Straus, Giroux, 1991.

———. "Clement and the Indians: Pastoral and History in *The Robber Bridegroom.*" *Eudora Welty: A Form of Thanks.* Ed. Louis Dollarhide and Ann Abadie. Jackson: UP of Mississippi, 1979. 25–45.

———. "Eudora Welty as Novelist: A Historical Approach." *The Late Novels of Eudora Welty.* Ed. Jan Nordby Gretlund and Karl-Heinz Westarp. U of South Carolina P, 1998. 3–17.

———. *Eudora Welty's Achievement of Order.* Baton Rouge: Louisiana State UP, 1980.

———. "*The Robber Bridegroom* and the Pastoral Dream." Bloom 135–48.

———. *Understanding Eudora Welty.* Columbia: U of South Carolina P, 1999.

Krupat, Arnold. *Ethnocriticism: Ethnography, History, and Literature.* Berkeley: U of California P, 1992.

Kugler, Paul. *The Alchemy of Discourse: An Archetypal Approach to Language.* London: Associated UPs, 1982.

Kupperman, Karen Ordahl. *Indians and English: Facing Off in Early America.* Ithaca, NY: Cornell UP, 2000.

Lacan, Jacques. *The Four Fundamental Concepts of Psycho-Analysis.* Ed. Jacques-Alain Miller. Trans. Alan Sheridan. New York: Norton, 1978.

Ladd, Barbara. "Dismantling the Monolith: Southern Places: Past, Present, and Future." S. W. Jones and Monteith 44–57.

———. *Nationalism and the Color Line in George W. Cable, Mark Twain, and William Faulkner.* Baton Rouge: Louisiana State UP, 1996.

———. "'Writing against Death': Totalitarianism and the Nonfiction of Eudora Welty at Midcentury." Pollack and Marrs 155–78.

Landess, Thomas H., ed. *The Short Fiction of Caroline Gordon: A Critical Symposium.* Irving: U of Dallas P, 1972.

Lauter, Paul, et al., eds. *The Heath Anthology.* Lexington, MA: Heath, 1990.

Lawrence. D. H. *Studies in Classic American Literature.* 1923. New York: Viking, 1961.

Lefebvre, Henri. *The Production of Space.* Trans. Donald Nicholson-Smith. Cambridge: Blackwell, 1991.

Limerick, Patricia Nelson. *The Legacy of Conquest: The Unbroken Past of the American West.* New York: Norton, 1987.

Littlefield, Daniel F., and James W. Farms. *The Chickasaw Freedmen: People without a Country.* Lanham, MD: Greenwood P, 1980.

——, eds. *Native American Writing in the Southeast: An Anthology, 1875–1935.* Jackson: UP of Mississippi, 1995.

Lott, Eric. *Love and Theft: Blackface Minstrelsy and the American Working Class.* New York: Oxford UP, 1995.

Lucas, Mark. *The Southern Vision of Andrew Lytle.* Baton Rouge: Louisiana State UP, 1986.

Lyon, Edwin A. *A New Deal for Southeastern Archaeology.* Tuscaloosa: U of Alabama P, 1996.

Lytle, Andrew Nelson. *At the Moon's Inn.* 1941. Tuscaloosa: U of Alabama P, 1990.

——. *The Hero with the Private Parts: Essays by Andrew Lytle.* Baton Rouge: Louisiana State UP, 1966.

——. "The Hind Tit." *I'll Take My Stand* 201–45.

——. *Stories: Alchemy and Others.* Sewanee, TN: U of the South P, 1984.

——. *The Velvet Horn.* 1957. Sewanee, TN: U of the South P, 1983.

——. *A Wake for the Living: A Family Chronicle.* Nashville: Sanders, 1992.

Maddox, Lucy. *Removals: Nineteenth-Century American Literature and the Politics of Indian Affairs.* New York: Oxford UP, 1991.

Makowsky, Veronica A. *Caroline Gordon: A Biography.* New York: Oxford UP, 1989.

Mallios, Peter Lancelot. "Faulkner's Indians, or The Poetics of Cannibalism." *Faulkner Journal* 18.1–2 (2003): 143–78.

Manning, Carol S. "Introduction: On Defining Themes and (Mis)Placing Women Writers." *The Female Tradition in Southern Literature.* Ed. Carol S. Manning. Urbana: U of Illinois P, 1993. 1–12.

Marrs, Suzanne. "The Conclusion of Eudora Welty's 'First Love': Historical Backgrounds." *Notes on Mississippi Writers* 13 (1981): 73–78.

Mason, Peter. *Deconstructing America: Presentations of the Other.* New York: Routledge, 1990.

Matsumoto, Valerie J., and Blake Allendinger, eds. *Over the Edge: Remapping the American West.* Berkeley: U of California P, 1999.

Matthews, John T. *The Play of Faulkner's Language.* Ithaca, NY: Cornell UP, 1982.

——. "Touching Race in *Go Down, Moses.*" *New Essays on* Go Down, Moses. Ed. Linda Wagner-Martin. Cambridge: Cambridge UP, 1996. 21–47.

McCaleb, Walter Flavius. *The Aaron Burr Conspiracy.* New York: Dodd, Mead, 1903.

McClintock, Anne. "The Angel of Progress: Pitfalls of the Term 'Postcolonialism.'" Barker, Hulme, and Iversen, *Colonial Discourse* 253–66.

——. *Imperial Leather: Race, Gender and Sexuality in the Colonial Contest.* London: Routledge, 1995.

——. "'No Longer a Future in Heaven': Gender, Race, and Nationalism." McClintock, Mufti, and Shohat 89–112.

McClintock, Anne, Aamir Mufti, and Ella Shohat, eds. *Dangerous Liaisons: Gender, Nation, and Postcolonial Perspectives.* Minneapolis: U of Minnesota P, 1997.

Melville, Herman. *Typee: A Peep at Polynesian Life.* 1846. London: Everyman, 1993.
Meriwether, James B., and Michael Millgate, eds. *Lion in the Garden; Interviews with William Faulkner, 1926–1962.* New York: Random House, 1968.
Michaels, Walter Benn. *Our America: Nativism, Modernism, and Pluralism.* Durham, NC: Duke UP, 1995.
Milanich, Jerald T. *Florida Indians and the Invasion from Europe.* Gainesville: UP of Florida, 1995.
Milanich, Jerald T., and Susan Milbrath, eds. *First Encounters: Spanish Explorations in the Caribbean and the United States, 1492–1570.* Gainesville: UP of Florida, 1989.
Mississippi: The WPA Guide to the Magnolia State. Intro. Robert S. McElvaine. 1938. Jackson: UP of Mississippi, 1988.
Moore, Gene M. "Chronological Problems in Faulkner's 'Wilderness' Stories." *Faulkner Journal* 18.1–2 (2003): 51–68.
——. "'European Finery' and Cultural Survival in Faulkner's 'Red Leaves.'" *William Faulkner's Short Fiction: An International Symposium.* Ed. Hans H. Skei. Oslo: Solum Forlag, 1997. 263–68.
——. "Introduction: Faulkner's Incorrect 'Indians'?" *Faulkner Journal* 18.1–2 (2003): 3–8.
Morris, Christopher, and Steven G. Reinhardt, eds. *Southern Writers and Their Worlds.* College Station: Texas A&M UP, 1996.
Morrison, Toni. *Playing in the Dark: Whiteness and the Literary Imagination.* Cambridge: Harvard UP, 1992.
Muldoon, James. *The Americas in the Spanish World Order: The Justification for Conquest in the Seventeenth Century.* Philadelphia: U of Pennsylvania P, 1994.
Muller, Gilbert H. "The Descent of the Gods: Faulkner's 'Red Leaves' and the Garden of the South." *Studies in Short Fiction* 11.3 (1974): 243–49.
Murra, John. "Cloth, Textile, and the Inca Empire." Starn 55–69.
Nabokov, Peter, ed. *Native American Testimony.* Foreword by Vine Deloria Jr. New York: Penguin, 1991.
Nelson, Dana D. *National Manhood: Capitalist Citizenship and the Imagined Fraternity of White Men.* Durham, NC: Duke UP, 1998.
Nolan, Charles J., Jr. *Aaron Burr and the American Literary Imagination.* Westport, CN: Greenwood P, 1980.
Norrell, Brenda. "Clinton Addresses Indian Country in Phoenix." *Indian Country Today* 5 July 2000: A1, A3.
O'Brien, Michael. *The Idea of the American South, 1920–1941.* Baltimore: Johns Hopkins UP, 1979.
——. Introduction. Morris and Reinhardt 3–8.
Owens, Louis. *Other Destinies: Understanding the American Indian Novel.* Norman: U of Oklahoma P, 1992.
Parker, Robert Dale. "Red Slippers and Cottonmouth Moccasins: White Anxieties in Faulkner's Indian Stories." *Faulkner Journal* 18.1–2 (2003): 81–100.

Parmet, Herbert S., and Marie B. Hecht. *Aaron Burr: Portrait of an Ambitious Man.* New York: MacMillan, 1967.

Parry, Benita. "Resistance Theory/Theorising Resistance, or Two Cheers for Nativism." Barker, Hulme, and Iversen, *Colonial Discourse* 172–96.

Pearce, Roy Harvey. *Historicism Once More.* Princeton, NJ: Princeton UP, 1969.

———. *The Savages of America: A Study of the Indian and the Idea of Civilization.* 1953. Baltimore: Johns Hopkins UP, 1965.

———. *Savagism and Civilization: A Study of the Indian and the American Mind.* Berkeley: U of California P, 1988.

Perdue, Theda. *Cherokee Women: Gender and Culture Change, 1700–1835.* Lincoln: U of Nebraska P, 1998.

———. *Slavery and the Evolution of Cherokee Society, 1540–1866.* Knoxville: U of Tennessee P, 1979.

Philip, Kenneth R. *John Collier's Crusade for Indian Reform: 1920–1954.* Tucson: U of Arizona P, 1977.

Phillips, Jerry. "Cannibalism qua Capitalism: The Metaphorics of Accumulation in Marx, Conrad, Shakespeare, and Marlowe." Barker, Hulme, and Iversen, *Cannibalism* 183–203.

Polenberg, Richard D. *The Era of Franklin D. Roosevelt, 1933–1945.* Boston: Bedford/ St. Martins, 2000.

Polk, Noel. "Andrew Nelson Lytle: A Bibliography of his Writings." *Mississippi Quarterly* 23 (1970): 435–91.

Pollack, Harriet, and Suzanne Marrs, eds. *Eudora Welty and Politics: Did the Writer Crusade?* Baton Rouge: Louisiana State UP, 2001.

Poma, Huaman (Don Felipe Huaman Poma de Ayala). *Letter to a King: A Peruvian Chief's Account of Life under the Incas and Under Spanish Rule.* Ed. Christopher Dilke. New York: Dutton, 1978.

Prakash, Gyan. Introduction. *After Colonialism: Imperial Histories and Postcolonial Displacements.* Ed. Gyan Prakash. Princeton: Princeton UP, 1995. 3–20.

Pratt, Mary Louise. "Transculturation and Autoethnography: Peru 1615/1980." Barker, Hulme, and Iversen, *Colonial Discourse* 24–46.

Prenshaw, Peggy Whitman, ed. *Conversations with Eudora Welty.* Jackson: UP of Mississippi, 1984.

———, ed. *Eudora Welty: Thirteen Essays.* Jackson: UP of Mississippi, 1983.

Prescott, William H. *History of the Conquest of Peru.* Vol. 1. New York: Harper, 1847.

Quinones, Ricardo J. *The Changes of Cain: Violence and the Lost Brother in Cain and Abel Literature.* Princeton, NJ: Princeton UP, 1991.

Rabate, Jean-Michel. *Jacques Lacan: Psychoanalysis and the Subject of Literature.* New York: Palgrave, 2001.

Ragland, Ellie, ed. *Critical Essays on Jacques Lacan.* New York: Hall, 1999.

Ransom, John Crowe. "Reconstructed but Unregenerate." *I'll Take My Stand* 1–27.

Rhodes, Karen. "The Grotesque Economics of Tragicomedy: Cultural Colonization in Faulkner's 'Red Leaves.'" *Faulkner Journal* 18.1–2 (2003): 69–80.

Richter, David H. *The Critical Tradition.* Boston: Bedford Books, 1998.

Ritter, Alexander. "Natchez in the Fiction of Three Centuries: Variants of Literary Regionalism in Chateaubriand, Sealsfeld, and Welty." *Southern Quarterly* 35.1 (1996): 13–28.

Robbins, William G. *Colony and Empire: The Capitalist Transformation of the American West.* Lawrence: U of Kansas P, 1994.

Roberts, Elizabeth Madox. *The Great Meadow.* 1930. Nashville: Sanders, 1992.

Roediger, David R. *Toward the Abolition of Whiteness: Essays on Race, Politics, and Working Class History.* London: Verso, 1994.

———. *The Wages of Whiteness: Race and the Making of the American Working Class.* London: Verso, 1991.

Rogin, Michael Paul. *Fathers and Children: Andrew Jackson and the Subjugation of the American Indian.* New York: Knopf, 1975.

Romine, Scott. *The Narrative Forms of Southern Community.* Baton Rouge: Louisiana State UP, 1999.

———. "Where Is Southern Literature? The Practice of Place in a Postsouthern Age." S. W. Jones and Monteith 23–43.

Rosaldo, Renato. "Social Justice and the Crisis of National Communities." Barker, Hulme, and Iversen, *Colonial Discourse* 239–52.

Rowe, John Carlos. *Literary Culture and U.S. Imperialism: From the Revolution to World War II.* New York: Oxford UP, 2000.

———. *The New American Studies.* Minneapolis: U of Minnesota P, 2002.

Rowlandson, Mary White. *The Sovereignty and Goodness of God.* Ed. Neal Salisbury. Boston: Bedford Books, 1997.

Rubin, Louis D., Jr. Introduction. *I'll Take My Stand* xi–xxxvi.

Rubin, Louis D., Jr., and Robert D. Jacob. *Southern Renascence: The Literature of the Modern South.* Baltimore: Johns Hopkins UP, 1953.

Rusco, Elmer R. *A Fateful Time: The Background and Legislative History of the Indian Reorganization Act.* Reno: U of Nevada P, 2000.

Said, Edward. *Culture and Imperialism.* New York: Knopf, 1993.

———. *Orientalism.* New York: Random House/Vintage, 1979.

Sarcone, Elizabeth. "Andrew Lytle: A Modern Traditionalist." Winchell 153–62.

Satz, Ronald N. *American Indian Policy in the Jacksonian Era.* Lincoln: U of Nebraska P, 1975.

———. *Tennessee's Indian Peoples: From White Contact to Removal, 1540–1840.* Knoxville: U of Tennessee P, 1979.

Sayre, Robert Woods. "Faulkner's Indians and the Romantic Vision." *Faulkner Journal* 18.1–2 (2003): 33–50.

Seed, Patricia. "'Failing to Marvel': Atahualpa's Encounter with the Word." *Latin American Research Review* 26.1 (1991): 7–32.

Seshadri-Crooks, Kalpana. "The Comedy of Domination: Psychoanalysis and the Conceit of Whiteness." *The Psychoanalysis of Race.* Ed. Christopher Lane. New York: Columbia UP, 1998. 353–79.

Shanks, Michael. "Culture/Archaeology: The Dispersion of a Discipline and Its Objects." Hodder, *Archaeological Theory Today* 284–305.

Shay, Frank. *The Incredible Pizarro: Conqueror of Peru.* New York: Mohawk P, 1932.

Simpson, Lewis P. *The Dispossessed Garden: Pastoral and History in Southern Literature.* Athens: U of Georgia P, 1975.

Skaggs, Merrill Maguire. "The Uses of Enchantment in Frontier Humor and *The Robber Bridegroom*." *The Critical Response to Eudora Welty's Fiction.* Ed. Laurie Champion. Westport, CN: Greenwood P, 1994. 57–63.

Slemons, Stephen. "Bones of Contention: Post-Colonial Writing and the 'Cannibal' Question." *Literature and the Body.* Ed. Anthony Purdy. Amsterdam: Rodoi, 1992. 163–77.

Slotkin, Richard. *The Fatal Environment: The Myth of the Frontier in the Age of Industrialization, 1800–1890.* New York: Atheneum, 1985.

———. *Gunfighter Nation: The Myth of the Frontier in Twentieth-Century America.* New York: Atheneum, 1992.

———. *Regeneration through Violence: The Mythology of the American Frontier, 1600–1860.* New York: Harper Perennial, 1996.

Smith, Carl S., et al., eds. *Law and American Literature.* New York: Knopf, 1983.

Smith, Sherry L. *Reimaging Indians: Native Americans through Anglo Eyes, 1880–1940.* New York: Oxford UP, 2000.

Spivak, Gayatri Chakravorty. "'Can the Subaltern Speak?': Speculations on Widow Sacrifice." *Marxism and the Interpretation of Culture.* Ed. Cary Nelson and Lawrence Grossberg. London: Macmillan, 1988. 271–313.

———. "Sex and History in the Prelude." *Poststructuralist Readings of English Poetry.* Ed. Richard Machin and Christopher Norris. Cambridge: Cambridge UP, 1987. 193–226.

Spurr, David. "New Mexico: Landscapes of the Colonizing Imagination." *Empire: American Studies.* Ed. John G. Blair and Reinhold Wagenleitner. Tübingen: Gunter Narr Verlag, 1997. 13–33.

Starn, Orin, ed. *The Peru Reader: History, Culture, Politics.* Durham, NC: Duke UP, 1995.

Stewart, George R. *Names on the Land: A Historical Account of Place-Naming in the United States.* New York: Random House, 1945.

Stoler, Ann Laura. "Making Empire Respectable: The Politics of Race and Sexual Morality in Twentieth Century Colonial Cultures." McClintock, Mufti, and Shohat 344–73.

Strong, Pauline Turner. *Captive Selves, Captivating Others: The Politics and Poetics of Colonial American Captivity Narratives.* Boulder: Westview P, 1999.

Stuckey, William J. *Caroline Gordon.* New York: Twayne, 1972.

Sullivan, Walter. *A Requiem for the Renascence: The State of Fiction in the Modern South.* Athens: U of Georgia P, 1976.

Swanton, John R. *The Indians of the Southeastern United States.* Part 1. 1942. St. Clair Shores, MI: Scholarly P, 1976.

———. *Indian Tribes of the Lower Mississippi Valley and Adjacent Coast of the Gulf of Mexico.* Smithsonian Institution: Bureau of American Ethnology. *Bulletin* 43 (1911).

Tate, Allen. "Remarks on Southern Religion." *I'll Take My Stand* 155–75.

Taylor, Walter. "Yoknapatawpha's Indians: A Novel Faulkner Never Wrote." *The Modernists: Studies in a Literary Phenomenon: Essays in Honor of Harry T. Moore.* Ed. Lawrence B. Gamache and Ian S. MacNiven. Rutherford, NJ: Fairleigh Dickinson UP, 1987. 202–09.

Thomas, Julian. "Archaeologies of Place and Landscape." Hodder, *Archaeological Theory Today* 165–85.

Thompson, Victor H. "Aaron Burr in Eudora Welty's 'First Love.'" *Notes on Mississippi Writers* 8 (1976): 75–83.

———. *Eudora Welty: A Reference Guide.* Boston: Hall, 1976.

Thornton, Russell. *American Indian Holocaust and Survival: A Population History since 1492.* Norman: U of Oklahoma P, 1987.

———. *The Cherokees: A Population History.* Lincoln: U of Nebraska P, 1990.

Todorov, Tzvetan. *The Conquest of America: The Question of the Other.* New York: Harper & Row, 1982.

Trilling, Lionel. "American Fairy Tale." W. C. Turner and Harding 31–32.

Turner, Frederick Jackson. "The Significance of the Frontier in American History." *Rereading Frederick Jackson Turner.* Ed. John Mack Faragher. New York: Henry Holt, 1994. 31–60.

Turner, W. Craig, and Lee Emling Harding, eds. *Critical Essays on Eudora Welty.* Boston: Hall, 1984.

Verrill, A. Hyatt. *Great Conquerors of South and Central America.* New York: D. Appleton, 1929.

Volpe, Edmund L. "Faulkner's 'Red Leaves': The Deciduation of Nature." *Studies in American Fiction* 3.2 (1975): 121–31.

Wald, Priscilla. *Constituting Americans: Cultural Anxiety and Narrative Form.* Durham, NC: Duke UP, 1995.

Wallace, Anthony F. C. *Jefferson and the Indians.* Cambridge: Belknap P of Harvard UP, 1999.

Warren, Robert Penn. "The Love and Separateness in Miss Welty." W. C. Turner and Harding 42–51.

Warrior, Robert Allen. *Tribal Secrets: Recovering American Indian Intellectual Traditions.* Minneapolis: U of Minnesota P, 1995.

Watkins, Floyd C. "Sacrificial Rituals and Anguish in the Victim's Heart in 'Red Leaves.'" *Studies in Short Fiction* 30 (1993): 71–78.

Weaver, Jace. *Other Words: American Indian Literature, Law, and Culture.* Norman: U of Oklahoma P, 2001.

Wells, Mary Ann. *Native Land: Mississippi, 1540–1798.* Jackson: UP of Mississippi, 1994.

Welty, Eudora. *The Collected Stories of Eudora Welty.* San Diego: Harcourt Brace Jovanovich, 1980.

———. *The Eye of the Story.* New York: Vintage, 1990.

———. *The Robber Bridegroom.* 1942. New York: Harcourt Brace, 1978.

———. *The Wide Net and Other Stories.* 1941. New York: Harcourt Brace, 1971.

Weston, Mary Ann. *Native Americans in the News: Images of Indians in the Twentieth Century Press.* Westport, CN: Greenwood P, 1996.

White, Hayden. *Tropics of Discourse: Essays in Cultural Criticism.* Baltimore: Johns Hopkins UP, 1978.

Williams, Jerry M., and Robert E. Lewis, eds. *Early Images of the Americas.* Tucson: U of Arizona P, 1993.

Williams, Patrick, and Laura Chrisman, eds. *Colonial Discourse and Post-Colonial Theory: A Reader.* New York: Columbia UP, 1994.

Williams, Robert A., Jr. *The American Indian in Western Legal Thought: The Discourses of Conquest.* Oxford: Oxford UP, 1990.

Williams, William Carlos. *In the American Grain: Essays by William Carlos Williams.* 1925. New York: New Directions, 1933.

Williamson, Joel. *William Faulkner and Southern History.* New York: Oxford UP, 1993.

Wilson, Charles Reagan. "The Invention of Southern Tradition." Hönnighausen and Lerda 3–21.

Winchell, Mark Royden, ed. *The Vanderbilt Tradition: Essays in Honor of Thomas Daniel Young.* Baton Rouge: Louisiana State UP, 1991.

Winston, Jay S. "Going Native in Yoknapatawpha: Faulkner's Fragmented America and 'the Indian.'" *Faulkner Journal* 18.1–2 (2003): 129–42.

Womack, Craig S. *Red on Red: Native American Literary Separatism.* Minneapolis: U of Minnesota P, 1999.

Wood, Sally, ed. *The Southern Mandarins: Letters of Caroline Gordon to Sally Wood, 1924–1937.* Foreword by Andrew Lytle. Baton Rouge: Louisiana State UP, 1984.

Yaeger, Patricia. *Dirt and Desire: Reconstructing Southern Women's Writing, 1930–1990.* Chicago: U of Chicago P, 2000.

Young, Thomas Daniel, and Elizabeth Sarcone, eds. *The Lytle-Tate Letters: The Correspondence between Andrew Lytle and Allen Tate.* Jackson: UP of Mississippi, 1987.

Index